Managing Flow

Also by Ikujiro Nonaka

THE KNOWLEDGE-CREATING COMPANY: How Japanese Companies Create the Dynamics of Innovation *(with H. Takeuchi)*

ENABLING KNOWLEDGE CREATION: How to Unlock the Mystery of Tacit Knowledge and Release the Power of Innovation *(with G. Von Krogh and K. Ichijo)*

KNOWLEDGE CREATION AND MANAGEMENT: New Challenges for Managers *(with K. Ichijo)*

HITOTSUBASHI ON KNOWLEDGE MANAGEMENT *(with H. Takeuchi)*

Managing Flow
A Process Theory of the Knowledge-Based Firm

Ikujiro Nonaka
Ryoko Toyama

and

Toru Hirata

In collaboration with Susan J. Bigelow, Ayano Hirose and Florian Kohlbacher

© Ikujiro Nonaka, Ryoko Toyama and Toru Hirata 2008
Cover designed by Tom Kamegai, GravityOne Inc.
Foreword © David J. Teece 2008
Softcover reprint of the hardcover 1st edition 2008 978-0-230-55376-7

All rights reserved. No reproduction, copy or transmission of this publication may be made without written permission.

No paragraph of this publication may be reproduced, copied or transmitted save with written permission or in accordance with the provisions of the Copyright, Designs and Patents Act 1988, or under the terms of any licence permitting limited copying issued by the Copyright Licensing Agency, 90 Tottenham Court Road, London W1T 4LP.

Any person who does any unauthorised act in relation to this publication may be liable to criminal prosecution and civil claims for damages.

The authors have asserted their rights to be identified as the authors of this work in accordance with the Copyright, Designs and Patents Act 1988.

First published in 2008 by
PALGRAVE MACMILLAN
Houndmills, Basingstoke, Hampshire RG21 6XS and
175 Fifth Avenue, New York, N.Y. 10010
Companies and representatives throughout the world.

PALGRAVE MACMILLAN is the global academic imprint of the Palgrave Macmillan division of St. Martin's Press, LLC and of Palgrave Macmillan Ltd. Macmillan® is a registered trademark in the United States, United Kingdom and other countries. Palgrave is a registered trademark in the European Union and other countries.

ISBN 978-1-349-36356-8   ISBN 978-0-230-58370-2 (eBook)
DOI 10.1057/9780230583702

A catalogue record for this book is available from the British Library.

10 9 8 7 6 5 4 3 2 1
17 16 15 14 13 12 11 10 09 08

Transferred to Digital Printing in 2013

Contents

List of Figures and Tables	vii
Foreword: From the Management of R&D to Knowledge Management	ix
Acknowledgements	xviii

Introduction: Why We Need a New Theory of the Knowledge-Based Firm		**1**
1	**The Characteristics of Knowledge**	**6**
1.1	Knowledge is subjective	7
1.2	Knowledge is process-relational	9
1.3	Knowledge is aesthetic	12
1.4	Knowledge is created through practice	13
1.5	Towards a process theory of the knowledge-based firm	14
2	**The Theoretical Framework**	**18**
2.1	The SECI model	18
2.2	A dynamic model of knowledge as the creating process	26
3	**Leading the Knowledge-Creating Firm**	**53**
3.1	The abilities that constitute *phronesis*	55
3.2	Exercising *phronesis*	65
3.3	Conclusion	66
4	**Vision and Driving Objectives: Values for the Common Good**	**70**
4.1	Eisai Co., Ltd	70
4.2	Honda Motor Co., Ltd	87
4.3	Implications	103
5	***Ba***	**107**
5.1	Mayekawa Manufacturing Co., Ltd	107
5.2	KUMON Institute of Education Co., Ltd	120
5.3	Implications	133

6	**Dialogue and Practice: Leveraging Organizational Dialectics**	**138**
	6.1 Seven-Eleven Japan Co., Ltd	138
	6.2 Ryohin Keikaku Co., Ltd – Muji	156
	6.3 Implications	170
7	**Dynamic Knowledge Assets in Process**	**174**
	7.1 YKK Corporation	174
	7.2 JFE Steel Corporation	185
	7.3 Implications	201
8	**Leadership: Fostering Distributed Excellence in the Organization**	**206**
	8.1 Canon Inc.	207
	8.2 Toyota Motor Corporation – Prius project	220
	8.3 Implications	231
9	**Conclusions**	**241**
	9.1 New developments	241
	9.2 Future challenges	244

Notes on Authors   246

Index   247

List of Figures and Tables

Figures

2.1	The knowledge-creating process: SECI model	19
2.2	A process model of the knowledge-based firm	27
2.3	*Ba* as shared context in motion	35
2.4	*Ba*: interpenetration of environment, structure, and agent	40
2.5	Organization as organic configuration of *Ba*: the knowledge ecosystem	41
3.1	Soichiro Honda watching motor cycle racing	59
3.2	Soichiro Honda drawing a sketch on the ground	61
4.1	Profits as a result of providing customer benefits	72
4.2	Empathizing with patients: Researchers indwelling with the elderly	75
4.3	The concept of a Knowledge Creation Department	82
4.4	Results of the Knowledge Survey	84
4.5	Honda's net sales and other operating revenue/operating margins	88
4.6	Honda's income/return on equity (ROE)	89
4.7	R&D system in Honda R&D Co., Ltd	100
4.8	LPL system to distribute practical wisdom (*phronesis*)	102
5.1	Mayekawa's business areas	109
5.2	Mayekawa as an organic configuration of doppos and blocks	111
5.3	Simplified model *of kigyouka keikaku*	115
5.4	Enrollment trends in the KUMON Centers	122
5.5	Self-learning system of the KUMON method	123
5.6	The process of learning in the KUMON method	125
5.7	Expansion of KUMON activities	129
5.8	Co-creation of *ba* between Mayekawa and a customer	134
6.1	The knowledge-creating process of Seven-Eleven Japan	139
6.2	Conceptual diagram of product positioning of Muji products	161
6.3	Muji advertisement: Muji bowl in a traditional Japanese *Shoin* room (left) and Zen garden (right) at Ginkakuji (Jishoji) temple in Kyoto	169
6.4	The view of Muji as an empty container	171
7.1	YKK management principles	176
7.2	Overview of the JFE group	187
7.3	Exchanging personnel at the JFE West Japan Works	194

7.4 JFE Holding's net sales and other operating revenue/operating margin — 198
7.5 JFE holding's debt outstanding — 198
7.6 Simplified model of the JFE merger — 200
7.7 YKK Cycle of Goodness and Spiral of Value Creation — 203
8.1 Canon's net sales and other operating revenue/operating margin — 208
8.2 Canon's debt outstanding — 208
8.3 Image of cell production system — 213
8.4 Canon's organic configuration of "multi-layers of *ba*" — 218
8.5 Various *ba* of the Toyota Prius project — 238

Tables

4.1 Number of *hhc* projects by division in 2005 — 77
6.1 Sales and profits of major convenience store franchisers in Japan — 140
7.1 Comparison of operating profit over sales (%) — 199
8.1 Distributed leadership at the Prius project — 222

Foreword: From the Management of R&D to Knowledge Management

Some contributions of Ikujiro Nonaka to the field of strategic management

Introduction

There is no one who in recent years has done more to shape the field of management than Ikujiro Nonaka. The body of work produced over the past two decades has been very influential, both in theory development and in management practice.

Ikujiro Nonaka is a University of California, Berkeley graduate who has been the Xerox Distinguished Professor at the Haas School of Business for almost a decade. But it is not his UC Berkeley lineage that causes me to give praise to a great colleague and friend. Rather, it is his deep insights into the management of the new product development process, and his efforts to help us understand the role of both leaders and middle management in knowledge creation.

Ikujiro Nonaka has become, for many of us, the new Peter Drucker – offering a deep intuitive understanding of management and the ability to see gaps and deficiencies in existing theories, as well as emerging trends which will impact on the nature of the business enterprise and its management. In what follows, I give a selective and perhaps personal history of the field of knowledge management, and try to position his important contributions.

The emergence of knowledge management

Were one to have stood here in Philadelphia 40 years ago and tried to talk to an audience about knowledge management, one would have received mainly blank stares. To get any traction, the conversation would have had to segue into the topic of the management of industrial research and development, as that was the rubric under which one could have a dialog about the new product development process. In 1967 Professor Edwin Mansfield at the Wharton School was only five to ten years into the very first serious scholarly research program aimed at improving understanding of technological innovation and the nature of corporate industrial research in the US (Mansfield, 1968). From that scholarship came a deep understanding of the nature of industrial research projects, the resource expenditures required at various "stages" in the R&D process, the nature of the technical and market risks involved with technological innovation, the role of patents in appropriability, the cost of patent workarounds, and the factors that drove variation in R&D spending within industries. By 1980, this work had become international in its flavor. Important studies were completed on international technology transfer and the global organization of research. This work showed that the role of offshore R&D at the time was mainly geared to adaptation to local markets.

Mansfield's work was both descriptive and analytical. Prescription was rare. Business and management scholars at that time puzzled over a limited set of matters such as how to get research from the laboratory to the market, the optimal scale of R&D activities, and the diffusion rates for new technologies. There was very little understanding around how firms generated new knowledge, other than through spending more money on R&D.

The 1980s and 1990s brought a sea change with respect to the innovation process and the nature and scope of competition faced by both domestic and multinational enterprises. This sea change required the development of new conceptual frameworks to understand innovation. Indeed, the study of R&D management gradually morphed into the study of knowledge creation and knowledge management. While Peter Drucker had begun talking about "knowledge workers" as early as 1959, and while Mansfield and others were tabulating the employment rolls of those engaged in science and technology, it was not until much later that the deep importance of skilled personnel and creative talent began to be fully appreciated, and the implications for the management of innovation explored.

Several developments occurred about this time which required a new view of the innovation process:

1. There was a belated recognition in both the scholarly community and in management circles that the creation and maintenance of competitive advantage was not just about scale and scope; it also required continuous innovation by the business enterprise. Hence, the management of intangible assets and of technical and business knowledge was critical to marketplace success in an open and competitive global economy.
2. Rapid economic growth outside the US, and especially in Japan and the Asian newly industrialized countries, meant that the sources of new knowledge were becoming geographically dispersed. Even before the 1980s, innovation had been significantly global. British and German companies had played major roles in the development of jet aircraft. Swiss, German, and British companies had for decades played major roles in the development of pharmaceutical and industrial chemicals. Swedish and Japanese companies had played significant roles in telecommunication and microelectronics. However, globalization amplified as the decades

of the twentieth century ticked by, and the outsourcing of components and assemblies accelerated. As the new millennium began, research and development was itself beginning to be outsourced offshore, especially in software development.
3. The development of low cost and high speed computer and information technologies for use at both the individual and the organizational levels enabled very large amounts of information to be collected, stored, analyzed, and transmitted, all at low cost. The introduction of personal computers, cell phones, PDAs, and web portals assisted connectivity and collaboration. These tools changed the speed and cost of information transfer and processing, as well as data storage. This in turn enabled new organizational processes and opened up knowledge transfer needs and opportunities. Vendors of computer equipment and "knowledge management" tools became active promoters of the need to better manage knowledge.

In the 1990s, Ikujiro Nonake burst onto this new landscape, with new frameworks to help managers understand how to develop intellectual capital and share knowledge inside the enterprise. His approach was informed by the study of new product development, particularly in Japan. At the time, Japanese firms, especially in autos and electronics, has achieved global pre-eminence in the development of new products and also in manufacturing. Nonaka's view was that:

> the traditional disciplines of management do not lend themselves to knowledge management and should be revised so that the knowledge based competence of a corporation can be managed effectively and efficiently. Traditional notions about strategy, human resource management, finance, and marketing should be re-examined and revised in order to manage knowledge for competitive advantage. (Ichijo and Nonaka, 2007: 7)

In particular, Nonaka has been offering an alternative knowledge-based theory of the firm. In what follows, I endeavor to review some of his contributions and indicate how they contribute to our understanding of management theory and practice.

The knowledge-creating firm and the SECI process

In the neoclassical theory of the firm managers are absent, except inasmuch as they are agents of the shareholders. Ikujiro Nonaka rejects this view and has put the manager back into the theory of the firm. He has advanced the proposition that firms differ not just because they have heterogeneous resources, but because managers have different visions of the firm's future. "Put simply, firms differ because they want and strive to differ. They evolve differently because they envision different futures – and structures to realize their futures" (Nonaka and Toyama, 2005: 2). In short, knowledge creation is about both ideas and ideals.

Nonaka also critiqued the view that firms are information processing machines. Rather, the firm should be seen more as a knowledge creating entity that reshapes the environment and itself through knowledge creation.[1]

In Nonaka's (and Toyama's) conception of the firm, individuals matter. They interact with each other to transcend their own boundaries and as a result change themselves. Subjective tacit knowledge held by an individual is externalized into objective explicit knowledge to be shared and synthesized. Tacit and explicit knowledge complement each other. Knowledge is socially created through the synthesis of the different views of different people.

Through Nonaka's SECI (socialization, externalization, combination, internalization) process, knowledge keeps expanding. The company's vision for what it wants to become and the products it wants to produce inspires the passions of employees. The company's vision for the future must go beyond goals defined by financial metrics alone.

The SECI process is a routine with a difference. It is a creative routine or "*kata*." Kata is about frame-breaking routines that lead to self-renewal. Good leaders help the organization to synthesize contradictions. They also provide vision, and the vision needs to be shared and accepted.

In short, Nonaka's theory of the knowledge-creating firm views the business enterprise as an entity to create knowledge by synthesizing contradictions. True breakthroughs occur by exploiting and managing what Kuhn (1996) would call a creative tension between the old paradigms and the new. Organizations don't just solve problems, they create and define them (Nonaka et al., 2000: 3). Leaders and individuals matter. Creativity requires their complementary skills.

The SECI process is the engine that drives Nonaka's knowledge-creating process. It is not just a mechanical process. Vision, organizational structure, incentives, corporate culture, and metaphors are all in some way implicated. Nonaka recognizes that employees, if they don't identify with the organization, won't necessarily help convert tacit knowledge to explicit knowledge. Leadership matters a great deal. Good leaders can accelerate the SECI process and make it more productive.

Middle-up-down management

Another major contribution from Ikujiro Nonaka is that he has resurrected the middle manager in management theory. In his framework, middle managers play a key role in knowledge creation inside the organization by bringing together the visionary ideas of top management and the chaotic realities of front line workers. Top management creates the dream, middle managers help deliver it by solving the tensions between where things are and where they need to be for top management's vision to be realized. Put simply, knowledge is created by middle managers. They are essential players in the SECI process.

With middle-up-down management, middle managers are not useless drones, as they are sometimes portrayed in the management literature. Nor have they been made obsolete by information technology. Indeed information technology allows the assembly of more information and data, thereby giving middle managers more tools. The middle managers play an integrating role, not unlike the system engineers in predivestiture AT&T.

Jiro's approach is both informed by and relevant to the context of innovation inside middle and large scale (Japanese) organizations. These contexts are not necessarily apt for understanding entrepreneurial start-ups; however, they are apt for helping to understand how the enterprise can sense and seize new opportunities. In that sense, Nonaka's framework is also a useful elaboration of how a large organization can build and maintain dynamic capabilities.

Phronesis (practical wisdom)

Another characteristic of the firm that is necessary for its continued success, according to Nonaka, is Aristotelian *phronesis*. Strategic analysis is unable to "specify exactly how a firm finds a way to create value by finding an unfilled customer need or a new way of fulfilling an existing need" (Nonaka and Toyama, 2007: 371). Part of the reason seems to be Nonaka's belief, which I share, that value creation begins when new opportunities are sensed.

However, strategic planning will not generally help the organization sense opportunities. Rather, "strategy is a process of creating the future" (ibid.: 372). Nonaka's view is compatible with Mintzberg et al.'s (1998) who sees strategy as something more than planning; strategy emerges, possibly alongside planning. Value flows from the ability to adapt to continuous change. Nonaka notes that Weick (2001) calls this process "just in time strategy."

Value creation relies on the ability of the organization to improvise a strategy to capture opportunities at the right moment. The firm can shape its environment while it is being shaped by it. Heterogeneity amongst firms in the same industry flows in part because firm's envision (sense) different futures, and respond differently to (seize) those opportunities.

The ability to understand and bring to fruition that which is considered good by individual customers in specific times and situations is what Nonaka calls *phronesis*. It is not purely a utilitarian concept, as practical wisdom also involves value judgments about what customers and society really want. It is a skill which needs to be distributed throughout the organization.

Reflections

There are a few concluding and comparative reflections I would like to make on Nonaka's important contributions to our understanding of the knowledge-creating firm.

I observe that Nonaka gives little attention to the allocation of resources to R&D. Such expenditures appear to be assumed. The core of the model is a set of processes which engage R&D personnel, designers, marketing and operations, as well as top management. There is a holistic view of innovation that transcends the typical R&D project-setting of much of the work in the innovation studies field.

The framework is different from, but compatible with, dynamic capabilities (Teece, 2007). With dynamic capabilities, the broader set of skills which establish and maintain competitiveness are sensing, seizing, and reconfiguring. This triad has obvious overlaps with SECI as sensing involves using tacit knowledge and making knowledge explicit so that there can be a basis for action. Seizing involves systemizing and applying explicit knowledge. It also involves combining co-specialized assets to exploit economies and address necessary complementarities; reconfiguring involves adapting to changing markets and competition as well as the internal growth of the enterprise.

The framework does not fully embrace the open innovation (Chesbrough, 2007) view of the enterprise. As Nonaka notes, "the firm needs to build its own knowledge assets, and that takes time" (Nonaka and Toyama, 2002: 998). In order not to be left behind, the firm must be good at synthesizing. This may not be all that different from the combinational capabilities stressed by Bruce Kogut and others. On the other hand, Nonaka's frameworks recognize the importance of shared context or place (what Nonaka calls "*ba*"). "*Ba*" need not be limited to a single organization – it can embrace suppliers, customers, governments, and competitors. Perhaps it's a half-open model of innovation. No doubt future writings will bring clarification.

The framework is overtly at odds with the neoclassical theory of the firm (with its emphasis on optimization against known constraints). The essence of Nonaka's enterprise is creativity and innovation. This involves quests and missions, not optimization. It has this in common with much of the new literature on the management of innovation. Nonaka clearly also rejects conceptualizations of the firm that portray the firm as a response to information problems (e.g., Coase, 1937; Alchian and Demsetz, 1972); he embraces instead a knowledge-based theory of the firm, in-line with Penrose (1959) (who sees the firm's planners as image creators rather than information processors), Fransman, and others.

Whether Nonaka's framework is a testable theory is yet to be fully flushed out. At present, the framework is not formulated with testable propositions articulated; but in my view it lends itself to hypothesis formulation and testing.

Testable propositions might be: (i) firms that follow the SECI process have higher R&D productivity; (ii) firms where top management has a clearly articulated knowledge vision perform better; (iii) large firms with engaged middle managers are more innovative; (iv) firms without widely articulated superordinate goals will perform poorly; and (v) strategic planning is neither necessary or sufficient for financial success. No doubt the battalions of doctoral students in the field can refine these hypotheses and begin the audacious and important task of empirical testing. I have high confidence that some statistically significant results will be forthcoming.

I'm not sure the framework fully captures network effects, entry timing, the role of industry architecture, and complementarities and co-specialization – yet these are all important to capturing value from innovation (Teece, 1986, 2006). Perhaps we should take Nonaka literally when he frames his theory around knowledge creating, and not knowledge commercialization. In this regard, I believe that the theory of knowledge creation needs to be married to a theory of knowledge utilization and value capture if it is to become a robust theory to guide management decisions.

The framework recognizes that individuals matter – although methodological individualism isn't especially deep in Nonaka's framework. The SECI process is anchored by middle managers, and is orchestrated by leaders. Socialization – transforming individual tacit knowledge to group tacit knowledge – is part of knowledge creation.

Nonaka's knowledge creating firm and the SECI process is very definitely Japanese. The emphasis is very much on group creativity, and listening to the advice of those with more experience. Age and experience give rise to wisdom, which also has a moral dimension. However, the approach does raise the question of whether Ikujiro Nonaka's leadership model embraces entrepreneurial leadership, and whether the SECI process is fully transferable to US and European contexts. I suspect it is for many large well-established firms; but it may not be fully transferable to new ventures.

So where does this leave my assessment? Note that some of Nonaka's writings have a deep philosophical bent, which makes it hard for some of us to understand. At the same time, this philosophical patina helps us better appreciate that management isn't just about the numbers.

I believe that Nonaka's work has deeply illuminated our understanding of innovation and new product development. His work helps us understand how great companies are led to create great products, and how management matters – not just top management, but middle management too. With the loss of two giants in management in the past 12 months – first Peter Drucker and then Alfred Chandler – we are all lucky to have a third giant amongst us. We want from Nonaka Peter Drucker's long years of productivity and insightful trend spotting; and we need from Nonaka Al Chandler's deep encyclopedic knowledge of the evolution of business in America, Europe, and Japan. We would of course like to see India and China added to the scholarly canvas too.

Jiro, you have more work to do! We salute you for your accomplishments, and we thank you for your contributions.

Remarks delivered in Philadelphia on the Occasion of the Award of the Booz, Allen and Hamilton Distinguished Scholar in International Management.

August 6, 2007

DAVID J. TEECE
*Director, Institute of Management,
Innovation and Organization
Professor, Haas School of Business
University of California, Berkeley*

Note

1. See Fransman (1994).

References

Alchian, A. and Demsetz, H. (1972). "Production, information costs, and economic organization," *American Economic Review*, 62: 777–95.

Chandler, A. (1990). *Scale and Scope: The Dynamics of Industrial Capitalism*. Cambridge: Harvard University Press.

Chesbrough, H. (2007). *Open Business Models: How to Thrive in the New Innovation Landscape*. Cambridge: Harvard Business School Press.

Coase, R.H. (1937). "The nature of the firm," *Economica*, 4 (16), 386–405.

Fransman, M. (1994). "Information, knowledge, vision and theories of the firm," *Industrial and Corporate Change*, 3: 713.

Ichijo, K. and Nonaka, I. (2007). "Introduction: Knowledge as competitive advantage in the age of increasing globalization," *Knowledge Creation and Management: New Challenges for Managers*. Oxford: Oxford University Press.

Kuhn, T.S. (1996). *The Structure of Scientific Revolutions*. Chicago: The University of Chicago Press.

Mansfield, E. (1968). *Industrial Research and Technological Innovation*. New York: WW Norton.

Mintzberg, H., Ahlstrand, B. and Lampel, J. (1998). *Strategy Safari: A Guided Tour Through the Welds of Strategic Management*. New York: Free Press.

Nonaka, I. and Toyama, R. (2002). "A firm as a dialectical being: Toward a dynamic theory of a firm," *Industrial and Corporate Change*, 11(5): 995–1009.

Nonaka, I. and Toyama, R. (2005). "The theory of the knowledge creating firm: Subjectivity, objectivity and synthesis," *Industrial and Corporate Change*, 14(3): 419–36.

Nonaka, I. and Toyama, R. (2007). "Strategic management as distributed practical wisdom (phronesis)," *Industrial and Corporate Change*, 16 (3): 372–94.

Nonaka, I., Toyama, R., and Nagate, A. (2000). "A firm as a knowledge creating entity: A new perspective on the theory of the firm," *Industrial and Corporate Change*, 9 (1): 1–20.

Penrose, E. (1959). *The Theory of the Growth of the Firm*. Blackwell: Oxford.

Teece, David J. (1986). "Profiting from technological innovation," *Research Policy*, 15 (6): 285–305.

Teece, David J. (2006). "Reflections on profiting from technological innovation," *Research Policy*, 35 (8): 1131–46.

Teece, David J. (2007). "Explicating dynamic capabilities: The nature and microfoundations of (sustainable) enterprise performance," *Strategic Management Journal*, 28: 1319–1350.

Weick, K.E. (2001). *Making Sense of the Organization*. Oxford, UK: Blackwell.

Acknowledgements

This book is the fruit of our quest to understand the significance of knowledge as a resource for business management. The quest began in 1982, when we presented research on innovation processes at Japanese companies to a symposium at Harvard Business School. During discussions at the symposium, we realized that these companies were not just processing information, but creating knowledge organizationally. This new perspective led us to pursue research on the process in which organizations create knowledge. The work resulted in a series of articles and books, including *The Knowledge Creating Company* by Nonaka and Takeuchi in 1995, in which we proposed the SECI model to describe a process of creating organizational knowledge from individual knowledge through human interaction. We believe the model had a big impact because it offered the new perspective that management is based on knowledge resources rather than physical resources, and on tacit knowledge in particular.

It has been 13 years since *The Knowledge Creating Company* was published, and the environment for firms has drastically changed. Firms in developed economies today, such as in the United States, Europe, and Japan, need to find a way to sustain growth through continuous innovation while also acting as responsible members of society. Firms in the so-called BRICs, or newly developing economies, have to find a way to set rules for managing their energies to realize sustainable development. In the era of the interconnected global economy, where activities in one country more immediately affect those of another, the firm has a responsibility to show that it has a reason for existing and a purpose in society other than for profit maximization. This calls for theory that can explain the process in which firms set their goals and implement strategies to achieve them.

In this book, we propose a new theory of the firm as a knowledge-based entity. Building on knowledge-creation theory and incorporating process philosophy, we re-examine the role of human beings in an organization from an ontological and epistemological point of view, based on the understanding that knowledge is a resource that is created by human beings in relationships. We argue that knowledge as a management resource cannot be understood without understanding the interactions of the human beings who create it. This is predicated on our view that each human being is a unique collection of experiences and is in a constant state of *becoming* to create a future through embracing and managing of contradiction. In this interactive process, individuals continually change themselves and their environments, and management of the firm becomes a reflection of this activity.

We chose the book title, *Managing Flow*, because our interest is in the *process* in which a firm creates its future by changing itself and its environment through knowledge creation. All things flow in continuous interaction and relation to each other, and this applies to human beings, firms, and the larger environment. Knowledge also flows and is in continuous change. Hence, all firms face the inherent contradiction of needing both stability and change to survive in the flow. We believe that the firms in our case studies overcome this contradiction by managing flow.

We would like to thank several people for their help in writing and editing this book. Professor David Teece at the Haas School of Business, University of California Berkeley, gave us tremendous intellectual stimulation and suggestions for building the theory through the many discussions we have had over the years. We also learned many things from discussions with Professor Dick Ellsworth of the Drucker School at Claremont Graduate University, where Ikujiro Nonaka currently serves as the first Distinguished Drucker Scholar. Hirotaka Takeuchi, dean of the Graduate School of International Corporate Strategy at Hitotsubashi University, gave us much support in conducting the research. Our research was also supported with funds from the Japan International Cooperation Agency (JICA). Working with JICA helped us to think about the role of the firm in society in other countries in Asia. In completing the book, we owe a lot to the following three persons. Susan J. Bigelow served as general editor, providing critical analysis and original writing to help us articulate the core concepts of the theory. Ayano Hirose translated the cases into English, contributing both writing and editing. Florian Kohlbacher helped us review the literature and contributed writing in part of one case. Critical comments, suggestions, and encouragement from professors Noboru Konno of Tama University, Tokyo, Georg von Krogh of the Swiss Federal Institute of Technology, Zurich, and Professor Zhichang Zhu at the University of Hull Business School, Hull, helped us make our way forward. Without these contributions, we would not have been able to finish the work. Finally, we thank Virginia Thorp and Emily Bown at Palgrave Macmillan for their efficient and supportive way of working with us. We extend our deepest appreciation to all.

Writing the book was itself an interesting and meaningful process of externalizing our own tacit knowledge accumulated through years of research. We learned many things about the potential and creativity of human beings. It is our sincere hope that the book communicates the essence of the knowledge-based firm to our readers.

May, 2008

IKUJIRO NONAKA
RYOKO TOYAMA
TORU HIRATA
Tokyo

Introduction: Why We Need a New Theory of the Knowledge-Based Firm

We are currently in the midst of great change, a condition which Lester Thurow (2003) called the third industrial revolution. It is a shift towards a knowledge-based economy, where knowledge is the most important resource, superseding the traditional management resources of land, capital, and labor (Drucker, 1993). This has stimulated more active discussion about the theory and practice of "knowledge management." Yet most firms still have serious difficulty understanding the knowledge resource, and we still lack an effective theoretical framework for understanding the operations of the firm in the knowledge-based economy.

In the world of business practice, knowledge management first took the form of heavy investment in information technologies (IT), an approach that turned out to be painfully ineffective, if not a downright failure. This was the result of the major misunderstanding that knowledge management is only about the efficient storage, transfer, and use of information, and the term "management" itself was misconstrued as the simple administration or supervision of information systems. In fact, knowledge is different in nature from information or physical resources, and unless we understand the essential nature of knowledge, we cannot share it or use it, and, more importantly, create it effectively.

In the academic world, the dominant management theories continue to be based on a view of the firm as a stable, atomic entity that operates according to a set of universal principles, and research is directed towards clarifying what these universal principles are and trying to make them more precise. While this theoretical approach can explain in hindsight why firms have been successful or unsuccessful in profiting from knowledge and protecting knowledge assets, it cannot effectively explain how firms create the particular knowledge that is unique to their practice.

To understand the paradigm shift to the knowledge society we have to make an equivalent paradigmatic shift in the way we think about knowledge and its management. Rather than conventional knowledge management, what we need is *knowledge-based management* derived from a comprehensive theory of the firm that explains the complex process of how knowledge is created and utilized organizationally through interaction with the environment. This book is our attempt to build such a theory. We believe it is unique in dealing with the subjective, process-relational, practical, and aesthetic aspects of knowledge creation and management in a holistic framework. In the knowledge economy, the firm doesn't just plan for the future, it continuously creates the future. What differentiates firms from one another is their vision of the future and their practical ability to act to realize that future by using their aesthetic sensibilities to create knowledge.

Since knowledge is created by human beings, we cannot theorize knowledge creation apart from human subjectivities, such as individual thoughts and feelings, ideas, hunches, and dreams. And we cannot understand how firms create knowledge that is unique to them unless we understand the role and function of human subjectivity in that process. The dominant theories of the firm have tended to avoid this side of management in the effort to pursue "good science," which is defined as excluding subjectivity in the search for objective "facts" and universal rules that govern how these facts connect. This neglect of the human factor has resulted in management theories that treat human beings as just another resource, like land and capital. They fail to account for the significance of human instinct and emotion and context in the management process, while bypassing altogether the human process of knowledge creation. As Christensen and Raynor (2003: 178) bluntly state: "Resources are usually people or things – they can be hired and fired, bought and sold, depreciated or built."

Our theory parallels the process-relational view of the firm, derived from the process philosophy of Alfred North Whitehead. This recognizes the ever-changing, interrelated nature of knowledge creation. It is contrary to the conventional view of knowledge as a self-contained substance and of the firm as a static, information-processing machine: the machine takes in information from the environment, processes it, and sets output levels to *adapt* to the environment. Such a view cannot conceptualize the actual process of knowledge creation. Knowledge is not a static substance or thing but an ever-changing process of interaction in an ever-expanding field of relations. So, to understand knowledge, we have to examine the process of human interaction and change. The theory of knowledge creation views knowledge as a dynamic process and the firm as a dialectical entity in active relationship with its environment. The existence of knowledge and of the firm is not independent of the environment but *in* the environment in relation with others, emerging in interaction with others, and reshaping itself and others and the environment through these interactions. Knowledge-creation theory is based on a view of the world and all things in it as in continuous "flow." The relationship with the environment is characterized by the active creation of change rather than the passive reaction to change. To understand this dynamic process, we need a theory of the knowledge-based firm that can explain how firms perceive and interpret realities, interact with various players both inside and outside the organization, and synthesize various subjective interpretations into a collective knowledge that becomes objectified and validated as a universal knowledge asset of the firm.

Our theory is practical in that it deals with real-life management practice as it is. Knowledge and its management must be concerned with the subjective time that is "here-now" and the value judgments made according to each particular situation or context. These situations cannot be distilled into a universal formula for the operation of the firm. They are simply the realities that each firm has to deal with. This book is not a "how to" of management practice. Rather, our aim is to theorize management not only as science but also as art, and build a theory that grasps the essential reality of life in the firm.

Since knowledge and its management is an accumulation of value judgments, management theory necessarily involves issues of aesthetics and ethics. In the era of the knowledge society, the question has shifted from one of quantity (how much should we produce?) to quality (what and why should we produce?). It is people's values and value-based decisions that determine the way of life in an organization, its *raison d'être*, and the value the organization creates. Hence, the knowledge-creating firm creates value by constantly asking and answering on a daily operational basis the human ontological question "why do we exist?" and the aesthetic question "what is good?". We draw on Aristotle's concept of *phronesis* – prudence or practical wisdom – to show how values, aesthetics, and ethics enter into the process of organizational knowledge creation. In our view, the essence of business is not about bettering the competition to maximize profit. It is about the relentless pursuit of the firm's own standard of excellence. Excellence emerges only with an unyielding commitment and practice to serve the common good of the company, its employees, its customers and other stakeholders, and the larger society, based on the company's own vision and values. Values are created through the continuous effort of doing one's best and creating knowledge and innovation to realize the future one has envisioned. Profit is a result of such value creation, not a purpose in itself.

While our theory draws on the philosophical works of Aristotle, Nishida, Polanyi and Whitehead, we are not concerned with philosophical speculation. We are neither philosophers nor interpreters of philosophy. Rather, we aim to integrate these philosophical ideas and concepts to develop a process theory of the knowledge-based firm. In Chapter 1, we discuss the nature of knowledge and why existing theories do not adequately explain the knowledge-creating process. In Chapters 2 and 3, we present the theoretical framework of the book. Subsequent chapters discuss the main elements of the theory and illustrate them with real-life examples from companies engaged in knowledge-based management. Both the theory and the practical examples emphasize the creative capabilities of the human being and how this leads to innovation on an organizational level. In the spirit of Whitehead's *Adventures of Ideas* (1933), we aim to contribute a theory of the firm in the knowledge society that integrates philosophy with the actual behavior and circumstances of knowledge-creating firms.

We use case study because the essence of process cannot be captured using the traditional scientific method of analyzing substance. Flyvbjerg (2006: 379) has pointed out that case study, precedent, and exemplars provide a method of research most appropriate to phronetic organizations, noting that "history is central to phronetic organization research [...] as narrative containing specific actors and events." The human being is a story-telling animal, and the notion of history is as fundamental as the notion of action (MacIntyre, 1984: 214, 216). Narrative is the act of description and explanation in story form, consisting of a beginning, middle, and end (Aristotle, 2002; Danto, 1985). It is an effective approach to understanding organizational complexity because it makes it possible to maintain contextuality, reflexivity, purpose and motives, and temporal sensitivity for grasping and explaining actuality (Tsoukas and Hatch, 2001). Furthermore, narrative is effective in explaining not only "why," by describing the causality between events, but also in explaining the dynamic question "how" – not "how to" but "how has this come to be" – because it is based on value judgment and practical reasoning about means-ends relationships. Practical reasoning occurs as a sequence of thoughts and actions toward a goal, establishing a means to realize that goal with the recommended action and performance of that action. Thus, the essential question in phronetic management concerns what action to take, and this can only be answered by the question, "What story or stories do I find myself a part of?" In this book, we have attempted to describe and explain the particular organizational events with interesting and focused narrative detail that allows us to abstract and articulate universals that explain the "how."

Knowledge is created through the synthesis of contradictions. The book title itself, *Managing Flow*, posits the seeming contradiction that if "all is in flux" we can manage nothing. The intention of Heraclitus was not to suggest that everything flows randomly without intention, but to stress the necessity of discerning and understanding the rules behind the flow, be it an attractor in chaos or a law of the universe. To do this, we have to be able to look at the process to grasp the essence of the actual. However, just seeing the essence is not enough. To survive in the constant flow of unceasing change and interrelatedness, we cannot be mere observers or reactors. We have to take *action* when facing a particular situation in order to change the flow. *Phronesis* is the ability to grasp the essence of a situation in process and take the action necessary to create change. This book is our attempt to build theory to explain how firms manage flow by exercising *phronesis* so they are able to continue to create knowledge in an ever-changing world.

References

Aristotle. (2002). *Nicomachean ethics* (S. Broadie & C. Rowe, Trans.). New York: Oxford University Press.

Christensen, C.M. and Raynor, M.E. (2003). *The Innovator's Solution: Creating and Sustaining Successful Growth*. Cambridge, MA: Harvard Business School Press.

Danto, A. C. (1985). *Narration and knowledge*. New York: Columbia University Press.

Drucker, P.F. (1993). *Post-Capitalist Society*. New York, NY: Harper Business.

Flyvbjerg, B. (2006). Making organization research matter. In S. Clegg, C. Hardy, T. Lawrence & W. Nord (Eds.), *The SAGE handbook of organization studies, second edition* (pp. 370–387). Thousand Oaks: SAGE publications.

MacIntyre, A. (1984). *After virtue: A study in moral theory* (2nd ed.). Notre Dame: University of Notre Dame Press.

Thurow, L.C. (2003). *Fortune Favors the Bold: What We Must Do to Build a New and Lasting Global Prosperity*. New York, NY: HarperCollins.

Tsoukas, H. and Hatch, N. J. (2006). Complex Thinking, Complex Practice: The Case for a Narrative Approach to Organizational Complexity. In R. MacIntosh, D. MacLean, R. Stacey and D. Griffin (eds.), *Complexity and Organization: Readings and Conversations*. Oxson: Routledge. 247–276.

Whitehead, A.N. (1933). *Adventures of Ideas*. New York, NY: Free Press.

1
The Characteristics of Knowledge

In this chapter, we discuss the nature of knowledge and how it differs from other resources. This will explain why we need a new theory of knowledge and its management. The issue of knowledge in theories of the firm has been addressed mainly in the resource-based view of the firm, where it has been treated as one of the important resources that lead to above average returns (Winter, 1987; Prahalad and Hamel, 1990; Nelson, 1991; Kogut and Zander, 1992; Leonard-Barton, 1992; Teece et al., 1997). The central questions in this view have been concerned with what kind of knowledge resources bring above average returns, how a firm can realize potential profit from the knowledge it owns, and how a firm can protect such knowledge as a resource. Although this view recognizes the dynamic capability of the firm (Teece et al., 1997; Teece, 2007), many of the arguments tend to focus on the utilization of resources, rather than on the dynamics in which the firm continuously builds resources through interaction with the environment. What is missing in the resource-based approach is a comprehensive framework that shows how various parts within and across organizations interact with each other over time to create something new (for a detailed critique see, e.g., Priem and Butler, 2001). The so-called knowledge-based view of the firm (Grant, 1996; Spender, 1996; Nonaka and Toyama, 2005) that grew out of the resource-based view tries to overcome this weakness. As Spender observed, "knowledge-based theory of the firm can yield insights beyond production-function and resource-based theories of the firm." He calls knowledge-based theory "a platform for a new view of the firm as a dynamic, evolving, quasi-autonomous system of knowledge production and application" (Spender, 1996: 59).

Further, in the resource-based view of the firm knowledge is treated as one of many revenue-generating resources. The intangibility of knowledge as a resource is well recognized and discussed, but this is still insufficient for understanding the role of knowledge in management and the process in which knowledge is created. The nature of knowledge as a management resource differs greatly from that of physical resources. The attributes of knowledge are such that it does not lose value when used by a large number of people, so it is a revenue-increasing resource; it transcends time and space, whether in the form of objects, writing, or traditions passed on through generations, so it is an infinite resource; it is produced and consumed simultaneously, making knowledge production and consumption interconnected and inseparable; and its value is born of the creation of new types and combinations of knowledge, creating value through recategorization (cf. Toffler, 1980; Romer, 1986; Bell, 1995; Nonaka and Takeuchi, 1995; Burton-Jones, 1999). In other words, while physical resources such as capital, raw materials, and manufacturing equipment can only be used by their owner and depreciate with use, knowledge does not decline in value, can be reproduced and shared by multiple users, and is broadly available. Moreover, the value of physical resources can increase when combined with knowledge.

Some of the characteristics of knowledge are common to information. Take for example the following features of information. It can be copied and is reproducible at low cost; it has externality, meaning its value depends on the number of people who possess it; it is indivisible or systemic rather than fragmented; its quality is uncertain, making its value difficult to determine; and its transaction is irreversible, such that, once someone knows information, it is impossible to "un-know" it (Stigler, 1961; Macho-Stadler and Pérez-Castrillo, 2001). However, knowledge is more than just a simple collection of information. The most prominent feature of knowledge, compared with physical resources and information, is that it is born of human interaction. It is not a self-contained substance waiting to be discovered and collected. Knowledge is created by people in their interactions with each other and the environment. Hence, to understand knowledge, we must first understand the human beings and the interactive processes from which knowledge emerges.

Because human interactions are the source of knowledge creation, knowledge is subjective, process-relational, aesthetic, and created in a practice. Our view of knowledge and the knowledge creation process is people-centered, action-oriented, and rooted in the philosophical traditions of Nishida in the East, and Aristotle, Polanyi, and Whitehead in the West, all of whom explain the nature of knowledge and human existence in an ever-changing, interrelated world.

1.1 Knowledge is subjective

For a long time, management scholars have been trying to exclude subjectivity from management in order to build an "objective" theory that can be applied universally to any situation that managers face. Despite this "rational" effort, it is impossible to completely exclude subjectivity from management. As Flyvbjerg (2001) points out, social science cannot be freed from subjective factors because it is about issues of subjectivity, such as values, contexts, and power. We have to deal with the issue of subjectivity in management, not only because it is impossible to exclude it, but because it is the very thing we have to examine to build a theory of the firm based on knowledge and its creation.

As stated in the previous section, knowledge is created by people in their interactions. Therefore we need to understand more about the nature of human beings to understand knowledge. What we should understand first is that human beings have different subjective viewpoints, and these differences are necessary for the creation of knowledge. Physical resources and information do not, and cannot, differ depending on their user. Organizational and information systems theories to date have tended to view the organization as an information-processing machine. In this view, the variances in human perspective and capability are considered weaknesses or "noise" to be overcome to run the machine efficiently. While mass production, assembly-line systems typical of the Ford factory, have been the foundation of modern capitalism, they are, in fact, systems trying to produce standardized products with the same level of quality regardless of the varying degrees of the capability of the labor. Information systems are developed in such a way that the information transmitted conveys the same meaning regardless of the sender or recipient. Bureaucracy defines authority and responsibility in a clear chain of command to ensure uniform operation, even though the people occupying these positions have varying levels of ability.

Management theories have tried to weed out these differences, but it is these differences in perspective and capability that give birth to new knowledge. The traditional Greek definition of knowledge as "justified true belief" suggests that knowledge is something that is objective, absolute, and context-free. This view of knowledge as a "truth" existing independent of us and beyond our experience, and at the same time waiting to be discovered by us, drawing our attention away from the essential meaning of knowledge. Rather, we should focus on "belief" as the starting point to an understanding of knowledge, because it is belief that is the source of all knowledge, and it is human beings who hold and justify such belief. Quoting St Augustine, Polanyi (1969) stressed the importance of belief for understanding knowledge: "Unless ye believe, ye shall not understand."

Knowledge cannot exist without human subjectivities and the contexts that surround human beings because "truth" differs according to who we are and from where we view it. Knowledge is information that is meaningful, and, as John Dewey observed, meaning is not a fixed quality associated with a specific event, but is the variety of possible ways in which the event might influence our future activities and our shared understanding (Dewey, 1916). It is subjectivity that interprets the significance of information. In other words, knowledge requires value judgment to be knowledge. New meaning is created and leads to the creation of new value precisely because subjective viewpoints differ from person to person, dependent on the context. Hence, we need a management theory that tackles head-on the issue of differences in individual subjectivity, such as how we view the world and what we value, rather than theory that treats human beings as replaceable parts of an organization and attempts to weed out human subjectivity as "noise" in the "machine."

Our view of knowledge is based on Michael Polanyi's concept of knowledge (Polanyi, 1958). Polanyi stands in opposition to the objective, analytical view that sees knowledge as something human beings obtain by analyzing the object as a thing that exists separately and beyond the self. He argues that human beings obtain new knowledge through their individual, active, and subjective shaping and integration of experience, which he calls "tacit knowing." For Polanyi, objective, analytical, explicit knowledge is a logic void of meaning that is no more than "knowledge without a knowing subject" (Popper, 1972), although he does not deny the significance of objective, explicit knowledge. Knowledge is first and foremost an issue of how we, as individuals, respond to reality and how we position that reality within ourselves. In other words, it is the issue of how we exist as individuals. It is in relation to this personal knowledge that we actively integrate our experiences and, in the process, create new knowledge and new meaning.

A few management scholars and practitioners have begun to point out that management theories have to be based on the experience of human beings, who have intentions and values (Yu, 2003). In the analysis of the environment or the firm's resources, Weick (1979) argues that an organization does not merely react to the environment but *enacts* the environment by interpreting it through a subjective framework. Contrary to the structuralist view, as in Michael E. Porter, Professor at Harvard Business School, reality does not have "objective" existence. It is *created* by an organization that perceives it as *real*. This means that organizations differ from each other not just in terms of the framework they use to *react* to a reality, but also in terms of the framework they use to *perceive* a reality, and that framework, in its turn, is formed through the interpretation of that reality. Such differences are the source of the different values that each organization can create.

1.2 Knowledge is process-relational

Our worldview is consistent with that of process philosophers such as Alfred North Whitehead.[1] In process philosophy, the world is an organic web of interrelated processes or series of events in which everything exists in relation. A human being is viewed as a complex spatiotemporal society of events (Jungerman, 2000). Although human beings tend to view the world as substance, nothing, not even the self, exists as self-contained substance through time. Rather, what we think of as substantial entities are momentary events occurring at a particular time and space. As Heraclitus said, *panta rhei*, all is in flux. "The river is not an object, but a continuing flow" (Rescher, 2003: 5). From this perspective, the tradition of science that views matter as substance is no longer valid. Instead, we must consider the interrelatedness and interdependence of entities in process and how the process changes as "flow" in space-time.

Theories and practice of knowledge management to date have treated knowledge as substance. Rather than substance, we should understand knowledge primarily as process, created and used in relation with the knowledge of other human beings who exist in relation with others. Even when knowledge seems to take a concrete or substantial form such as in a product, it embodies past processes of product development by the manufacturer and it *becomes* new knowledge when it is *experienced* by customers, which triggers another new knowledge-creation process. However, we do not deny the merits of comprehending knowledge as substance. To some extent, this is inevitable because it is generally beyond human capability to comprehend existence as pure process. We can only understand existence by abstracting or freeze-framing a part of the process as an understandable entity at a particular point in time. However, we should be aware that this abstraction that we engage in to make sense of the world is also an aspect of the process. As Whitehead warns, we should be careful not to fall into the trap of the fallacy of misplaced concreteness, that is, to misunderstand the abstracted process itself as concrete reality. Bearing this caution in mind, there are instances when we understand knowledge better in the form of substance and instances when we understand it better in the form of process. Like the process of noun-verb conversion, we obtain a better understanding of the actual in the process of conversion, rather than seeing it simply as either verb or noun.

Knowledge emerges from experience, which is a subjective process of feeling, and from grasping essence to interpret the world. We should note that the "subjective" in our meaning differs from that of traditional Western philosophy stemming from Descartes and Kant, where the subject is considered a stable center of the universe. In process philosophy, the subject is considered to emerge in interaction with the world, rather than the world emerging from the subject as in Kant (Whitehead, 1978).[2] Rather than existing as a self-contained, atom-like substance, we exist, or come into being, as an integrated process in the world through our interactions with that world.

In Whitehead's view, the human being as "actual entity" is a complex society of events occurring as a series of unique occasions or experiences. This means the "actual entity" is that which is experienced. What we have experienced up until the present moment creates what we are both at that moment and as we move into the next moment. The world is made up of events or occasions of experience rather than of *things* that endure; of entities constituted largely by their relations (Cobb, 2007: 571).[3] Every experience is momentary and has unique features. We unify present experience with our past experience and the experience of other individuals and we become a new self. In Whitehead's terms, "the many become one and increased by one." This unitary reality is a creation. In this regard, "to experience is to create, to create is to experience," and at "each moment I am a new experience" (Hartshorne, 2007: 77, 81). When we make a decision, we incorporate, directly or indirectly, all past experiences. With decision, the event is actualized and becomes an object that is available for experience by future entities. Our experiences are not self-contained substance, but a process involving relationships (Jungerman, 2000: 1–14). In short, we are what we have experienced so far, and how we relate to the world is based on who we are. In the process view, the human is always in the state of *becoming*, where *being* is but one aspect of *becoming*.

This does not mean that we are passive beings defined and formed by the environment. On the contrary, we are active beings seeking to define ourselves and redefine and reform the environment through our interactions with it. Our individual purpose defines our emergence in the world because it shapes how we relate to the world and create meaning, and how we form that world in turn. Heidegger stated that the future, which presents the potentiality-for-being, is the most important temporal dimension because as we project our future in the present, both our present exercise and past experience can be seen in a different light (Heidegger, 1962). For example, when a woman projects a future as a novelist, her past becomes a source of stories for her and "the world opens up as a place filled with fellow artists, audiences, publishers and so on. Her future and her past give rise to her present" (Polt, 1999: 97). Humans are purposeful beings who will act to realize their dreams and ideals – and these are beyond mere preference (Rescher, 2003). Human beings transform themselves and the environment that surrounds them by questioning their own existence, by asking the question: "for what purpose do we live?" Creativity plays a role in the relationship between human beings and the world. In the process of organizational knowledge creation, individuals interact with each other to transcend their own boundaries and realize their vision of the future. As a result, they change themselves and others, the organization, and the environment.

Process philosophy has been incorporated into the work of a few management scholars. Among them, Chia and Tsoukas (2003) propose a "rhisomic" model of organizational change based on the philosophy of Deleuze. Critically, they have grasped the essential weakness of existing models of organizational change as trapped in a Parmenidean intellectual legacy, "which implicitly elevates performance over change, discreteness over immanent interconnectedness, linear progress over heterogeneous becoming, and equilibrium over flux and transformation" (Chia and Tsoukas, 2003: 218).

In the process theory of the knowledge-based firm, we have defined knowledge as "a dynamic human/social process of justifying personal belief towards the truth" (Nonaka and Takeuchi, 1995: 58). Knowledge is created by people in their interactions with each other and the environment. It is a process in which the individual's subjective thoughts are justified through social interaction with others and the environment to become objective "truth." Justification of belief through social interaction is necessary and possible precisely because the meaning derived from a phenomenon varies with each individual. Knowledge is born of the multiple perspectives of human interaction. Through this multiple perspective one is able to see various aspects of a phenomenon in different contexts that, viewed together, approach an understanding of the essence or truth of the whole phenomenon in each. Hence, the knowledge-creating process is a social process of validating truth (Nonaka, 1994; Nonaka and Takeuchi, 1995). Recent philosophers, such as Richard Rorty, claim that group validation produces knowledge that is not private and subjective (Rorty, 1979). Knowledge is created socially in the synthesis of differing views held by a variety of people.

Hence, to understand knowledge, we have to understand the process in which humans are interrelated. In the substance thinking of conventional economic theory, where the person is viewed as *homo economicus*, individual relationships are defined in contracts for satisfying people's desires only in terms of the possession and consumption of goods and the accumulation of wealth. There, there is no community, only individuals who exist apart from others. A contract-based view of external relationships cannot grasp the social process of knowledge creation.

1.3 Knowledge is aesthetic

As stated earlier, knowledge is created from one's belief, and for a belief to become knowledge it has to be justified as truth. Polanyi says knowledge has to be judged in terms of its significance. Knowledge emerges in a series of value judgments. Such a judgment depends on how we perceive truth, goodness, and beauty. In other words, it depends on our aesthetic sense. As Whitehead states, "in the absence of Beauty, Truth sinks to triviality. Truth matters because of beauty" (Whitehead, 1933: 267). Further, he views harmonious experience as the most concrete form of beauty.

As Taylor and Hansen (2005) point out, historically, organizational theory has concerned itself primarily with the instrumental questions of efficiency and effectiveness. As the study of business aesthetics makes its way into the mainstream, attention is shifting from the purely instrumental to include the moral sphere and the aesthetic. Broadly speaking, "aesthetics is concerned with knowledge that is created from our sensory experiences" (Taylor and Hansen, 2005: 1212). Strati (2003) argues that aesthetic knowing is a form of knowledge that persons acquire by activating the specific capacities of their sensory-perceptive faculties to make aesthetic judgments in their day-to-day lives within organizations (Strati, 2003: 54). Since

Nietzsche (1967), there has been broad philosophical agreement on the notion of aesthetic knowing through experience and on the argument that other forms of knowing derived from rational thought depend on and grow out of aesthetic experience (Dewey, 1934; Gagliardi, 1996). Aesthetic knowledge offers fresh insight and awareness that may not be possible to put into words, but nevertheless enables us to see in new ways (John, 2001).

Aesthetic sense is necessary not only for judging the knowledge that is being created, but also for determining what kind of knowledge to create. We create knowledge according to our values and ideals. Firms differ from each other because they envision different futures and strive to realize them (Nonaka and Toyama, 2007). A firm's new opportunities, new markets, new technologies, or new business models are based on its vision of the future, and it is the values, ideals, and aesthetic sense of the organizational members that determine this vision. In other words, the ontology of the firm, which defines "how the organization should exist in the world," first sets the firm's vision of the future and then defines the firm's existence, the knowledge it creates, and, eventually, the environment in which it operates.

1.4 Knowledge is created through practice

Because knowledge is subjective, process-relational, and aesthetic, it can only be created in the actual practice of dealing with each particular situation. How we relate to others and how we perceive the world that surrounds us changes according to the situation, since both we and the world are in a state of constant change. Thus, there is a need for theory that explains the process in which knowledge is created in practice by individuals making value judgments according to their particular context and situations, through interactions with the particular environment that surrounds them.

In the effort to make business management a science, management theorists have sought universal rules by analyzing the firm's resources or the environment in which it operates. The particular problems that a firm faces in specific situations are viewed merely as initial conditions to be entered into the strategic planning formula. In this view it is believed that the right "rules" will naturally lead to the right answer and that these will optimize performance in the end. But the particular situations that practitioners face everyday are not just "initial conditions." They are the real problems that change day-to-day and have to be dealt with.

Some theorists have discussed the problem of viewing management as a set of universal rules (Mintzberg et al., 1998). They note that management is not formulated by analysis based on universal rules, but emerges through practices devised to deal with the particular problems that a firm faces. They argue that the source of competitive advantage is in the ability to adapt, in practice, to continuous change, rather than the ability to draw up a precise analytical plan (Chia, 2004; Whittington, 2004). In this view, management is more art or craft than science because it is based on insight, vision, and intuition, and relies on experience (Mintzberg, 2004). It is the social ability to improvise, which is the ability to react quickly and appropriately to an unpredictable situation (Weick, 2001). However, this analysis stops short of explaining the process in which such ability actually emerges in practice.

1.5 Towards a process theory of the knowledge-based firm

In the previous section, we have argued that the most important characteristic of knowledge is that it is created by human beings through their interactions and that, therefore, knowledge is subjective, process-relational, aesthetic, and created in practice. To understand knowledge-based management we need a theory of the firm based on this view of knowledge, in contrast to conventional management theories that view the firm as an indifferent, self-contained entity in which human subjectivities are "noise" that should be excluded from the analysis. The view of knowledge as subjective, process-relational, aesthetic, and practical action reveals how knowledge is continuously created to change the firm and the environment, and how this creative capacity develops in interactions with the environment. What defines the firm and the knowledge it creates is its practical ability to make value judgments in each particular situation to realize its vision of the future. This ability was described by Aristotle as an essential habit of mind that grasps the truth. It is the intellectual virtue he called *phronesis*, roughly translated as prudence, practical wisdom, and practical rationality.

The concept of *phronesis* is generally understood as the ability to determine and undertake the best action in a specific situation to serve the common good. *Phronesis* takes into account contextual circumstances, addresses particulars, and shifts aims in process when necessary (Eisner, 2002). *Phronesis* is concerned with values. It goes beyond analytical, scientific knowledge (*episteme*) and technical knowledge or know-how (*techne*) and involves judgments and decisions made in the manner of a virtuoso social actor (Flyvbjerg, 2001: 370). In other words, it is the high-quality tacit knowledge acquired from practical experience that enables one to make prudent decisions and take timely action appropriate to each situation, guided by values and ethics. *Phronesis* is acquired through the pursuit of excellence, the effort to perfect one's craft, which makes one a virtuous artisan (MacIntyre, 1984).

With *phronesis* as the synthesizing glue, we can explain the subjective, process-relational, aesthetic, and practical aspects of the knowledge-creating process in the firm. *Phronesis* synthesizes "knowing why" as in scientific theory, and "knowing how" as in practical skill, with "knowing what" as a goal to be realized. In the next chapter, we present a theoretical model to explain the dynamic process of organizational knowledge creation and how it develops the creative capacity called *phronesis*.

Notes

1. Leading exponents include Heraclitus, Leibniz, Bergson, Peirce, James, and Whitehead (Rescher, 2000). Here, we focus exclusively on Whitehead. Whitehead himself does not use the term "process philosophy," but "philosophy of organism."
2. Hence, Whitehead uses the term "superject" instead of "subject" (Whitehead, 1978).
3. Process philosophy has an affinity with Buddhist philosophy and Taoism. In Buddhism, it is said that "everything arises out of multiple other things and has no existence apart from its relations to them" (Cobb, 2007: 568). According to Hartshorne, Whitehead's doctrine has the merits of Buddhist thought but with considerably more clarity and consistency as it draws on more than a thousand years of intellectual process and the stimulus of Western science and logic (Hartshorne, 2007: 82).

References

Bell, D. (1995). *Chishiki Shakai no Shogeki* [The impact of intellectual society]. Tokyo: TBS Britanica.
Burton-Jones, A. (1999). *Knowledge Capitalism: Business, Work, and Learning in the New Economy*. New York, NY: Oxford University Press.
Chia, R. (2004). "Strategy-as-practice: Reflections on the research agenda," *European Management Review*, 1, 29–34.
Chia, R. and Tsoukas, H. (2003). "Everything flows and nothing abides: Towards a 'Rhisomic' model of organizational change, transformation and action," *Process Studies*, 32 (2), 196–224.
Cobb, J.B., Jr. (2007). "Person-in-community: Whiteheadian insights into community and institution," *Organization Studies*, 28 (4), 567–88.
Dewey, J. (1916). *Democracy and Education: An Introduction to the Philosophy of Education*. New York, NY: Free Press.
Dewey, J. (1934). *Art as Experience*. New York, NY: GP Putnam's Sons.
Eisner, E.W. (2002). "From episteme to *phronesis* to artistry in the study and improvement of teaching," *Teaching and Teacher Education*, 18, 375–85.
Flyvbjerg, B. (2001). *Making Social Science Matter: Why Social Inquiry Fails and How it Can Succeed again* (S. Samplson, Trans.). Cambridge: Cambridge University Press.
Gagliardi, P. (1996). "Exploring the aesthetic side of organizational life," in S.R. Clegg, C. Hardy and W.R. Nord (eds.). *Handbook of Organization Studies*. London: Sage.
Grant, R.M. (1996). "Toward a knowledge-based theory of the firm," *Strategic Management Journal*. 17:109–122.
Hartshorne, C. (2007). "The idea of creativity in American philosophy," in H.F. Vetter (ed.). *Hartshorne: A New World View*. Cambridge, MA: Harvard Square Library, pp. 66–83.
Heidegger, M. (1962). *Being and time*. (J. Macquarrie and E. Robinson Trans.). Malden, MA: Blackwell Publishing.

John, E. (2001). "Art and knowledge," in B. Gaut and D. Lopes (eds). *The Routledge Companion to Aesthetics*. London: Routledge, pp. 329–52.

Jungerman, J.A. (2000). *World in Process: Creativity and Interconnection in the New Physics*. Albany: State University of New York Press.

Kogut, B. and Zander, U. (1992). "Knowledge of the firm, combinative capabilities, and the replication of technology," *Organization Science*, 3 (3), 383–97.

Leonard-Barton, D. (1992). "Core capabilities and core rigidities: A paradox in managing new product development," *Strategic Management Journal*, 13, special issue, 111–25.

Macho-Stadler, I. and Pérez-Castrillo, J.D. (2001). *An Introduction to the Economics of Information: Incentives and Contracts*, tr. R. Watt. Oxford: Oxford University Press.

MacIntyre, A. (1984). *After Virtue: A Study in Moral Theory*, 2nd edn. Notre Dame: University of Notre Dame Press.

Mintzberg, H. (2004). *Managers not MBAs: A Hard Look at the Soft Practice of Managing and Management Development*. San Francisco: Berrett-Koehler Publishers.

Mintzberg, H., Ahlstrand, B., and Lampel, J. (1998). *Strategy Safari: A Guided Tour through the Wilds of Strategic Management*. New York, NY: Free Press.

Nelson, D.B. (1991). "Conditional heteroskedasticity in asset returns: A new approach," *Econometrica*, 59 (2), 347–70.

Nietzsche, F. (1967). *The Will to Power* (W. Kaufmann & R.J. Hollingdale, Trans.). New York, NY: Random House.

Nonaka, I. (1994). "A dynamic theory of organizational knowledge creation," *Organization Science*, 5 (1), 14–37.

Nonaka, I. and Takeuchi, H. (1995). *The Knowledge-Creating Company*. New York, NY: Oxford University Press.

Nonaka, I. and Toyama, R. (2005). "The theory of the knowledge-creating firm: Subjectivity, objectivity and synthesis," *Industrial and Corporate Change*, 14, 419–36.

Nonaka, I. and Toyama, R. (2007). "Strategic management as distributed practical wisdom (phronesis)," *Industrial Corporate Change*, 16 (3), 371–94.

Polanyi, M. (1958). *Personal Knowledge: Towards a Post-Critical Philosophy*. Chicago: University of Chicago Press.

Polanyi, M. (1969). *The Logic of Tacit Inference, Knowing and Being*. Chicago: University of Chicago Press.

Polt, R.F. (1999). *Heidegger: An Introduction*. Ithaca, NY: Cornell University Press.

Popper, K.R. (1972). *Objective Knowledge: An Evolutionary Approach*. Oxford: Oxford University Press.

Prahalad. C.K. and Hamel, G. (1990). "The core competence of the corporation," *Harvard Business Review*, June–July.

Priem, R.L. and Butler, J.E. (2001). "Is the resource-based theory a useful perspective for strategic management research?" *Academy of Management Review*, 26 (1), 22–40.

Rescher, N. (2000). *Process Philosophy: A Survey of Basic Issues*. Pittsburgh: University of Pittsburgh Press.

Rescher, N. (2003). *Rationality in Pragmatic Perspective*. Lewiston, NY: Edwin Mellen Press.

Romer, P.M. (1986). "Increasing returns and long-run growth," *Journal of Political Economy*, 94: 1002–37.

Rorty, R. (1979). *Philosophy and the Mirror of Nature*. Princeton, NJ: Princeton University Press.

Spender, J.C. (1996). "Making knowledge the basis of a dynamic theory of the firm," *Strategic Management Journal*, 17, winter special issue), 45–62.
Stigler, G.J. (1961). "The economics of information," *The Journal of Political Economy*, 69(3), 213–25.
Strati, A. (2003). "Knowing in practice: Aesthetic understanding and tacit knowledge," in D. Nicolini, S. Gherardi, and D. Yanow (eds). *Knowing in Organizations: A Practice-Based Approach*. New York, NY: M.E. Sharpe.
Taylor, S.S. and Hansen, H. (2005). "Finding form: Looking at the field of organizational aesthetics," *Journal of Management Studies*, 42 (6), 1211–31.
Teece, D.J. (2007). "Explicating dynamic capabilities: The nature and microfoundations of (sustainable) enterprise performance," *Strategic Management Journal*, 28(13), 1319–50.
Teece, D.J., Pisano, G., and Shuen, A. (1997). "Dynamic capabilities and strategic management," *Strategic Management Journal*, 18(7), 509–33.
Toffler, A. (1980). *The Third Wave*. New York, NY: Morrow.
Weick, K.E. (1979). *The Social Psychology of Organizing*, 2nd edn. Reading: Addison-Wesley.
Weick, K.E. (2001). *Making Sense of the Organization*. Malden, MA: Blackwell.
Whitehead, A.N. (1933). *Adventures of Ideas*. New York, NY: Free Press.
Whitehead, A.N. (1978). *Process and Reality*, corrected edn. New York, NY: Free Press.
Whittington, R. (2004). "Strategy after modernism: Recovering practice," *European Management Review*, 1, 62–8.
Winter S.G. (1987). "Knowledge and competence as strategic assets," in D.J. Teece (ed.). *The Competitive Challenge: Strategies for Industrial Innovation and Renewal*. Cambridge, MA: Ballinger. 159–184.
Yu, F.T. (2003). "A subjectivist approach to strategic management," *Managerial and Decision Economics*, 24, 335–45.

2
The Theoretical Framework

As discussed in the previous chapter, knowledge is created in the dynamic interaction between subjectivity and objectivity. Knowledge emerges from the subjectivity of actors embedded in a context and is objectified through the social process. Knowledge is created from the synthesis of thinking and action by individuals interacting both within and beyond organizational boundaries. This knowledge then forms a new praxis for interaction that becomes the basis for generating new knowledge again, through the knowledge-creation spiral.

In this chapter, we offer a framework that captures the dynamic process of knowledge creation. First, we examine the SECI model of knowledge creation (Nonaka, 1991, 1994; Nonaka and Takeuchi, 1995), which illustrates the continuous process of conversion between subjective, tacit knowledge and objective, explicit knowledge.

2.1 The SECI model

New knowledge is created from the continuous interaction of tacit and explicit knowledge. Polanyi asserted that all knowledge is either tacit or rooted in tacit knowledge, and that no knowledge is completely explicit (Polanyi, 1969). According to Polanyi, human awareness deepens through the continuous process of alternating between tacit knowledge integration and recomposition. However, he did not theorize the process of knowledge creation. While we agree with Polanyi on the importance of tacit knowledge, we believe that it is the process of interaction between tacit and explicit knowledge that is the source of knowledge creation. Tacit and explicit knowledge do not exist separately, but rather, like the visible and submerged portions of an iceberg, form a continuum. Because they are opposite in character, they interact in a creative, dialectical process that is dynamic. It is within this dynamic that new knowledge is born.

The process is illustrated in our model, which consists of four modes of knowledge conversion: socialization, externalization, combination, and internalization (see Figure 2.1). We call this the SECI Model (Nonaka and Takeuchi, 1995). In the SECI spiral, the tacit knowledge possessed by individuals is externalized and thereby transformed into explicit knowledge so it can be shared with others and enriched by their individual viewpoints to become new knowledge. It is then internalized once more by a larger number of individuals as a new, richer, subjective knowledge that becomes the basis for starting another new cycle of knowledge creation.

As stated in the previous chapter, knowledge is process, not substance. The term "conversion" might be misunderstood as implying that knowledge is substance that can be processed in the same way as physical resources. As Whitehead observed, human thinking ascribes substance to process by taking a snapshot of events in progress at a particular time and place as a way to grasp and constitute meaning. We must first stabilize the process to be able to grasp what it is. "According to Whitehead, we freeze processes into entities, precisely in order to makes sense of the fluid 'real' world" (Bakken and Hernes, 2006: 1602) in the form of substance. Substance in the form of nouns and products, as in Baird's *Thing Knowledge* (2004), is a crystallization of the process at that particular context of time-space. The SECI model is our framework or snapshot of the process of continuous creation of knowledge, which enables analysis and evaluation to make sense of the flowing real world.

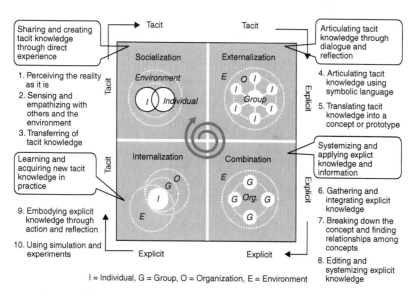

Figure 2.1 The knowledge-creating process: SECI model

The SECI model is a process model. It starts with socialization of individuals, moving to externalization within groups, combination in organizations, and then back to internalization in individuals. The important point is that individuals, groups, and organizations are themselves transforming in the knowledge-creating process since they themselves are collections of processes.

2.1.1 Socialization

In this stage, individual tacit knowledge is shared through shared experiences in day-to-day social interaction to create new tacit knowledge. Since tacit knowledge is difficult to formalize, and is often specific to a particular time and space, it can only be shared among individuals through shared, direct experience that engages the five senses. Usually, this requires that the individuals spend a great deal of time together or live in the same environment. The apprenticeship system is a typical method of transferring knowledge through socialization, where the apprentice observes the master to acquire know-how through imitation and practice. On-the-job training in corporations is a variation of this.

By living in a particular world or *indwelling*, individuals share and accumulate tacit knowledge about the world around them. For example, one can have tacit knowledge about customer preferences through one's own experience as a customer. In socialization, individuals embrace contradictions rather than fighting them, absorbing knowledge in their social environment through action and perception. One can share the tacit knowledge of customers, suppliers, and even competitors by empathizing with them through shared experience. In the end, this will help to reach a new awareness. At the Honda Motor Co. Ltd, the fundamental way of thinking about product development is encapsulated in the phrase *"sangenshugi"* or the "three *gen* principle." These are: *genba*, go to the actual place; *genbutsu*, know the actual situation; and *genjitsu*, be realistic. The implications of the three *gen* principle are that one indwells with the product in *gen* or the "here-now", in the place where it is made and used, to understand its essential reality. Thus, when Honda was developing its Fit vehicle, initially envisioned for the European market, the development team first went to Europe to observe, with their own eyes, the types of cars in use in each region and how they were being used. The team did not solicit the views either of Honda people working in Europe or others knowledgeable about the European market, because they wanted to observe directly and without preconceptions the various situations of users. As one team member said:

> If all we had wanted was research data, we could have gotten it from our people in Europe. But we experienced for ourselves the weight and bulk of carrying six bottles of wine by hand; we pushed our own shopping

carts in the supermarkets, experiencing the hot or cold weather at the time just like the local people. The goods they loaded into their cars varied by country, but we learned that regardless of the country, it was important that a full shopping cart of items fit into the car. By observing reality at the frontline and thinking with your body, you can dispel the image that you've created in your head. (Ui, 2002: 52)

What the Honda team tried to obtain through experience was not just concrete information about cars, but the feel of the place, which could only be obtained by experiencing the customers' lifestyles and values. Socialization is not mere observation, but a process in which the observer abandons preconceived beliefs to enter into a shared feeling of experience with the other that precludes subject/object relations, so the self and the observed are experienced as one. In the socialization process, the method of seeing is phenomenological, which means that one suspends one's preconceived values and ideas, or puts them in brackets, in order to observe reality simply as it is (cf. Husserl (1962) for the concept of *"epoché"* or "bracketing"). Taking this a step further, socialization is a process of sharing knowledge with others through commitment, discovery, and action.

To express the present fact or state, we will use the words "reality" or "actuality." These words are similar in denoting the state of happening, or real existence. The difference is in cognition versus action. According to Kimura (1994: 29), the word "reality" originates in the Latin *"res"* meaning substance. Thus, reality was an existing substance or object that could be observed. "Actuality" originates in the Latin *"actio"* meaning action or activities. Thus, it is a situation in progress that can only be grasped by those committed to and dwelling in the actual, situated experience. Actuality is sensed with the five senses and through empathy with others. The most committed of experiences comes closest to truth. This means actuality is the origin of knowledge creation.

What is important is the quality of the experience and the degree to which one is able to observe while in the experience. As a concept this is partly explained by Dewey's notion of undifferentiated "primary experience," in which both active and passive experience are a necessary whole; and by William James's and Kitaro Nishida's notion of "pure experience," which exists prior to the division of subject and object. In Whitehead, the term "concrescence" describes the feeling or direct experience of the present. "Realness is felt before it is known. Knowing comes later" (Brown, 2003: 51). In all of these descriptions, "experience" is the unified and concrete whole, where interpretation or analysis by the "self" or consciousness has not yet taken place. It is an active, pre-state or "magma" of knowledge from which the interactions between subjectivity and objectivity emerge in the process of making sense of the experience.

2.1.2 Externalization

Tacit knowledge gathered in the socialization stage is articulated as explicit knowledge through the externalization process. While socialization fosters the creation of knowledge through direct sharing of the same experience, in externalization the tacit knowledge of individuals is made explicit through language, images, models, and other modes of expression, and then shared with the group.

Examples of externalization would be a research and development team trying to explain a new product concept, or seasoned frontline workers trying to describe their tacitly understood skills in a training manual or in a proposal to management for *"kaizen"* or improvements in efficiency. It is not unusual to be unaware of the tacit knowledge one possesses because it has no visible form. Through externalization, the firm can communicate acquired knowledge more efficiently to many more people than it can if the knowledge remains tacit. Furthermore, new realizations occur in the process of externalizing, and new knowledge is created once again.

As discussed in the previous chapter, we must stabilize the process to be able to grasp what it is. Stated in terms of language, it is like converting verb into noun. "We make nouns *from* processes in order to make sense *of* processes" (Bakken and Hernes, 2006: 1601). Hence, abstraction of action into substance is not apart from actual experience at a particular time and space, but is inextricably linked with that experience.

In externalization, the tacit knowledge of individuals is verbalized in a two-way dialogue and further conceptualized and refined. Plato in Greek philosophy stressed the importance of dialogue as a process of clarifying the essence of things in the search for new knowledge. The philosophical foundation of the externalization process is idealism, since tacit knowledge is articulated by pursuing the essence of one's subjective experience to realize one's ideal. Here, dialogue is an effective method to articulate one's tacit knowledge and share the articulated knowledge with others (Nonaka, 2005).

Verbalizing an ideal and a prototype is a process of conceptualizing an invisible essence (for a detailed discussion of prototypes, see Rosch, 1978). Externalization at its finest produces what Husserl termed *"eidetic intuition,"* or insight into an essence. It is the ability to grasp and express an *eidos* or a form and therefore requires great strength of imagination. This is the essence of poetry. As Whitehead said, philosophy is like a poem (Whitehead, 1925). It must be founded on universal principles and at the same time explain the most particular and concrete facts. A poem is a contradictory art that utilizes words which, themselves, are abstracted and thus apart from the "actual," but which yet also express the "actual" itself, beyond the limitations of one's experience of it.

Where deductive or inductive logical analysis fails to arrive at a viable form of expression to make hidden concepts or mechanisms accumulated in tacit knowledge more explicit, the more effective tools are metaphor and analogy, the abduction of hypotheses, and the use of narrative to give context and time frame. Metaphor is particularly useful in dialogue for converting tacit knowledge into explicit knowledge because it enables us to understand and experience one thing in terms of another (Lakoff and Johnson, 1980). For example, the development team for the Honda Accord van used the metaphor of the falcon, the fastest bird, to conceptualize their prototype, using the image of the falcon's wings to express speed and the falcon's body to express solidity. When the product development team at Matsushita Electric was working on its fast-drying centrifugal-force dryer, it used the metaphor of the Chinese wok to come up with the technical concept of a wok-shaped dryer drum rotating in quick, short bursts (Nonaka and Katsumi, 2004).

2.1.3 Combination

Explicit knowledge is collected from inside or outside the organization and then combined, edited, or otherwise processed to form more complex and systematic sets of explicit knowledge. We call this the combination stage. The new explicit knowledge is then disseminated across the organization. Specific examples of this are revealed in the design process for transforming a concept into concrete product specifications, or in the analysis of combinations of data for specific meaning. The combination mode can also include the "breakdown" of concepts. Breaking down a concept, such as a corporate vision, into business or product concepts creates further systematic, explicit knowledge. Here, contradictions are solved through logic. In the combination stage, rationalism, or scientific methodologies based on logical analysis originating from the time of Descartes, are the most useful for combining, editing, and breaking down explicit knowledge. But tracking, evaluating, and combining information costs money, and combination is not just the simple combining of existing knowledge. The whole is not only the sum of its parts. The validity of the knowledge whole created varies widely depending on how well it has been organized. Creative use of computerized communication networks and large-scale databases can facilitate this mode of knowledge conversion. Many IT-based methods of knowledge management are aimed at improving this stage through more efficient and effective combination.

Unprecedented developments in information technology and the Internet in recent years have made it possible for large numbers of people to gain access to information simultaneously in real time, in a free exchange of explicit knowledge unfettered by constraints of time and space. Open-source computer programming of the type that resulted in the creation of the Linux operating system illustrates how hundreds or even thousands of people can cooperate in a digital network, sharing program source codes and working in parallel to speed up development, reducing the costs of knowledge creation drastically. Such large-scale, open development combines a broader pool of human resources and knowledge more efficiently and effectively compared with development behind closed doors by a small group of people. Open-source cooperation is based on the sharing of a standardized algorithm, a logical procedure following a finite set of operating principles, that enables participants to combine their explicit knowledge faster and more effectively.

2.1.4 Internalization

Explicit knowledge is created and shared throughout an organization and is converted into embodied, tacit knowledge during the internalization process. Reading books, for example, can put us in contact with a vast array of explicit knowledge. However, it is rare that we are able to make that explicit knowledge our own just by reading it. It is only by reflecting on it or putting it into practice that we are able to connect it to our own context or to the knowledge that we already possess, and grasp its essential meaning. This stage can be understood as praxis, where knowledge is applied and used in practical situations and becomes the basis for new routines. Thus, explicit knowledge, such as product concepts or manufacturing procedures, has to be actualized through action, reflection, and practice so it can be internalized as knowledge of one's own. For example training programs can help trainees to understand themselves as part of their surrounding organization. By reading and reflecting deeply on information in documents or manuals about their jobs and the organization, trainees can internalize this explicit knowledge and enrich their own tacit knowledge. Explicit knowledge can also be embodied through simulations or experiments.

Internalization is not only a process of putting something into practice, but of doing so with a conscious mind. Consciousness is critical, as there is a wide gap between conscious and unconscious implementation. Organizational psychologist Donald Schon (1983) has described those people who have the ability to communicate things that are hard to explain as "reflective practitioners." Internalization is the process by which we reflect on the meaning of what we have learned from our actions and simultaneously convert explicit knowledge into skill that can be used at will. This process is explained by the philosophy of pragmatism, particularly by Dewey's notion of "secondary experience" as intellectual experience that includes reflection, and by Schon's idea of "reflection in action."

When the thoughts and skills of the individual are crystallized into a performance, a product, or service, and marketed, the ensuing interaction with customers, competitors, cooperators, other regions and other entities further enriches the tacit knowledge of the entire group. This enriched, internalized tacit knowledge can be shared again through socialization, starting another new SECI process.

Product development provides a useful illustration of how the SECI process of knowledge creation works. Tentative and partial knowledge based on an individual's values and experiences becomes justified when it is shared by members of the organization. It then becomes the basis for the creation of new knowledge, perhaps in the form of a new product. The knowledge embodied in the product then goes through the justification process again in the marketplace, and knowledge is created anew in the synthesis of views from the market.

It is important to understand that movement through the four modes of knowledge conversion proceeds in a *spiral*, not a circle. Knowledge creation is a future-creating activity, and the future is always open. Nothing is stable. Human beings keep changing or *becoming* by exercising their creativity in choosing among alternatives to create their future. In the spiral of knowledge creation, interaction between tacit and explicit knowledge is amplified through the four modes of knowledge conversion. The spiral increases in scale as knowledge moves up through the ontological levels: from individual to individual (socialization), from individual to group (externalization), from group to organization (combination), and from organization back to the individual (internalization). Knowledge created through the SECI process can trigger a new spiral of knowledge creation, expanding horizontally and vertically as it moves through communities of interaction that transcend sectional, departmental, divisional, and even organizational boundaries. Knowledge can be transferred beyond organizational boundaries, and the knowledge of different organizations interacts in the knowledge-creating process (Badaracco, 1991; Nonaka and Takeuchi, 1995; Inkpen, 1996). Knowledge created by an organization from the dynamic interaction of individuals can trigger the mobilization of knowledge held by outside constituents such as consumers, affiliated companies, universities, and distributors. For example an innovative new manufacturing process may bring about changes in a supplier's manufacturing process, which, in turn, triggers a new round of product and process innovation in the original organization. Another example is in the articulation of the tacit knowledge of customers, which they themselves have not been able to articulate. A product can elicit this tacit knowledge as customers give meaning to the product by purchasing, adapting, using, or not purchasing it. A product can also trigger changes in customer behavior in terms of their worldview and may eventually reconstruct their environment. Customer reactions are then reflected in the innovation processes of the organization, starting a new spiral of knowledge creation. Organizational knowledge creation is a never-ending process that upgrades itself continuously.

With the progress of IT and various knowledge management tools, it is now possible to externalize tacit knowledge into explicit knowledge and combine explicit knowledge more efficiently and effectively. However, just relying on externalization and combination will not give a firm sustainable competitive advantage. Katsuaki Watanabe, the president and CEO of Toyota Motor Corporation, emphasizes the importance of the "spiral up of tacit knowledge and explicit knowledge," and warns of the danger of stopping at the point of externalizing tacit knowledge. He says that unless tacit knowledge is grown, explicit knowledge will not grow either. If one relies only on explicit knowledge such as manuals or expert systems and does not think about the tacit knowledge behind it, there will be no progress and the knowledge base will be lost in the end (Watanabe, 2008).

This dynamic process is a dialectical movement between tacit and explicit knowledge, and between creativity and efficiency. The interaction between tacit and explicit knowledge is a continuous movement back and forth between the subjective and the objective. In the subjective viewpoint, the self plays a central role as observer. In the objective viewpoint we step back from the self to observe. It is a continuous round trip between the subjective and the objective, moving toward the truth.

2.2 A dynamic model of knowledge as the creating process

As discussed in the previous section, new knowledge is created in the conversion between tacit and explicit knowledge. Ideally, knowledge increases in quality and quantity in an upward spiral as it is transferred from the individual to the group and from the group to the organization. However, the quality and quantity of knowledge can also plummet in a downward spiral if one of the four modes in the SECI process is impeded for any reason.

Research to date shows that several enablers are required to rotate the SECI spiral effectively and link it to an organization's collective strengths (von Krogh, Ichijo and Nonaka, 2000). These enablers are related to how an organization motivates the people who create knowledge, and how relationships are created between people, and between people and the environment.[1] We offer a dynamic model based on the SECI process that illustrates the various factors that enable knowledge creation (Nonaka, Sasaki, and Senoo, 2004; Nonaka, Toyama, and Konno, 2004; Nonaka and Toyama, 2005b). The model is dynamic because it involves the continuous synthesis of abstraction and actual experience in particular contexts to build universal theory. Contradiction is, therefore, inherent. There is always a gap or contradiction because it is impossible to convert all tacit knowledge into explicit knowledge, and it is equally impossible to convert all explicit knowledge into practice. While there are a wide variety of enabling factors, only the company that organically combines and synthesizes these factors to continuously and consistently create knowledge can truly actualize knowledge-based management.

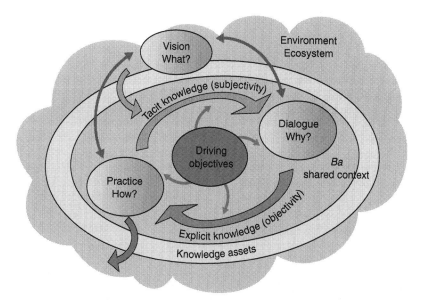

Figure 2.2 A process model of the knowledge-based firm

Figure 2.2 shows the model of a knowledge-creating firm, where knowledge is created through dynamic interaction with the environment. The model consists of seven basic components: the SECI process of *dialogue* and *practice*; the *knowledge vision* and *driving objectives*, which gives direction and energy to the SECI process; *ba*, a space-time nexus for the SECI process to occur; *knowledge assets*, which are the inputs and outputs of the SECI process; and the *environment*, as an ecosystem of knowledge and multilayered *ba*.

2.2.1 Knowledge vision

The knowledge vision of a firm arises from confronting the fundamental questions: "Why do we exist?" "What do we want to be?" and "Why do we do what we do?" This kind of questioning revisits the founding knowledge of the company that is its domain and mission. As explained in the previous chapter, firms differ because they envision different futures. The possibilities for attaining a future praxis are manifested at each organizational level by answering the live question "why do we exist?" (Heidegger, 1962). A knowledge vision, which is based on the company's aesthetic value of truth, goodness, and beauty, defines the kind of future that the company imagines for itself and determines the collective ideal mission and domain. It gives the firm direction and focus concerning the knowledge to be created beyond its existing products, capabilities, organizational structure, and markets. Therefore the vision determines how the firm evolves in the long term.

In conventional economics, the ultimate goal of any company is to maximize profit. But in the knowledge society, a corporate vision has to transcend such an objective and be based on an absolute value that goes beyond financial matrices (Collins, 2001). For example, Drucker (1954) states that the only valid definition of business purpose is to create a customer. The Honda Motor Co. has the stated objective of "providing the customer with a good car." While this objective ultimately leads to the realization of profit, it is not just a method for maximizing profit. It is an absolute objective in itself, articulating the kind of entity that Honda wants to be. It is this kind of knowledge vision that gives the knowledge spiral its direction. It transcends the boundaries of the company's products, divisions, organization, and even markets, and determines the essence of its knowledge base, which remains focused on the absolute value that the company is pursuing and the direction in which it is evolving.

The vision, or how the company defines its reason for existence, also questions the commitment to the future of the people in the organization, and inspires the intellectual passion of organizational members so that they are encouraged to create knowledge. The nobleness of the cause is intrinsically motivating and helps raise the moral aspirations of organizational members (Ellsworth, 2007). It also defines a consistent value system for evaluating and justifying knowledge created in the organization. As we stated earlier, the social process of knowledge justification is essential for combining individual, subjective knowledge with the knowledge of others to create new knowledge. For this justification process to occur, the company must have its own coherent standard of truth, goodness, and beauty.

A knowledge vision is an ideal picture of how we want to be, and that ideal is not something that is easily achieved. Rather, as a vision of the future that gives meaning to the past and present, it is a self-transcending objective aimed at getting the organization to surpass itself. In the pragmatic idealism of Nicholas Rescher, even an objective that appears impossible to attain plays an important role in moving thought and action in the direction of the ideal. The values and ideals inherent in the objective provide a sufficient rational basis for maximizing the effect of substantive human action (Rescher, 1994).

The Japanese company Olympus has a vision of "Social-IN," which, they claim, is a more advanced concept than "Market-IN", since it is based on the idea that Olympus would create values based on the viewpoints of people who live in the society. At Honda, value is expressed absolutely as "the joy of buying, the joy of selling, and the joy of creating" rather than just beating the competition. As we will explain in Chapter 4, the Japanese pharmaceutical company Eisai has a knowledge vision that articulates absolute value as "human health care" (*hhc*). This vision sends the message to every individual in the organization that Eisai embraces a coherent value that seeks to understand and share the feelings of patients and their families and to contribute to patients' well-being, rather than simply trying to please the doctors and pharmacists who are Eisai's direct customers. Everyday, employees at all levels of the company ponder anew the question of what it means to contribute to the well-being of patients and their families and what Eisai can do as a pharmaceutical company to deliver this. This mobilizes the collective wisdom of all employees in knowledge-creating activities designed to help patients and their families.

As we will see in Chapter 6, the management philosophy of Seven-Eleven Japan is articulated in its two principles "adaptation to change" and "getting the basics right". These express *how the company wants to be* as a knowledge vision, although such visions are not easily achieved. Indeed, it is precisely because this is difficult to achieve that both head office and the stores can continue to push the knowledge-creation process forward as they thoroughly cover the basics while trying to respond to ongoing changes in customer demand. A knowledge vision is just a set of empty words if it doesn't have a context and a concrete mechanism for turning the vision into reality. While the philosophy of rational idealism asks why we seek truth, beauty, and goodness, pragmatic idealism requires the addition of practice to achieve the ideal.

2.2.2 Driving objectives

A firm has to have a mechanism for realizing its knowledge vision. The mechanism is a concrete concept, goal, or action standard that connects the vision to the knowledge-creation process of dialogue and practice. We call this the *driving objective* because it drives the knowledge-creation process.

The driving objective is the engine that drives the entire organization. It synthesizes contradictions to create knowledge through questioning that seeks the essence of things. The Japanese motorcycle company Suzuki expressed its driving objective for a new scooter as "1cc = 1,000 yen." This was not meant to express a preference for cost cutting but was a concrete articulation of their vision "to sustain a Japanese manufacturing heritage." This objective galvanized the entire company to create knowledge by asking the question: "What is the essence of a scooter?" To realize the objective of 1cc per 1,000 yen it was not enough for Suzuki engineers to ask simply, "Is this part or task really necessary to the making of a scooter?" Instead, what they had to ask was: "What is a scooter to begin with?" Such fundamental questioning led to the development of the *Choinori* scooter based on a new approach of adding to a bare frame only the most essential parts, rather than removing all unnecessary parts from an existing model (Nonaka and Katsumi, 2004). "The most essential parts" did not mean they were low cost. On the contrary, the new scooter was built with costly, state-of-the art technologies, but these ultimately reduced costs by cutting the total number of parts needed. The firm's driving objective became the engine that motivated departments such as research and development, manufacturing, and marketing to transcend their differences by focusing on the same goal.

At Japan-based Canon Inc. the driving objective is "cash flow." Despite this clear financial focus, it is not the typical financial management objective aimed at securing profit. As a concept, cash flow can be understood easily and grasped intuitively and is therefore a good mantra for motivating all individuals in the organization to think about how they can make the sources of competitive advantage at the company evident in their own work: how they can contribute in their work to improving cash flow in the organization. It is not enough to just do your best in your own job. To do your job well in a way that improves cash flow overall, you have to consider many more factors in various time frames and in relation to the work of others.

Reaching for the unattainable ideal serves the regulative function of driving the organization in a way that prevents it from contending with imperfect realities and keeps it moving closer to the ideal, even if only by one step at a time (Rescher, 2003). Looking at the case of Seven-Eleven Japan in Chapter 6, the driving objective of this convenience store chain is to "cut opportunity losses." This means that when customers come to a store they must be able to find what they want, or the store has lost an opportunity to sell them something. Unlike losses resulting from unsold inventory, opportunity losses are invisible. Seven-Eleven has refined a cycle of creating, testing, and implementing hypotheses about daily stock requirements, making it possible to provide customers with what they want, when they want it. Although this is a clear, concrete goal, there is no clear end to it, nor is there a clearly defined route to achieving it. It can only be achieved through relentless pursuit of knowledge creation. Hence, it keeps driving the organization in a positive direction toward unattainable perfection and excellence. This is Seven-Eleven's source of sustainable competitive advantage.

In summary, to foster organizational knowledge creation it is not enough just to set the vision and driving objective. Slogans are meaningless if they are not shared and accepted by all members of the organization. To achieve this, leaders in the organization have to facilitate constant dialogue and practice to "evangelize" the knowledge vision and driving objectives across the organization.

2.2.3 Dialogue and practice (dialectic of thought and action)

As discussed previously, knowledge is created in the continuous round trip between subjectivity and objectivity. In concrete terms, the synthesis of contradiction that occurs in this process is achieved through dialectical thinking and action. Dialectical dialogue is a very powerful method of converting tacit knowledge that is difficult to express into the formal language of explicit knowledge in the stage of the SECI process called externalization. Dialogue is also effective in the creation of new explicit knowledge by linking, deepening, and refining the variety of existing explicit knowledge in the combination stage of SECI. Practice lays a foundation for the sharing of tacit knowledge through shared experience (socialization), and also enables the embodiment of explicit knowledge by reconnecting it to a specific act or context and fleshing it out as tacit knowledge (internalization). Through continuous dialogue and practice, process is converted into substance in order to be grasped and understood, and a new process emerges out of this substance. In other words, it is a continuous process of verb–noun conversion.

Knowledge creation is guided by the synthesis of contradictions (Nonaka and Toyama, 2002, 2003). The world is filled with contradictions; duality is an essential aspect of reality. By accepting duality and synthesizing it, one can move beyond simple dichotomies of "either or" and create new knowledge to resolve contradiction.

Synthesis is achieved through dialectical thinking and action (cf. Hegel, 1969). Here, the concept of "soft dialectic," which embraces contradiction and incorporates conflicting viewpoints as interrelated processes, can be used along with Hegel's dialectic of thesis, antithesis, and synthesis. In the soft dialectic typical of Eastern philosophy, everything is viewed in context and in relation to the whole rather than in terms of absolute truth (Nisbett, 2003). The metaphor of the world as a jigsaw puzzle is an insightful illustration. The world is a puzzle consisting of various pieces that recognize and accept the existence of various other pieces, all of them trying in a pluralistic manner, to find the best position or match. Each and every piece has, in their very existence, a common ground that is the basis of the whole world. Unlike the process of negation in Hegelian dialectics, each piece of the world puzzle admits the variety and diversity of all the other pieces, recognizing and having the common relationship residing at the base of the whole, and achieving self-recognition in relationship to the whole. Thus, the shape of each piece in the puzzle is determined by the shapes of the surrounding pieces and the relationships among the pieces. The pieces maintain their interrelationships in a certain frame and thereby structure the whole. In knowledge creation, the whole and its parts are not external to each other but are internally related, and new solutions are found in the contradictions in those relationships.

Dialogue: the synthesis of thought

The dialectical synthesis of knowledge occurs through dialogue that pursues essence, or the essential meaning of things. While something may appear to be a paradox and contradictory, by pursuing its essence and creating new contexts that incorporate the viewpoints of others through dialogue we abandon our preconceptions and are able to find new resolution in the contradictions.

In dialogue one shares an existential context in the form of deep thoughts and emotions. Martin Buber's (1958) I–Thou relationship is a direct, highly personal form of reaching out to others and opening oneself to them.

Dialogue is effective as the basis for knowledge creation because it enables us to understand that there are views that are different from our own, and it helps us to accept and synthesize these views. To engage in effective dialogue we must be able to articulate our thoughts in a way that is simultaneously assertive and modest. Knowledge creation requires the kind of dialogue where we pit our views against those of others in a way that makes us realize that we make mistakes and which pushes us to a higher plane in pursuit of the essence of things. This kind of dialogue requires an open mind and the ability to be both self-assertive and modest.

What matters more in such dialogue is not the form of logic it takes but the meaning it creates. For example, using the simple, logical form of the syllogism we can reach the conclusion that "Socrates dies" from the premises that "every human is mortal" and "Socrates is human." But despite its correctness, this logical form cannot add any new meaning to the original premises. On the other hand, if we pursue inquiry about the essence of being human or the essence of death, we may reach the new conclusion that "Socrates as a thought is immortal."

At Toyota, dialogue that pursues essence is encouraged in daily operations at every organizational level through a practice called "Ask why five times." It is not so difficult to come up with a reason that explains why you do a certain thing. However, when you are asked again and again to explain the basis for the reason you came up with, you inevitably start to think more about the essential reason behind your thought or action. Such existential dialogue enabled Toyota to synthesize many contradictions in a way that goes beyond mere compromise. For example, the contradictions between cost and quality are no longer contradictions at Toyota. By pursuing the essence of both quality and cost, it has created a new system of manufacturing that makes it possible to lower costs by raising quality.

At Honda, contradictions are resolved dialectically by asking questions at three levels of inquiry. The first is level A, and is a question about design specifications. For example, many contradictions have to be resolved to reach a final decision on engine specifications, such as fuel efficiency versus power, or safety versus speed. Engineers at Honda try to resolve such contradictions not by finding the best balance or compromise between contradictory conditions, but by asking a question at the next higher level. The second level is called A0 and is a question about concepts. Engineers go back to the question of what is the concept of the engine for the particular car, and then decide on the specifications necessary to realize that concept. If the contradictions cannot be resolved with A0 level questions, then inquiry moves to the third level, called A00. This is an existential question related to why or what for. For example, what is Honda's purpose in making that particular car? Or, even, why does Honda exist in the first place? "What is your A00?" is a commonly heard refrain in daily operations at Honda.

It may seem that such questions are too philosophical and have little to do with business. However, deciding on specifications without thinking about essential purposes only leads to a choice among existing options. To come up with a new solution that goes beyond the contradictions one has to answer existential questions that pursue essence based on one's own values and the values of the organization.

Practice: synthesis of action

In knowledge creation, contradictions that cannot be resolved solely by logical analysis are synthesized through practice. By practice, we do not only mean action. Knowledge-creating activities require us to think deeply about the essential meaning of our actions and their outcomes while we are performing them, and to use the results of this reflection to correct them. This process of "reflection in action" is emphasized by Schon (1983), who was influenced by Dewey's concept of pragmatism. Of course, this self-reflection incorporates thorough, logical analysis, and in the continuous movement between subjectivity and objectivity one's subjective experience grows into knowledge through action and practice (cf. MacIntyre, 1984; Bourdieu, 1998). This viewpoint is a metacognition that synthesizes the viewpoints of insiders and outsiders.

Contradictions that cannot be solved through objective analysis alone can be solved by synthesizing subjective views and intuition accumulated through practice. To do this, one has to discard preconceived notions to observe and experience the particular reality as it is. For example, when the Japanese beverage company Suntory developed its new sports drink, DAKARA, the members of the development team discarded the concept for the first product derived from logical analysis of the market at the time. That concept was a sports drink that "gives the working man that one extra push." The development team started by going out into the field to observe how sports drinks were being consumed. After thorough observation they determined that most consumers were tired and in need of healing rather than "one extra push." This finding led to the new concept of "a drink to preserve your health when life gets tough" (Nonaka and Katsumi, 2004).

To reflect on action is to think hard about the essential meaning of an action and its outcome so as to revise it in process. In the case of Seven-Eleven Japan, it is not enough to use sales data to check whether a hypothesis is right or wrong. Employees are encouraged to think thoroughly about why an action was right or wrong so they can produce more effective hypotheses next time. Reflection on action combines logical, objective analysis with subjective observation and experience. It is a metacognitive understanding that synthesizes insiders' and outsiders' viewpoints. Through dialogue and practice, subjective views are objectified to expand the knowledge resource.

2.2.4 *Ba*

Knowledge depends on context because it is created in situated action (Suchman, 1987). Knowledge is also context specific in that it depends on a particular time and space (Hayek, 1945). Therefore the knowledge-creating process is necessarily context specific in terms of time, space, and relationships with others. Knowledge cannot be created in a vacuum, but it needs a place or context that enables the interpretation of information to construct meaning and become knowledge.

In the theory of organizational knowledge creation, Nonaka and his associates have identified the importance of the physical or virtual space of interaction called *"ba,"* that is, the context for knowledge creation (Nonaka and Konno, 1998; Nonaka et al., 2000; Nonaka et al., 2001). It is a shared context in motion, that is "an existential place where participants share contexts and create new meanings through interactions" (Nonaka and Toyama, 2003: 7). Like a Petri dish for the cultivation of ideas, the *ba* is a temporary container for creative interaction guided by a particular worldview that establishes the conditions for participation. It can also be seen as a "shared space for emerging relationships" (Nonaka et al., 2006: 1185) among individuals, and between individuals and the environment.

This notion of *"ba,"* which translates literally into English as "place," "space," or "field," originates in the concept of *"basho,"* developed by the Japanese philosopher Kitaro Nishida (1926; cf. Abe, 1988; Heisig, 2001; Wargo, 2005) and later refined by Hiroshi Shimizu (1995). While it has been applied frequently in the Japanese management literature (e.g. Itami et al., 2000; Shimizu et al., 2000; Yamada, 2005; to mention but a few), it should not be mistaken as a uniquely Japanese way of thinking. The importance of place in human cognition and action has been identified by Western philosophers dating from Plato's *"chora"* or "receptacle" as a place of genesis and Aristotle's *"topos"* as the place of physical existence, to Heidegger's *"Ort"* as the place of human existence (Nonaka and Toyama, 2003; Nonaka, 2005; cf. Casey, 1997, for a philosophical history of the concept of place).

We define *ba* as a shared context in motion, in which knowledge is shared, created, and utilized. *Ba* is the foundation for knowledge-creating activity. It is the place where one engages in dialectical dialogue and practice to implement the vision and driving objectives of the firm. Although it may be easier to see *ba* as a physical space, such as a meeting room, it should be understood as a multilevel interactive state that explains the *interactions* that occur at specific time-spaces. In Japanese, the word *ba* refers not just to a physical place, but a specific time and space, or the character of relationships in a specific time and space. *Ba* can emerge among individuals, in working groups, project teams, informal circles, temporary meetings, in virtual space such as email groups, and at the frontline in contact with the customer. *Ba* is an existential place where participants share their contexts and create new meanings through interaction. In *ba*, participants share their and build "here-now" relationships. Moreover, the right context and the right timing for interaction are crucial for knowledge creation. A typical informal *ba* can be found in a gathering of people in a pub, where participants talk in a friendly and open atmosphere about their "here-now" concerns in a way that sometimes triggers insight and resolution.

We define *ba* as a shared context *in motion* because *ba* are constantly moving and changing. Participants bring their own contexts to a *ba* and interact with others and the environment, changing their own contexts, the context of the *ba*, and the environment (see Figure 2.3). New knowledge is created through such change in meanings and contexts. In *ba*, the future, or the knowledge to be created, is connected with the past, or the contexts that participants bring to the present, in an emerging relationship that shapes a shared context and perspective. In Whitehead's terms, this is the state of "prehension," or the way in which what was "there-then" becomes "here-now." It is the way in which one momentary experience incorporates its predecessor (Cobb, 2007). The emerging relationship in *ba* is in continuous change as the contexts of individual members in the *ba* change. Hence, a *ba* has the quality of the "here-now." *Ba* synthesizes clock time or *chronos* with timely time or *kairos* (Rämö, 2004a, 2004b), making it possible to take action that is timely according to the particular situation. While *ba* makes it possible for participants to share time and space, *ba* itself transcends time and space.

Ba as a shared context means that subjective views are understood and shared in their *relationship* with others. Modern science has been based on the premise that subjectivity cannot be shared between individuals. Consistent with this premise, some see knowledge creation mainly as an individual activity. For example, Simon (1991) said, "All learning takes place inside individual

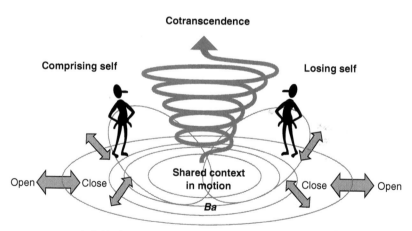

Individual contexts are shared in *Ba*, and the shared context and individual context expand them selves through such interaction

Figure 2.3 *Ba* as shared context in motion

human heads" (p.125), while Grant (1996) views knowledge creation as an individual activity, and the primary role of firms as applying existing knowledge. As we have argued, subjectivities have to be shared in interaction in order for knowledge creation to occur. *Ba* supports such sharing and synthesizing of subjectivity. To participate in a *ba* is to get involved and transcend one's own limited perspective. *Ba* is a place of cotranscendence, requiring an intentional self-involvement with the other persons, object, or situation by transcending subject/object distinctions to experience the immediate present directly (Nishida, 1960). Nishida states that the essence of *ba* is "nothingness." This does not mean that nothing exists in *ba*. It means that in *ba*, one exists in relationship with others rather than in the atomistic sense of absolute self. In *ba*, one can lose oneself to be open to others. In a similar vein, others have observed the loss of self-consciousness in flow (Csikszentmihalyi, 1990; Nakamura and Csikszentmihalyi, 2002). Through relationships in *ba*, one can see oneself in relation to others and embrace others' views and values, enabling an understanding and sharing of subjective viewpoints. In that sense, *ba* is what Whitehead called *"extensive continuum,"* a field of interconnected and interrelated events in space-time. Such interrelatedness is latent (Cooper, 2005) and emerges through *ba*. In *ba* the individual's internal viewpoint resonates in tandem with the external viewpoint of the other, or the group. It is not an either/or proposition, but both/and. *Ba* supports such sharing and synthesizing of subjectivity, which is necessary for knowledge to be created. In Chapter 5 we show how interactions with customers and the sharing of tacit knowledge in *ba* enabled the employees of Mayekawa Manufacturing Ltd to grasp the latent needs and wants of its customers and realize them from multiple perspectives.

It is in *ba* that knowledge emerges for the first time through a shared perception and cognition of mutual existence. According to Kozlowski and Klein (2000), emergence is bottom-up and interactive as well as shaped and constrained. Informal patterns of interaction – social interaction that transcends formal boundaries and work flows – shape emergence. *Ba* thus fosters and generates emergence, most specifically the emergence of knowledge and a fundamental understanding. In a sense, this leads to the building of the social capital of an organization.

Although the concept of *ba* has some similarities with the idea of "communities of practice" (Lave and Wenger, 1991; Wenger, 1998), there are important differences. While a community of practice is a place for learning, *ba* is a place for knowledge creation. While the boundaries of a community of practice are firmly set by the task, culture, and history of the community, the boundaries of *ba* are fluid and can change quickly. While membership in a community of practice is fairly stable, and it takes time for a new member to learn about the community and become a full member in practice, membership in *ba* is not fixed; participants come and go. *Ba* is created, functions, and disappears according to the needs of the participants.

Whereas members of a community of practice belong to the community, the participants in *ba* relate to the *ba*.

Factors behind the activating knowledge emergence in ba

A *ba* does not necessarily arise because someone has provided the space and gathered the people. There are a variety of features of *ba* that must also be present in order for the *ba* to be an effective place for knowledge creation.

First, a *ba* must be self-organized and possess its own intention, objective, direction, and mission. Without intention, there is no way to direct the energy of the *ba*, and chaos will rule. A firm's knowledge vision can set direction, but each *ba* must establish actual work objectives and clarify intention, and middle management must be at the center of this activity. With such intention, the state of "one-to-many and many-to-one" is achieved as individual intentions synthesize and the intention of the *ba* becomes the intention of each participant.

Second, *ba* participants must establish a shared sense of purpose. The sharing of subjective, tacit knowledge and values helps develop intersubjectivity. Relationships are open-minded and empathetic and participants extemporaneously create a space of shared meaning that transcends individual subjectivity. When contexts are shared in motion within a *ba*, participants do not observe from a self-centered standpoint but reposition themselves in terms of their relationship with others.

Third, a *ba* requires participants with different types of knowledge. *Ba* is a shared situation or time-space nexus where the various subjective and historical dimensions of the members of the *ba* intersect and their heterogeneous experiences interact. New knowledge is created in the synthesis of subjective viewpoints, and is enriched by the diversity of contexts and perspectives. However, just bringing it all together is not enough to trigger the creation of new knowledge. The principle of emergence is the process whereby a structure comes into existence from a set of conditions, and that structure is beyond the expected outcome. It is a process of generating a whole that has a different quality from the mere sum of its parts (Polanyi, 1966). Hence, emergence can only be realized in *ba* that supports simultaneous and spontaneous interaction of the parts and the whole. A process must develop for the sharing of views and contexts based on pre-established shared objectives. But this takes time and the active involvement of participants, and the more their contexts vary, the less efficient they are in knowledge creation. Effectively synthesizing the contradiction between creativity and efficiency is an issue of *ba* management.

Fourth, while a *ba* needs boundaries, these must be open. The possibilities for expanding contexts are limitless, so meaningful context-sharing requires boundaries. Therefore leaders should protect a *ba* from external contexts so that it can grow its own context, especially when the *ba* is aimed at creating the kind of knowledge that is outside the current norms of the organization.

It is often difficult for participants of a *ba* to see and accept the need to bring in contexts that are different from the one being shared in that *ba*. But the boundaries must be permeable, in keeping with the dynamic nature of *ba*, where shared context is in continuous change as individual participants come and go. Furthermore, the boundaries of a *ba* should be open to allow for connection with other *ba*. It is the important task of the leader who is outside the *ba* to find and build connections among the various *ba*. Legitimate power in an organization can be used effectively to protect the boundaries for cocooning, while ensuring they remain permeable.

Fifth, a *ba* requires the commitment of participants. Indeed, commitment is the basis of human knowledge-creation activity (Polanyi, 1966) and the source of energy driving interaction within the *ba*. Knowledge is formed when *ba* participants are both committed to the *ba*'s objectives and willingly engage in its events and activities, even contributing their own, personal time and energy. For this, the *ba* needs a process of mutual understanding, trust, and respect, as well as shared perceptions and active empathy. This accords with Naess (1987, 1989), whose concept of "self-realization" refers to the process of infinitely comprising subject and object through empathy, leading to unification.

Individuals who have accumulated the tacit knowledge that is the source of an organization's sustained competitive advantage are highly valuable. However, there may be occasions when such persons choose not to externalize their expertise, fearing it will reduce their relative value to the company. For example, a top salesperson may not want to share his or her exclusive know-how with others, fearing they might catch up. The cultivation of a sense of security among participants developed through trust and caring relationships, and shared commitment to the *ba* and the organization, countervails this tendency.

Research into the motivating factors behind knowledge creation reveals the importance of endogenous or internal, intrinsic motivation as a source of competitive superiority (Osterloh and Frey, 1997). While money is the archetypical exogenous or extrinsic motivator, typical endogenous motivators are personal aspiration and achievement. While exogenous motivation tends to be more effective over the short term in comparatively routine work, it can also produce the negative effect of work not getting done if there is not also some form of endogenous incentive over the long term. Therefore exogenous motivation does not necessarily encourage externalization of tacit knowledge in highly valued employees. In fact, in the worst case, extrinsic motivation might "crowd-out" (ibid.) intrinsic motivation and subsequently stall the SECI engine.

For endogenous motivation to function in an organization, the following conditions must be satisfied: creativity must be demanded; the work must be complex but broad in scope and require extensive knowledge; and tacit knowledge must be shared and created. In work of this nature, the existence or lack of endogenous motivation determines the quality of the results. Feelings of satisfaction and a sense of comradeship or belonging are important in the creation of tacit knowledge. Furthermore, appropriate conditions must be established for individuals to sustain endogenous motivation, such as high-quality learning experiences, a mentoring and coaching *ba*, and a varied and multidimensional incentive system, that encourages the transfer and creation of tacit knowledge. This helps to facilitate knowledge emergence in *ba*.

A good *ba* can be expressed as a sphere, where there is maximum surface area for a given volume (Nonaka and Toyama, 2002). A good *ba* can achieve the maximum external interface with the requisite variety. And every participant in the *ba* is at the same distance from the center. However, it should be noted that the meaning of "center" here is not as a fixed point. Since *ba* is a shared context in motion, the center can change as *ba* evolves, and any participant has the potential to be a center.

The organization as an organic positioning of diverse ba

A *ba* is not necessarily exclusive to one meeting or one project. In the theory of the knowledge-creating firm, the firm is viewed as an organic configuration of multilayered *ba*, where people interact with each other and the environment, based on the knowledge they have and the meanings they create.[2] When companies are viewed as organic configurations of *ba* rather than as organizational structures, it is possible to see what kind of knowledge should and can be created, who are the "right people" with embedded knowledge who can do this, and what kind of interactions are needed among them to create knowledge without being restricted by the conventional organizational structure. This explains the firm's suitability for both routine and non-routine tasks (Thompson, 1967). Formal exchanges defined by organizational command structures represent only a part of the interactions that occur to create knowledge. Informal, dialectical interactions between people inside the firm, and outside with others in the environment, also contribute to knowledge creation. Since all of these interactions contribute to knowledge, participation in *ba* must straddle multiple organizational levels and contexts, both internal and external. People in the organization learn to transcend their own subjective boundaries by participating in a variety of *ba* beyond the borders of the company, building layers of small-world networks (Watts, 2003) that ultimately link up to a larger *ba*. While the firm's formal hierarchy determines the *objective* allocation of power and resources, the informal pattern of social interactions enables actors to locate and utilize knowledge *subjectively* beyond formally defined information processing routes. This changes the nature of the boundaries that define a firm. No longer just a simple question of ownership (Arrow, 1974; Williamson, 1975), boundary setting in the knowledge-creating company becomes more complex. Interactions cannot be owned, and the knowledge arising from informal, subjective interactions "out there" might be vital to economic performance "in here" and cannot objectively be separated from the functioning of the organization.

40 *Managing Flow*

In conventional theory of organization, it is believed that the environment determines the structure of the firm and the structure of the firm determines the actions of the human/agents inside the firm in linear sequence. In fact, the structure of the firm does not always and directly determine the actions of the people inside it. Rather, environment and structure are activated and actualized by the people in the firm while simultaneously affecting them. Structure is an abstraction that is only made actual through interaction in *ba* where people share the same experiences of the actual, concrete, "here-now" situation. In other words, *ba* emerges at the point where environment, structure, and the agent intersect and interpenetrate to create new knowledge.

As discussed, *ba* is a process of indwelling in a "here-now" situation that transcends time and space. This means that *ba* emerges not only from the interpenetration of environment, structure, and agency in the dimension of space, but also from the simultaneous occurrence of past, present, and future in the dimension of time. A good *ba* both transcends and emerges in a time-space nexus (see Figure 2.4).

In the dialectical relationship between *ba* and structure, *ba* is the verb and structure is the noun, where structure is a stabilized form of *ba* as process. This makes it easier to see and manage the actual practice of knowledge creation and sharing. However, because structure inherently aims for stabilization it can impede the self-organizing process of the emerging and connecting *ba*. Therefore, the structural features of the organization should encourage the creation of *ba* both vertically and horizontally in the firm in order for knowledge to be created continuously. A synergy of *ba* and corporate

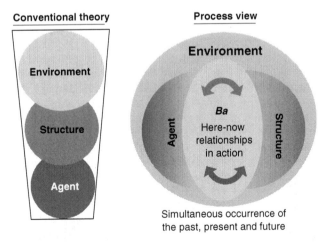

Figure 2.4 *Ba*: interpenetration of environment, structure, and agent

structure synthesizes the apparent contradictions of knowledge-creation versus efficiency, and freedom versus control in issues of power.

The key to responding to environmental uncertainty is the effective leveraging of both hierarchy and networks to enable flexibility and change in organizational structure when necessary. *Ba* that are organically configured to fit each situation make this possible. In highly innovative companies we see a multilayered structure or organic configuration of *ba* forming freely in accordance with the organization's overall objectives. Both *ba* for collective reflection and *ba* that act as connecting points with the outside world are embedded in the organization and effectively expand its boundaries in relation to customers and suppliers as well as with regional industrial clusters.

Hence, we need to reconsider exactly what the boundary of a firm is. A *ba* is not limited to the frame of a single organization but can be created across organizational boundaries. A *ba* can be built as a joint venture with a supplier, as an alliance with a competitor, or as an interactive relationship with customers, universities, local communities, or the government (see Figure 2.5). Members of an organization transcend its boundaries by participating in *ba*, and they transcend the boundaries of the *ba* when it connects to other *ba* that they participate in. In that regard, the legal boundaries of a firm are not as important as whether and how it synthesizes its various *ba*, both inside and outside the organization. Some *ba* have to be built within the company exclusively because they produce the knowledge that gives the firm its competitive advantage. But what is more important for the company is that it is able to build *ba* that give it the capability to synthesize. Knowledge creation is a dynamic human process, and managers and workers grow within that process. Managers become leaders and grow their capability to

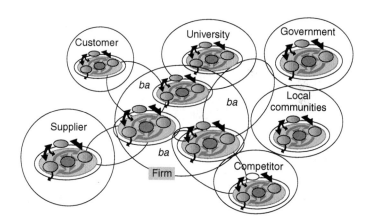

Figure 2.5 Organization as organic configuration of *Ba*: the knowledge ecosystem

synthesize different *ba* through their experience of participating in *ba*. We will return to this issue and discuss *ba* and its management in greater detail in Chapter 5.

2.2.5 Knowledge assets

We have explained how knowledge arises from the knowledge-creation process of dialogue and practice in *ba*. The knowledge that accumulates in that process becomes part of the organization's knowledge assets, which contribute to the generation of corporate value. Knowledge assets include patents, licenses, databases, documents, and other so-called knowledge capital, as well as skills, social capital, brand equity, design capability, organizational structures and systems, and organizational routines and cultures.

The term "knowledge assets" has affinities with the term "intellectual capital." The latter is commonly used and has a broad meaning (cf. Roos et al., 1997; Stewart, 1997; Sveiby, 1997; to name but a few). Edvinsson and Malone (1997) have defined intellectual capital as "knowledge that can be converted into value" and as consisting of two major components, *human resources* and *structural capital*, including intellectual assets (original emphasis). Human resources are the collective capabilities of employees, such as experience, know-how, and creativity. Structural capital or intellectual assets are the collections of tangible and transferable knowledge. Structural capital includes organizational structure and incentive systems, as does our term "knowledge assets."

Knowledge assets are both the output of the knowledge-creation process and the input of new knowledge creation. While it is possible to acquire existing knowledge assets through patent-use rights or by purchasing a company outright, the purchaser must already possess a certain level of knowledge and capability to fully exploit that acquisition. Much of the knowledge obtainable from outside a company is explicit. To be able to create knowledge continually, a company must accumulate its own tacit knowledge, and this takes time. As we have seen with path-dependent technologies, the kind of tacit knowledge assets that a company already possesses largely determines the kind of knowledge assets it will possess in the future, and this is an important factor in determining competitive advantage.

Unlike physical assets, knowledge assets are process rather than substance, and therefore in continuous change. They are an indispensable, internal resource for creating values that cannot be readily bought and sold (Konno, 1998; Teece, 2000). Much of a firm's economic value is measured in explicit knowledge assets, such as know-how, patents, copyrights, and brand image, because they are easier to measure. But, in fact, these are the results of past knowledge-creation endeavors. The more valuable asset is the underlying tacit knowledge that was needed to create them because that knowledge and its methodology are the source of knowledge-creation capability at the firm and therefore the gauge of future value.

Since knowledge arises from interactions among people, the knowledge assets that generate knowledge are the relationships in which knowledge is shared in the firm's *ecosystem* of knowledge workers, customers, suppliers, and universities, and this is the social capital that drives the organization forward. Robert Putnam describes social capital as the "features of social life – networks, norms, and trust – that enable participants to act together more effectively to pursue shared objectives" (Putnam, 1996: 56). It is also described as the "stock of active connections among people: the trust, mutual understanding, and shared values and behaviors that bind the members of human networks and communities and make cooperative action possible" (Cohen and Prusak, 2001). A person exists in relationships with others who constitute the community, and at the same time each person has unique characteristics and a unique experience of the community as a person-in-community (Cobb, 2007). However, it is often the case that in the substance thinking of economics a person is viewed as *"Homo economicus,"* where individual relationships are defined by contract. This builds external relationships only, rather than internal relationships, because the individuals do not share experiences. This means individuals exist apart from each other and there is no community.

One of the most important knowledge assets of a firm is its specific *"kata"* of dialogue and practice. *Kata* roughly means pattern or way of doing things. It is a traditional Japanese code of knowledge and describes a process of synthesizing thought and behavior in skilful action; the metacognition of reflection in action. Takashi Saito describes *kata* as the distilled essence of a program of behavior that is the ideal of master practitioners and excellent companies (Saito, 2001). *Kata* is the practice of perceiving essence in order to act in a way that is appropriate to the context. It involves the practiced ability to read a situation in motion and synthesize that observation in effective action. *Kata* is explained in Greek philosophy as the concept of *"phronesis"* or practical wisdom, which we will discuss later in this chapter.

Nelson and Winter (1982) emphasized the importance of a firm's routines in effectively maintaining and strengthening the firm's evolutionary process. Here, we focus on the "creative routines" of *kata*, which make knowledge creation possible by fostering creativity and preserving efficiency. *Kata* is different from a routine in that it contains a continuous self-renewal process. Feldman observes that continuous self-renewal is achieved by incorporating a high-quality feedback function that sharpens the senses and helps to notify and modify the differences between predicted outcomes and reality (Feldman, 2000). Thus, *kata* functions with a high degree of freedom to make continuous modifications based on real-time feedback from the situation as it unfolds. The practice of *kata* consists of learning and growing through the three stages of *Shu* (learn), *Ha* (break), and *Ri* (create). In *Shu*, one learns by following the instruction of a teacher, imitating his or her practice and embracing his or her values and techniques and mastering them as one's own. In the next stage, *Ha*, the practitioner breaks the teacher's mold and attempts to revise it using his or her own creative influence. In the final stage, *Ri*, the practitioner leaves the teacher and works to develop his or her own, unique approach. Thus, *kata* is not the wholesale adoption of another's method, but the practice of improving on it incrementally. It is a continuous tacit process of self-renewal, motivated by the pursuit of truth, goodness, and beauty.

Kata can also be explained by the concept of kinetics, as a process form of knowledge that is deeply engrained in the body and expressed in the unconscious actions of tacit knowledge (Fradette and Michaud, 1998). When *kata* or kinetics is shared, the synthesizing capability of an organization grows so that it is able to take action instantaneously in a situation without having to think it through as a logical procedure. *Kata* or kinetics is embedded in the organization as "creative routine." While conventional management systems standardize routines in manuals that must be followed explicitly, *kata* as a creative archetype requires a high degree of freedom because it embraces continuous self-renewal. It is perfection of the practice of making adjustments on the spot through real-time assessment of oneself in action. Seven-Eleven Japan's daily routine of creating, implementing, and verifying hypotheses about consumers has become a shared *kata* in the organization that is continuously repeated. While simple routine does not enable the organization to respond to continuous change in customer needs, a creative routine that incorporates a verification process does.

Just as *kata* enables the practitioner to correct inefficient action, practiced as an organization *kata* improves corporate performance and ensures efficient organizational management. In conventional management, an efficient organizational routine and culture in one environment can sometimes function in reverse, inhibiting knowledge creation in another environment. The failure to relinquish such a practice signifies an "overdependence on successful experiences" (Levitt and March, 1988; Leonard-Barton, 1992). In the routine of creative change that is *kata*, however, specific practices are in constant revision and renewal, so it is not those practices that are maintained but the underlying practice of continuous, improvisational change and innovation. This raises the quality of organizational kinetics in actualizing the knowledge vision, and enables continuous improvement on past successes.

In the American Major League, Japanese baseball player Ichiro Suzuki describes his *kata*, saying that he feels another "self" observing his form whenever he is at bat. This means that he is able to stand back and logically assess his actions while he is performing them, studying the gap between his movement and what he imagines to be his ideal form, and trying to close that gap. In doing so, he practices the simultaneous, objective observation and correction of action that is metacognition. It is the ability to quickly assimilate explicit knowledge by examining it logically and then internalizing it as our own.

2.2.6 Environment: an ecosystem of knowledge

Significant changes during the last two decades in the legal environment and in managerial and technological capabilities have made it easier for companies to collaborate, distributing a firm's operations across many organizations. As Iansiti and Levien (2004: 5–6) point out, this development has shifted many industries towards a network structure, where products or services are now the result of collaboration among many different organizations. Prahalad and Ramaswamy (2000: 81) also observe that "the unit of strategic analysis has moved from the single company, to a family of businesses, and finally, to what is called the "extended enterprise" consisting of a central firm supported by a constellation of suppliers." Firms operate in a business ecosystem, that is, "the community of organizations, institutions, and individuals that impact the enterprise and the enterprise's customers and suppliers" (Teece, 2007). In the network economy, no firm can be seen as isolated, and both value and innovation are generated through co-creation, overcoming the traditional, company-centric view in business.

This new environment lends itself to *ba*-centered strategic management practice that spans organizational boundaries. This can occur in various relationships, such as a joint venture with a supplier, an alliance with a competitor, or in interactive relationships with customers, universities, local communities, and government. This redefines the entity of the firm as an "organic configuration of multilayered *ba*," or a collection of *ba* in dynamic interaction.

All organizations now depend on a network of alliances, outsourcing, and knowledge-sharing to remain competitive. Such networks constitute a business ecosystem' (cf. Moore, 1996; Iansiti and Levien, 2004; Nonaka and Toyama, 2005b; Kohlbacher, 2007) and may also exist within a multi-unit firm (e.g. Eisenhardt and Galunic, 2000). Economic value in a knowledge-creating firm emerges from the interactions among knowledge workers, or between knowledge workers and their environment of customers, suppliers, or research institutes (Nonaka and Toyama, 2005b). The firm's knowledge base, then, includes its technological competencies as well as its knowledge of customer needs and supplier capabilities (Teece, 1998). As Prahalad and Ramaswamy (2000: 81) observe, business competence is now "a function of the collective knowledge available to the whole system" in an enhanced network of suppliers, manufacturers, partners, investors, and customers.

An ecosystem of knowledge consists of multilayered *ba* existing across organizational boundaries and continuously evolving. Firms create knowledge by synthesizing their existing knowledge with that of various players outside the firm, such as customers, suppliers, universities, and even competitors (Nonaka and Toyama, 2005b). Note that it is the human being that remains the most important intellectual entity in the business ecosystem, as the embodiment of the firm's rich tacit knowledge and deep relationships.

Knowledge is embedded not only in the organization, but in its customers, suppliers, competitors, university partners, and other actors in its environment. The organization combines the external knowledge of these players with its own to produce new knowledge. Just as an ecosystem of living organisms includes both kinematic chains and habitat segregation, the environment of the firm is an ecosystem of organic relationships among the variety of knowledge sources interacting both inside and outside the organization. Our view of the market as a reservoir of knowledge is close to that of the Austrian School of Economics. Hayek (1945, 1948a, 1948b), for instance, noted that all markets are distinguished by decentralized and dispersed knowledge and that the entrepreneur's ability to profit from competitors comes from his or her unique, local, and thus superior information. Hayek was also a pioneer in drawing attention to the importance of implicit, context-specific knowledge and argued that changing circumstances continually redefine the relative advantage of knowledge held by different individuals.

Our view of the market as a dynamic process also has similarities with the Austrian school, for example in Kirzner's (1973) theory of the market process as one of entrepreneurial discovery. As O'Driscoll and Rizzo (1996: 5, original emphasis) have noted, "all market activity...can be rendered intelligible as a *process of attempting* to correct errors and coordinate behavior." Obviously, knowledge and knowledge creation in that sense are the necessary means to overcome ignorance in individual actors and manage and control that process. Like the Austrian school, we propose a dynamic theory of the market and competition that challenges those models based solely on rationalism and equilibrium.

The business ecosystem evolves dynamically in a chain of multilayered *ba* that transcends organizational boundaries. The environment and the organization therefore should be viewed as interdependent and evolving together, rather than as separate entities. Positivism in economics and organizational management theory has made it difficult to grasp this concept of interdependency. In the contemporary view of cognition as embodied action, knowledge emerges through interaction with the environment, and both the actor and the environment are changed in the interaction. Viewed from the phenomenological perspective of the "lifeworld" (Husserl, 1970), the environment is not simply a pre-existing object of human, scientific observation, but is the meaning that arises from our experience of interacting with it. We operate in the everyday lifeworld with the common-sense knowledge that we possess about the world prior to theory. This daily practical consciousness absorbs society as physical knowledge and resolves dualistic conflicts dialectically in the process of action. In the same way, corporations set goals that both influence and are influenced by the environment. The resulting knowledge is absorbed, interpreted, and transformed into internal knowledge and reflected in the company's next product or service, so the environment is neither a fixed premise nor a conflicting relationship. At Seven-Eleven Japan, employees and store clerks are told not to *think for* customers but to *think as* customers. The moment one views the customer as an object of analysis, one becomes blinded by preconceptions and unable to see that customer as he or she really is.

The relationships in an ecosystem cannot be described by simple causality, as pointed out by Edward Lorenz in the early 1960s with the "butterfly effect," and by the work of many biologists seeking to explain the relationships between the food chain and environmental effects. It is difficult to identify all the relationships or links in the chain and prove causality. In reality, all living organisms coexist. An ecosystem can be compared to a three-dimensional jigsaw puzzle, where the pieces connect to each other directly, but also indirectly to pieces that are elsewhere in the puzzle (Ezaki, 2007). The puzzle may seem static, but if one piece changes, all the other pieces are affected, and so they dwell together in dynamic interaction. Not every piece of the puzzle is equally important; but some are key pieces. It is the same in the ecosystem where keystone species determine the coexistence of related species. All species in the ecosystem, no matter how selfish they may seem, live and let live to make up the jigsaw puzzle. Then, the question of coexistence becomes one of sensing the extent of relationships, and this makes sensitivity or "feeling" and imagination important.

The firm as a dynamic entity in an ecosystem of knowledge relationships can no longer be defined simply by ownership. And boundary setting that is based on reducing transaction costs is insufficient to understanding and managing economic value and competitive advantage. The knowledge-creating firm must manage multilayered *ba* stretching beyond the firm, while simultaneously protecting knowledge assets as its source of competitive advantage. Viewed in this context, the complete protection of knowledge assets is a complex, and arguably, almost impossible task.

The SECI model is a framework for overcoming the dualities of free will versus environmental determinism, and agency versus structure. The subject, situated in the world, engages in knowledge creation, and in making that knowledge whole gradually discloses it to the world. This process is not determined by environment or free will but occurs somewhere in between, in the dialectical relationship between the individual subject and the environment that emerges in dialogue and practice, in a dynamic synthesis that changes both.

Notes

1. For the list of empirical research concerning the SECI process and enablers, see Nonaka et al. (2006).

2. As a matter of interest, this view shows certain similarities with Kozlowski and Klein's (2000) view of organizations as multilevel systems.

References

Abe, M. (1988). "Nishida's philosophy of 'place,'" *International Philosophical Quarterly*, 28 (4), 355–71.
Arrow, K.J. (1974). *The Limits of Organization*. New York: Norton.
Badaracco, J.L. (1991). *The Knowledge Link: How Firms Compete through Strategic Alliances*. Boston: Harvard Business School Press.
Baird, D. (2004). *Thing Knowledge: A Philosophy of Scientific Instruments*. Berkley, CA: University of California Press.
Bakken, T. and Hernes, T. (2006). "Organizing is both a verb and a noun: Weick meets Whitehead," *Organization Studies*, 27 (11), 1599–1616.
Bourdieu, P. (1998). *Practical Reason: On the Theory of Action*. Stanford, CA: Stanford University Press.
Brown, F. (2003). "Value in mind and nature," in F.G. Riffert and M. Weber (eds). *Searching for New Contrast: Whiteheadian Contribution to Contemporary Challenges in Neurophysiology, Psychology, Psychotherapy and the Philosophy of Mind*. Frankfurt: Peter Lang, pp. 37–59.
Buber, M. (1958). *I and Thou*, tr. R.G. Smith. New York: Charles Scribner's Sons.
Casey, E.S. (1997). *The Fate of Place: A Philosophical History*. Berkeley: University of California Press.
Cobb, J.B., Jr (2007). "Person-in-community: Whiteheadian insights into community and institution," *Organization Studies*, 28 (4), 567–88.
Cohen, D. and Prusak, L. (2001). *In Good Company: How Social Capital Makes Organizations Work*. Boston: Harvard Business School Press.
Collins, J. (2001). *From Good to Great: Why some Companies Make the Leap and others Don't*. New York: HarperBusiness.
Cooper, R. (2005). "Peripheral vision: relationality," *Organizational Studies*, 26 (11), 1689–710.
Csikszentmihalyi, M. (1990). *Flow: The Psychology of Optimal Experience*. New York: Harper and Row.
Drucker, P.F. (1954). *The Practice of Management*. New York: Harper.
Edvinsson, L. and Malone, M. (1997). *Intellectual Capital*. New York: Harper Business.
Eisenhardt, K.M. and Galunic, D.C. (2000). "Coevolving: at last, a way to make synergies work," *Harvard Business Review*, 78 (1), 91–101.
Ellsworth, R.R. (2007). "Leading innovation with purpose and meaning," unpublished manuscript.
Ezaki, Y. (2007). *Seitaikei tte nani?* [What is ecosystem?]. Tokyo: Chukou Shinsho.
Feldman, M.S. (2000). "Organizational routines as a source of continuous change," *Organization Science*, 11 (6), 611–29.
Fradette, M. and Michaud, S. (1998). *The Power of Corporate Kinetics: Create the Self-adapting, Self-renewing, Instant-action Enterprise*. New York: Simon & Schuster.
Grant, R.M. (1996a). "Prospering in dynamically-competitive environments: organizational capability as knowledge integration," *Organization Science*, 7 (4), 375–87.
Grant, R.M. (1996b). "Toward a knowledge-based theory of the firm," *Strategic Management Journal*, 17(winter special issue), 109–22.

Halverson, R. (2004). "Accessing, documenting and communicating practical wisdom: the *phronesis* of school leadership practice," *American Journal of Education*, 111 (1), 90–121.
Hamel, G. (2003). *The Quest for Resilience.* Harvard Business Review, September issue.
Hayek, F.A. (1945). "The use of knowledge in society," *The American Economic Review*, 35 (4), 519–30
Hayek, F.A. (1948a). *Individualism and Economic Order.* Chicago: University of Chicago Press.
Hayek, F.A. (1948b). *The Meaning of Competition: Individualism and Economic Order.* Chicago: University of Chicago Press, 92–106.
Hegel, G.W.F. (1969) *Hegel's Science of Logic*, tr. A.V. Miller. New York: Humanities Press.
Heidegger, M. (1962). *Being and Time*, tr. J. Macquarrie and E. Robinson. New York: Harper & Row.
Heisig, J.W. (2001). *Philosophers of Nothingness: An Essay on the Kyoto School.* Honolulu: University of Hawaii's Press.
Husserl, E. (1970). *The Crisis of European Science and Transcendental Phenomenology: An Introduction to Phenomenological Philosophy.* (D.Carr, Trans.). Evanston: Northwestern University Press.
Husserl, E. (1962). *Ideas: General Introduction to Pure Phenomenology*, tr. B. Gibson. New York: Collier.
Iansiti, M. and Levien, R. (2004). *The Keystone Advantage: What the New Dynamics of Business Ecosystems Mean for Strategy, Innovation, and Sustainability.* Boston: Harvard Business School Press.
Inkpen, A.C. (1996). "Creating knowledge through collaboration," *California Management Review*, 39 (1), 123–40.
Itami, H., Nishiguchi, T., and Nonaka, I. (eds). (2000). *Ba no dainamizum to kigyo* [The Dynamism of Ba and the Corporation]. Tokyo: Toyo Keizai Shinposha.
Kimura, B. (1994). *Kokoro no byouri wo kangaeru* [Thoughts on Pathology of the Mind]. Tokyo: Iwanami Shoten.
Kirzner, I.M. (1973). *Competition and Entrepreneurship.* Chicago: University of Chicago Press.
Kohlbacher, F. (2007). *International Marketing in the Network Economy: A Knowledge-based Approach.* Basingstoke: Palgrave Macmillan.
Konno, N. (1998). *Chishiki shisan no keiei.* [Management by Knowledge Assets]. Tokyo: Nihon Keizai Shimbun Sha.
Kozlowski, S.W.J. and Klein, K.J. (2000). "A multilevel approach to theory and research in organizations: contextual, temporal, and emergent processes," *Multilevel theory, research, and methods in organizations: Foundations, extensions, and new directions*, 3–90.
Lakoff, G. and Johnson, M. (1980). *Metaphors We Live by.* Chicago: University of Chicago Press.
Lave, J. and Wenger, E. (1991). *Situated Learning: Legitimate Peripheral Participation.* New York: Cambridge University Press.
Leonard-Barton, D. (1992). "Core capabilities and core rigidities: a paradox in managing new product development," *Strategic Management Journal*, 13(special issue), 111–25.
Levitt, B. and March, J.G. (1988). "Organizational learning," *Annual Review of Sociology*, 14, 319–38.
MacIntyre, A. (1984). *After Virtue: A Study in Moral Theory*, 2nd edn. Notre Dame: University of Notre Dame Press.

Moore, J.F. (1996). *The Death of Competition: Leadership and Strategy in the Age of Business Ecosystems*. New York: HarperBusiness.

Naess, A. (1987). "Self-realization: an ecological approach to being in the world," *The Trumpeter*, 4(3), 35–42.

Naess, A. (1989). *Ecology, Community and Lifestyle: Outline of an Ecosophy*, tr. D. Rothenberg. Cambridge: Cambridge University Press.

Nakamura, J. and Csikszentmihalyi, M. (2002). "The concept of flow," in C.R. Snyder and S.J. Lopez (eds). *Handbook of Positive Psychology*. New York: Oxford University Press, pp. 89–105.

Nelson, R.R. and Winter, S.G. (1982). *An Evolutionary Theory of Economic Change*. Cambridge, MA: Belknap Press of Harvard University Press.

Nisbett, R.E. (2003). *The Geography of Thought: How Asians and Westerners Think Differently – and Why*. New York: Free Press.

Nishida, K. (1926). Basho (Topos). *Tetsugaku Kenkyu* [The Journal of Philosophical Studies], 123(June), 1–99.

Nishida, K. (1960). *A Study of Good*, tr. V.H. Viglielmo. Printing Bureau, Japanese Government.

Nonaka, I. (1990). *Chishiki souzou no keiei* [A theory of organizational knowledge creation]. Tokyo: Nihon Keizai Shimbunsha.

Nonaka, I. (1991). "The knowledge-creating company," *Harvard Business Review*, 69 (6), 96–104.

Nonaka, I. (1994). "A dynamic theory of organizational knowledge creation," *Organization Science*, 5 (1), 14–37.

Nonaka, I. (2005). "Managing organizational knowledge: theoretical and methodological foundations," in K.G. Smith and M.A. Hitt (eds). *Great Minds in Management: The Process of Theory Development*. New York: Oxford University Press, pp. 373–93.

Nonaka, I. and Katsumi, A. (2004). *Innovation no honshitsu* [The essence of Innovation]. Tokyo: Nikkei BP sha.

Nonaka, I. and Konno, N. (1998). "The concept of '*Ba*': building a foundation for knowledge creation," *California Management Review*, 40 (3), 40–54.

Nonaka, I., Konno, N., and Toyama, R. (2001). "Emergence of '*Ba*': a conceptual framework for the continuous and self-transcending process of knowledge creation," in I. Nonaka and T. Nishiguchi (eds). *Knowledge Emergence: Social, Technical, and Evolutionary Dimensions of Knowledge Creation*. New York: Oxford University Press, pp. 13–29.

Nonaka, I., Sasaki, K., and Senoo, D. (2004). "Jizokuteki seichou kigyou no sikou, koudou youshiki: risouteki pracmatism no takyuu" [The Thinking and Action Pattern of Sustainable Growth Firms: Pursuing Idealistic Pragmatism], *Think!*, winter, 92–101.

Nonaka, I. and Takeuchi, H. (1995). *The Knowledge-Creating Company: How Japanese Companies Create the Dynamics of Innovation*. New York: Oxford University Press.

Nonaka, I. and Toyama, R. (2002). "A firm as a dialectical being: towards a dynamic theory of a firm," *Industrial and Corporate Change*, 11 (5), 995–1009.

Nonaka, I. and Toyama, R. (2003). "The knowledge-creating theory revisited: knowledge creation as a synthesizing process," *Knowledge Management Research & Practice*, 1 (1), 2–10.

Nonaka, I. and Toyama, R. (2005a). "Phronesis toshite no senryaku" [Strategy-as-Phronesis], *Hitotsubashi Business Review*, 53 (3), 88–103.

Nonaka, I. and Toyama, R. (2005b). "The theory of the knowledge-creating firm: subjectivity, objectivity, and synthesis," *Industrial and Corporate Change*, 14 (3), 419–36.

Nonaka, I., Toyama, R., and Konno, N. (2000). "SECI, Ba and leadership: a unified model of dynamic knowledge creation," *Long Range Planning*, 33 (1), 1–31.

Nonaka, I., Toyama, R., and Konno, N. (2004). "Chishiki-beisu kigyo riron" [The knowledge-based theory of the firm: toward dynamic evolution of strategic management], *Hitotsubashi Business Review*, 52 (2), 78–93.

Nonaka, I., von Krogh, G., and Voelpel, S.C. (2006). "Organizational knowledge creation theory: evolutionary paths and future advances," *Organization Studies*, 27 (8), 1179–208.

O'Driscoll, G.P. Jr and Rizzo, M.J. (1996). *The Economics of Time and Ignorance*. London: Routledge.

Osterloh, M. and Frey, B. (1997). "Managing motivation: crowding effects in the theory of the firm," *Diskussionsbeitrag*, 31. Zurich: Institut für betriebswirtschaftliche.

Polanyi, M. (1966). *The Tacit Dimension*. New York: Doubleday.

Prahalad, C.K. and Ramaswamy, V. (2000). "Co-opting customer competence," *Harvard Business Review*, 78 (1), 79–87.

Putnam, R.D. (1996). "Tuning in, tuning out: the strange disappearance of social capital in America," *Political Science and Politics*, 288 (4), 664–83.

Rämö, H. (2004a). "Moments of trust: temporal and spatial factors of trust in organizations," *Journal of Managerial Psychology*, 19 (8), 760–75.

Rämö, H. (2004b). "Spatio-temporal notions and organized environmental issues: an axiology of action," *Organization*, 11 (6), 849–72.

Rescher, N. (1994). *Philosophical Standardism: An Empiricist Approach to Philosophical Methodology*. Pittsburgh: University of Pittsburgh Press.

Rescher, N. (2003). *Rationality in Pragmatic Perspective*. Lewiston, NY: Edwin Mellen Press.

Roos et. al. (1997). *Intellectual Capital: Navigating in the New Business Landscape*. New York: University Press.

Rosch, E. (1978). "Principles of categorization," *Etnolingwistyka* [Ethnolinguistics], 17, 11–35.

Saito, T. (2001). *Dekiru hito ha doko ga chigau noka* [What Makes Effective People Different?]. Tokyo: Chikuma Shobo.

Schon, D.A. (1983). *The Reflective Practitioner: How Professionals Think in Action*. New York: Basic Books.

Shimizu, H. (1995). "Ba-principle: new logic for the real-time emergence of information," *Holonics*, 5 (1), 67–9.

Shimizu, H., Kume, T., Miwa, Y., and Miyake, Y. (2000). *Ba to kyoso* [Ba and co-creation]. Tokyo: NTT Shuppan.

Simon, H.A. (1991). "Bounded rationality and organizational learning," *Organization Science*, 2 (1), 125–34

Stewart, T.A. (1997). *Intellectual Capital : The New Wealth of Organizations*. New York: Doubleday.

Suchman, L.A. (1987). *Plans and Situated Actions: The Problem of Human-machine Communication*. Cambridge: Cambridge University Press.

Sveivy, K.E. (1997). *The New Organizational Wealth: Managing and Measuring Knowledge-Based Assets*. Berrett-Koehler Publishers.

Teece, D.J. (1998). "Capturing value from knowledge assets: the new economy, markets for know-how, and intangible assets," *California Management Review*, 40 (3), 55–79.

Teece, D.J. (2000). *Managing Intellectual Capital: Organizational, Strategic, and Policy Dimensions*. New York: Oxford University Press.

Teece, D.J. (2007). "Explicating dynamic capabilities: the nature and microfoundations of (sustainable) enterprise performance", *Strategic Management Journal*, 28 (13), 1319–50.

Thompson, J.D. (1967). *Organizations in Action*. New York: McGraw-Hill.

Ui, Y. (2002). "Fujyoshiki no susume" [Promoting un-common]. *Leadership Strategy*, spring edition, 52.

von Krogh, G., Ichijo, K., and Nonaka, I. (2000). *Enabling Knowledge Creation: How to Unlock the Mystery of Tacit Knowledge and Release the Power of Innovation*. New York, NY: Oxford University Press.

Wargo, R.J.J. (2005). *The Logic of Nothingness: A Study of Nishida Kitarō*. Honolulu: University of Hawaii's Press.

Watanabe, K. (2008). "Monodukuri no shitsu wo hibi takameru" [Improving the quality of making product every day]. *Voice*, 362, 80–7.

Watts, D.J. (2003). *Six Degrees: The Science of a Connected Age*. New York: W.W. Norton.

Wenger, E. (1998). *Communities of Practice: Learning, Meaning, and Identity*. New York: Cambridge University Press.

Whitehead, A.N. (1925). *Science and the Modern World*. New York: Macmillan.

Williamson, O.E. (1975). *Markets and Hierarchies, Analysis and Antitrust Implications: A Study in the Economics of Internal Organization*. New York: Free Press.

Yamada, Y. (2005). *Basho no ronri ni yoru jigyokaikaku* [Business Innovation Based on the Logic of Place]. Tokyo: Hakutoshobo.

3
Leading the Knowledge-Creating Firm

In the previous chapter we discussed the dynamic model in which a firm creates knowledge through interactions with its environment. The driver of this entire dynamic process is leadership. Leadership plays a variety of roles in the knowledge-creating process, such as: providing knowledge-vision and a driving objective; developing and promoting the sharing of knowledge assets; creating, energizing, and connecting *ba*; and enabling and promoting the continuous spiral of knowledge creation through dialogue and practice. At the base of such leadership is *phronesis*, that is, practical wisdom to make the necessary decisions and take the appropriate action with the right timing to achieve a common good.

The concept of *phronesis* originates with Aristotle. In the *Nicomachean Ethics* (2002), he distinguishes between three types of knowledge: *episteme*, *techne*, and *phronesis*. *Episteme* is universal truth, corresponding to the universal validity principle in the practice of modern science. Based on the rational analysis of idealism, it is context-independent, objective (explicit) knowledge that focuses on universal applicability, independent of time or space. *Techne* roughly corresponds to technique, technology, and art. It is the know-how or practical skill required to be able to create. Based on instrumental rationality, it is context-dependent, practical (tacit) knowledge. *Phronesis* is an intellectual virtue. Roughly translated today as prudence, ethics, practical wisdom, or practical rationality, *phronesis* is generally understood as the ability to determine and undertake the best action in a specific situation to serve the common good. *Phronesis* takes into account contextual circumstances, addresses particulars, and shifts aims in process when necessary (Eisner, 2002). In other words, it is the high-quality tacit knowledge acquired from practical experience that enables one to make prudent decisions and take action appropriate to each situation, guided by values and ethics. *Phronesis* is acquired through the effort to perfect one's craft, which makes one a virtuous artisan.

In general, *phronesis* is the practical knowledge of ethical, social, and political life, which accounts for its development first in the field of political science. Politics is the art of the possible, which creates the future through a process of negotiation and coordination. *Phronesis* as political judgment is the ability to initiate action toward the future, based on a universal consensus about specific goals and measures reached through the shared judgment and conviction of individuals in each context (Beiner, 1983).

If the concept seems complicated, let's look at it using the example of the car. Anyone in possession of the necessary technology and parts can manufacture a car. But whether a user finds value in the car, that is, whether the car conforms to what the user would consider a "good" car, is another matter because the values of those who made the car and those who use it are different. A product, in this case a car, incorporates the values held by its makers at the time it is made. If *techne* is the knowledge of how to make a car well, *phronesis* is the knowledge of what a "good" car is (value judgment) and how to build such a car (realize the value judgment). A company cannot survive on *techne* alone because no matter how well it can make a car, if it is not a "good" car, the effort is meaningless. *Episteme* cannot answer the question of what a good car is either, since "good" is a subjective value whose definition depends on the person using the car, and this value cannot be a universal truth since it depends on the context, or who perceives that goodness, and that answer continuously changes. In short, *phronesis* in the firm is the ability to understand and bring to fruition that which is considered "good" by individual customers in specific times and situations.

With *phronesis* as the synthesizing glue, we can explain the practical, subjective, and future-creating aspects of the dynamic process of strategy building and execution in the knowledge-creating company. *Phronesis* is a concept that synthesizes "knowing why," as in scientific theory, with "knowing how", as in practical skill, and with "knowing what", as a goal to be realized. Unlike *episteme*, it emphasizes practices in particular contexts because the "goodness" one perceives has to be realized by a means suitable to each situation. However, *phronesis* is not just knowledge about a certain, particular context per se. Since it is knowledge to serve the common good, it has an affinity with universal principles. According to Dunne (1993), *phronesis* is characterized as much by perceptiveness with regard to concrete particulars as it is by knowledge of universal principals. As actions originate from particular situations, *phronesis* is the ability to synthesize a general, universal knowledge with the particular knowledge of a concrete situation.

Phronesis is concerned with value judgments about truth, justice, and beauty, or simply the common good that people strive for; and the ability to make *phronetic* judgments is necessary for knowledge conversion. Tacit knowledge does not translate directly into explicit knowledge but is converted in the context of the value judgments of the knower. In leadership, *phronesis* is manifested in the capacity to choose the appropriate goals and to successfully devise means to reach them (Halverson, 2004). Phronetic leaders use their sense of the details to "see" or "feel" the problems of their organizations as solvable within local constraints and develop successful plans to address the problems identified. In decision-making, *phronetic* leaders must be able to synthesize contextual knowledge, accumulated through experience, with universal knowledge gained through training.

Working in educational theory, Halverson (2004) states that leaders in organizations with collective *phronesis* create organizational structures that help them to shape the problems they are able to identify and the solutions to them. As a consequence, the organization develops shared practices through which it can detect and process various problems and solve them. The seemingly effortless integration of political and personal *phronesis* in expert practice is a characteristic of virtuoso performance (Dreyfus and Dreyfus, 1986).

3.1 The abilities that constitute *phronesis*

What exactly is *phronesis*, then, in the context of a knowledge-creating company? We argue that it consists of the following six abilities: (i) the ability to make a judgment about "goodness"; (ii) the ability to share contexts with others to create the shared space of knowledge we call *ba*; (iii) the ability to grasp the essence of particular situations/things; (iv) the ability to reconstruct particulars into universals and vice versa using language/concepts/narrative; (v) the ability to use well any necessary political means to realize concepts for the common good; and (vi) the ability to foster *phronesis* in others to build a resilient organization.[1]

The following sections explain these six abilities in detail, while bearing in mind the *phronesis* of Aristotle and how that concept has been developed in political science and pedagogy. Our work on this topic is still in progress and further research is required. The six abilities are ideal models. They are not necessarily equal, but allow for a broad range of variation depending on the situation and, therefore, should be judged on their overall coherence. Furthermore, we reiterate that the need for *phronesis* is not limited to top management. Knowledge creation is a process in which *phronesis* is practiced by a distributed leadership, where people at various organizational levels are able to exercise *phronesis* in their own situations.

The ability to judge goodness

Judging goodness refers to the ability to practice one's moral discernment on what is "good" and act on that judgment on a practical level according to the particular situation. It is the ability both to conceive an ideal and to pursue its realization. The judgment of "goodness" begins with individual values. Knowledge created in an organization depends upon the values of truth, goodness, and beauty possessed by the leader of the organization. Without a solid, philosophical foundation for their values, individuals cannot make judgments about what is good, and so a company is unable to produce value.

As Honda Motor Company founder Soichiro Honda argued, sound philosophy is absolutely essential to developing technologies and using them because it is people who create technology for the benefit of society. He wrote: "Philosophy is more important than technologies. Things like money and technologies are merely the means to serve people... There is no meaning in a technology if, at the base of it, it does not consider people... What drives a firm's growth is philosophy... A true technology is a crystal of philosophy. Therefore, even in a research lab, the philosophy of the people who work there should take precedence over the technology" (Honda, 1996: 61–62).

The values or philosophy that is the basis for judging goodness has to be one's own. It cannot be given by others. At Honda, the most important question asked of everyone is: What do *you* think? Honda recognizes that its value is a product of the values or philosophy of each individual in the company. Its management principle, "respect for the individual," acknowledges that every human being is different, and these differences are an important source of the values Honda creates. However, it does not mean that each individual should pursue what is good only for him or her. *Phronesis* is the ability to judge goodness for the *common* good. This kind of judgment requires a higher point of view to be able to see what is good for the whole, even though that view stems from one individual's values and desires.

Another principle that expresses Honda's fundamental beliefs is "The Three Joys." These are: the joy of buying, the joy of selling, and the joy of creating. The joy of creating things from one's own, original idea is important at Honda. Employees are told to create what gives them joy to create, based on their own values. Still, they are told that the product should not be something that only Honda engineers can enjoy. Those who sell the product and, above all, those who buy the product must enjoy it as well. This viewpoint sets the value standard for Honda employees to act for the common good.

When Honda was developing the CVCC engine, a low-emission engine that would meet a revised Clean Air Act in the United States in 1970, Soichiro Honda declared that it would put Honda in a position to beat the Big Three US auto manufacturers who opposed the new law. But Honda engineers objected to Soichiro's motives, saying that what they really wanted was to develop an engine that fulfilled their social responsibility as an automobile company to reduce harmful emissions. They said they were doing it for their children. As the story goes, Soichiro was so ashamed of himself when he heard this that he decided it was time to retire.

It is this kind of value of the common good, that gives a firm an absolute value to pursue, that is a goal in itself. It is not simply a means to enhance profit, which is the goal implicitly set by conventional management scholars in their theories of the firm. In his introduction to *Metaphysics*, Aristotle writes, "All men by nature desire to know," and in the *Nicomachean Ethics* he writes, "Every sort of expert knowledge and every inquiry, and similarly every action and undertaking, seems to seek some good" (2002: 95). In short, man pursues good for its own sake, not because such good leads to profit or advantage over others. It is not simply a means, but an absolute, self-sufficient good, such as happiness or, more specific to the firm, self-realization. Money is not goodness in itself, but a means to achieve a goal that is goodness. Profit is something gained as a result of pursuing *phronesis* rather than being the ultimate goal.

How then does one acquire *phronetic* judgment? The ability to make a judgment about goodness is fostered through life experiences. The importance of experience as a source of knowledge has been discussed, but the experience needed to foster *phronesis* goes beyond experiences at the workplace. According to Aristotle, *phronesis* is the character embodied in a good man. To foster goodness one needs experiences as a human being in every aspect of life. Especially important are aesthetic experiences and a culture of philosophy, history, literature, and the arts, which foster insights into historical and social situations. To cultivate critical *phronetic* leadership, an organization must provide a mechanism for learning through high-quality experiences. In the end, the ultimate goal for both individuals and organizations must be the relentless pursuit of excellence. Indeed, MacIntyre (1984) sees the ultimate goal of practice as achieving "standards of excellence," an idea that can also be found in Aristotle.

The ability to share contexts with others to create *ba*

As explained earlier, *ba*, which roughly means "place" in Japanese, is defined here as a shared context in motion, where knowledge is shared, created, and put to use. *Ba* as a shared context means that individual, subjective views are understood and shared so that one can see oneself in relation to others and accept others' views and values. It is the space where individuals share directly with each other the emotional underpinnings of their particular knowledge and expertise. To participate in a *ba* is to get involved and transcend one's own, limited perspective.

To function effectively in *ba*, one must have the ability to empathize, to put oneself in the position of the other and understand his or her feelings. Anticipating what customers value requires the ability to empathize, and understanding another's emotions requires imagination. The ability to mobilize people depends on one's imaginative capacity to understand and empathize with others and to elicit empathy in return. Being able to imagine others' emotions and the consequence of the actions of oneself and others is important to building and managing ever-changing contexts.

To do this, one needs an ability to "read" a situation and adapt to it quickly. Since *phronesis* is the ability to make a decision that is suitable for each situation, one has to be able to quickly recognize a situation and understand what is required in that context. Soichiro Honda once said: "Joking is very difficult. You have to grasp the atmosphere of the occasion and the opportunity. It exists only for that particular moment and not anywhere else. The joke is in the timing and it doesn't work at any other moment ... To joke is to understand human emotion" (Honda 1966: 56–57). The ability to share emotion is not just about understanding others' emotions but being able to communicate your own emotions in a way that others are able to understand. To do this, one has to cultivate social capital, through love, care, trust, and commitment.

A *phronetic* leader also must have the ability to engage in and cultivate sharing among participants in *ba*. Social capital such as care, love, trust, and a sense of security has to be cultivated to form *ba* (von Krogh et al., 2000). It is only in such an environment that individuals are able to transcend the self and connect with others. The same social capital is employed to link *ba* in multiple layers.

A knowledge-creating firm must be capable of immediate action in response to the various *ba* that emerge and disappear over time, both inside and outside the organization. In a fixed leadership company, this would be impossible. As knowledge is created in dynamic interaction with the environment, managing the knowledge-creating process requires the ability to foster and manage those interactions according to the situation. It is the responsibility of the leadership to mobilize knowledge that is unevenly distributed, while, at the same time, determining how to enhance the quality of knowledge on all levels and how to synthesize the diversity of knowledge. To do so, knowledge leaders must be able to connect various *ba* both inside and outside the organization to form a self-organizing ecosystem of knowledge. This is done through the formation of small-world networks (Watts, 2003) in which individuals, in many cases middle managers, are connected to each other at will and become tipping points for action or change (Gladwell, 2000).

The ability to grasp the essence of particular situations/things

What we gain from empathizing in *ba* is no more than a single experience unless we endeavor to understand the essential meaning of that experience, that is, the essence that makes it universally relevant as a constant, universal truth. Seeing essence is the ability to fathom intuitively the true nature and meaning of people, things, and events. It is the ability to quickly sense what lies behind phenomena and accurately project an image of the future based on this intuition. *Phronesis* is "a form of reasoning and knowledge that involves a distinctive mediation between the universal and the particular" (Bernstein, 1983: 146).

By recognizing the situation correctly and grasping the essence, one can envision the future and decide on the action to be taken to realize that future. To do this, one has to be able to see at both the micro- and the macrolevels simultaneously. Like the saying, "God is in the detail," the kind of consciousness that enables one to sense truth in individual details is the starting point of creativity. To borrow from Hayek, it is the everyday small changes that make up economic phenomena that are important (Hayek, 1945). A keen sensitivity to daily change and the ability to see the implications of that change in the bigger picture are essential attributes of *phronesis*. For Gadamer, understanding is a form of *phronesis* (Bernstein, 1983), and he emphasizes the importance of dialogue (Gadamer, 2006). He tells us that "it is only through the *dialogical* encounter with what is at once alien to us, makes a claim upon us, and has an affinity with what we are that we can open ourselves to risking and testing our prejudices" (Bernstein, 1983: 128–9, original emphasis).

The Automobile Hall of Fame in Detroit, which honors those who have made a significant contribution to the industry, has a corner devoted to Soichiro Honda. One of the photos in the exhibition shows him at a motorcycle race, squatting to put himself at eye level with the rider (see Figure 3.1). This pose captures the essence of the Honda way: the focus on place, the product, and the reality of experience – the three *gen* principle. Honda once said, "When I look at a motorcycle, I see many things. I see that I should do such and such to maneuver past the curve. And I think about the next generation machine: I think, if I do this, it will have more speed...I move naturally into the next process" (Honda, 1963). When one is able to perceive

Figure 3.1 Soichiro Honda watching motor cycle racing
Source: Honda Motor Co., Ltd.

universality through experience, to see the forest and the trees simultaneously, that is a *phronetic* experience. *Phronesis* enables one to perceive beyond the ordinary, to see essence. In the end, "what is required is an interpretation and specification of universals that are appropriate to this particular situation" (Bernstein, 1983: 54).

The ability to reconstruct the particulars into universals and vice versa using language/concepts/narrative

Traversing between the particular and the universal requires an ability to conceptualize and articulate subjective, intuitive ideas in clear language, to link these "micro" concepts to a macrohistorical context, and convincingly to articulate them as a vision and scenario for the future. In this process, both vertical methods of deductive and inductive reasoning, as well as horizontal methods of expression, such as metaphor, analogy, and narrative, are used. As stated earlier, *phronesis* requires more than just practical knowledge of a particular situation. It requires the ability to contemplate to grasp a universal "truth" from the particular in order to determine the best way to act for the common good. Hence, it requires continuous interaction between subjective insight and objective knowledge to identify the optimal way to behave. While Soichiro Honda was a strong believer in the importance of the front line of production, he also stressed the need to cross-pollinate front-line, subjective insights with objective knowledge. He said: "Action without philosophy is a lethal weapon; philosophy without action is meaningless" (Tagami, 2003: 87). While stressing the importance of seeing the actual situation or thing, the Honda Motor Co. also urges *respect for sound theory* (see Figure 3.2).

Drucker (2004: 15) said that "management is what tradition used to call a liberal art – liberal because it deals with the fundamentals of knowledge, self-knowledge, wisdom, and leadership; art because it deals with practice and application." The ability to understand relationships in the ecosystem with sensitivity and feeling would be nurtured in the liberal arts. Even if one is able to grasp an essence and conceptualize it, the concept remains buried inside the individual until it can be communicated to others. The essence grasped must be communicated in a universal language that everyone can understand and must be expressed as an aspiration or vision that motivates people. This requires rich imagination (or *"phantasia,"* cf. Noel, 1999), especially historical imagination, and an outstanding ability to create and communicate a vision of the future that captures the imagination of others, through effective use of metaphor, analogy, or simple storytelling.

The CEO of Canon Inc., Fujio Mitarai, is known for his ability to modify his message to fit the context of the interaction. Mitarai shares his management philosophy with Canon employees in ways that are easily understood, through annual visits to every Canon office and factory in Japan. During those visits, he speaks for about two hours at a time, then meets with every

Figure 3.2 Soichiro Honda drawing a sketch on the ground
Source: Honda Motor Co., Ltd.

employee in the smaller branch offices, and with everyone from assistant manager up in the larger offices. While sharing his knowledge, he is also able to acquire contextual knowledge, which he uses in strategic decision-making. Mitarai's concept of "cash-flow management and cost optimization" is Canon's driving objective (Nonaka and Toyama, 2005a). Unlike the simple entreaty, "increase sales!," Mitarai uses a basic accounting concept to express a more complex, multidimensional idea of how each individual employee can contribute in their own particular job to optimizing cost and cash flow in the organization as a whole. He encourages employees to think at a deeper level about how to synthesize their particular view on the job with the universal norms of the company, and this sensibility is cultivated in *ba*.

The political power to realize concepts for the common good

It is not enough to identify essence, share it, and communicate it to others. One must also be able to bring people together and spur them to action, combining and synthesizing everyone's knowledge and efforts in pursuit of the goal. To mobilize others to achieve the common good, *phronetic* leaders must choose and utilize the means suitable to each particular situation, including sometimes Machiavellian means, where shrewdness and determination can help to achieve "the good" result (Badaracco, 1997).

The issue of leadership is an issue of power, and not necessarily formal power stemming from hierarchical position. Knowledge itself can be a source of power, and therefore can exist outside of the hierarchy of the organization. Knowledge as a source of power also means that it is fragile and needs nurturing. The human attractiveness of a leader depends on his or her values and worldview, and often affects the efficiency and effectiveness of the knowledge-creating process more than the formal power the leader exercises. Research indicates that effective leaders have the capability to synthesize contradiction by understanding that contradictory ideas are a way of life. Leaders have to exercise their political power to energize the emotional and spiritual resources of the organization.

While it is difficult to provide an ideal example, we can say that the probable sources of effective enactment of political power are personal magnetism, consideration of others' viewpoints, and a sense of timing. The human attractiveness of a leader depends on his or her values and worldview and this often affects the efficiency and effectiveness of the knowledge-creating process more than the formal power the leader exercises. For Nietzsche, "[t]he will to power is not *Reich* but *Macht* and not supremacy but superiority" (Solomon, 2003: 130, original emphasis).

A sense of balance to achieve what Aristotle called the golden mean is also important in making political judgments. The golden mean here does not simply mean middle ground. It means to avoid extremes and to act to resolve contradiction, and with moderation. To do that, *phronetic* leaders think in the way of "both and," not "either or." Political power is the ability to understand the full complement of contradictions in human nature – good and bad, optimism and pessimism, civility and incivility, diligence and laziness – and to harmonize them in a timely fashion as each situation arises. It has been said that personal magnetism is hard to describe, but those who possess it have, in their own way, embraced the contradictions associated with human nature and have been able to synthesize them (Iizuka, 2003).

The reality of management is that it is dynamic and full of confusion and contradiction. Traditional management theories have tried to resolve contradictions through the design of organizational structures, incentive systems, routines, or organizational culture. In a knowledge-creating organization, contradictions are not obstacles to overcome but are necessary for the creation of knowledge. Rather than seeking optimal balance between contradictions, they are synthesized in dialectical thinking that negates the dichotomy and yields knowledge. By accepting contradiction, one is able to make the decision best suited to the situation without losing sight of the goodness to be achieved. The dialectical process of achieving the goal through social interaction is political, driven by the ability to make political judgments. *Phronetic* leaders exercise political judgment by understanding others' emotions in verbal and non-verbal communication day-to-day, and by giving careful consideration to the timing of their interaction with others (Steinberger, 1993). Such political power can also reduce the costs of knowledge creation (among other justification costs), be it knowledge within the organization or imported from outside (Nonaka and Toyama, 2002).

Mitarai exercised political power to transform Canon. He broke down the barriers between divisions and reduced inventory by introducing a cell system of production and a *meister* system to recognize masterful assembly workers. He synchronized research and development with production and sales to speed up the development of better products, and withdrew the company from several unprofitable businesses. Throughout this process it was critical that he maintained close communication with the front line and the labor union. In his description of the effort, Mitarai says it is the frequency of communication that is the key to persuading and convincing others to take an active role in the transformation (Mitarai and Niwa, 2006). In addition to his annual office and factory visits which take about one month to complete, he also meets with about 800 managers and with the labor union every month to discuss current, important topics and management policies.

The ability to foster *phronesis* in others to build a resilient organization

Phronesis as a strategy is not planned or implemented by a few select leaders in the organization. Rather, *phronetic* leadership is distributed in the organization, with various members assuming leadership roles according to the situation. Cultivating this kind of leadership requires mechanisms for fostering and transferring the existing *phronetic* capabilities of individuals in the organization to others, creating a system of distributed *phronesis* (Halverson, 2004). This will ensure that an organization has the resilience (Hamel, 2003) to respond flexibly and creatively to any situation to pursue its own good. It also lowers justification costs since the function of justifying the knowledge created is distributed throughout the organization rather than controlled by a select few. Johan Roos and others have argued that by cultivating practical wisdom in an organization, people can develop the "everyday strategic preparedness" needed to deal with a complex and uncertain world (Roos, 2006; Statler and Roos, 2007). However, their model is abstract and based on cognitive balance theory, thus differing in perspective from the theory of knowledge creation.

Leadership in a knowledge-creating company is not about fixed administrative control. It is a flexible and *distributed* leadership, where the leader is determined by the context. Schumpeter argued that innovation is brought about by entrepreneurial leaders. However, he viewed leadership as an activity of elites, and entrepreneurship as a matter of individual disposition (Peukert, 2003). Knowledge creation, on the other hand, implemented at every level of the organization through daily practice, demands the active commitment of every individual in the organization, not just a small group of elites, because knowledge is created through dynamic and diverse, human interaction.

This does not mean that everyone can start creating knowledge immediately. For knowledge leadership to work, the mechanism of middle-up-down is key. Middle managers break down the vision or driving objective into concrete concepts or plans, build *ba*, and lead dialogue and practice. They are also the tipping points in small-world networks (Gladwell, 2000; Watts, 2003). The ability to foster *phronesis* is a form of knowledge that enables the firm to cultivate the critical, next generation of employees. It is the ability to present the issues to be addressed, the ability to create the necessary *ba* for creative exchange and peak experience (Maslow, 1970) that is challenging, high quality, and direct, and the ability to constantly ask oneself what is good. It is important that leaders provide clear examples of the *phronetic* way of thinking in practice. People learn to understand what *phronesis* is through practice, accomplished in interaction. As Dobson (1999: 133, emphasis in original) states, "ethics is something that is *learned* through observation of others' behavior." *Phronesis* is distributed throughout the organization by *phronetic* managers who act as exemplars or what Dobson calls the aesthetic manager-as-artisan. *Phronetic* managers-as-artisans make effective use of improvisation, as in jazz or improvisational theater (cf. Weick, 1998; Vera and Crossan, 2005), and as a result achieve the necessary strategic preparedness and resilience to deal with the unexpected or the uncertain.

Honda's routine of constantly asking employees "what do you think?" is meant to encourage them to think deeply about their own values in relation to the values of Honda and society. The question also forces them to think about what *they* want to do in their work at Honda, since it is their thoughts that are to be put into practice. Honda emphasizes the importance of direct experience with its three *gen* principle: going to *genba* or the front line; knowing *genbutsu* or the actual elements and situation; and seeing essential reality or *genjitsu*. Thus, Honda created the Fit by sending its development team to Europe to experience the market there directly, without preconceptions. This is the dialogue and practice at Honda in which distributed *phronesis* is cultivated.

3.2 Exercising *phronesis*

How, specifically, is *phronesis* exercised? As we mentioned earlier, the practical syllogism of Aristotle is more effective for exercising *phronesis*.[2] In contrast, the logical syllogism, which has been the typical way of thinking in scientific research, comprises a major premise (e.g. "all men die"), a minor premise describing a specific event, fact, or action (e.g. "Socrates is a man"), and a conclusion that leads, deductively, to an event or truth (e.g. "Socrates will die"). The syllogism is thus a methodology in which two or more premises (major and minor) lead to a necessary conclusion. The relationship between the premises and the conclusion is conceptual. This method of formal logic is deductive, such that if the two premises are true then the conclusion must also be true. However, since the conclusion is already contained within the premises, the potential of this method to create new knowledge is limited.

In contrast, the practical syllogism aims to elicit actions as conclusions, each with concrete individual implications. *Phronesis* is the ability to gain insight into the events of the minor premise immediately facing the observer and choose the best action. In the process, the minor premise and conclusion can become the major premise. The strength of Aristotle's practical syllogism is that it begins with the minor premise, the intention or objective of *what needs to be done right now*, and, while continuing discussion at the universal level, realizes the best action, not through logic, but by traversing back and forth between the particular (practice) and the universal (theory) in "good practice." Unlike the logical syllogism, the conclusion gained through the practical syllogism is not necessarily "right," since it often cannot answer such questions as whether something is absolutely right or wrong. Because of this ambiguity, the practical syllogism can promote the relentless pursuit of perfection, if one has the vision of an ideal to pursue.

When we decide what action to take, we do not deductively follow a given principle to the specific outcome but, rather, we begin with intention and, while maintaining a balance with the particular context, we take action that satisfies both the objective and the situation. Thus, the difference between the logical syllogism and the practical syllogism is that the former logically judges whether the proposition is true, while the latter judges whether the action can be justified. In this regard, the practical syllogism is close to the method of abduction, which freely combines the vertical logic of deduction with the horizontal, analogous reasoning of induction to achieve the objective through hypothesis building and testing (Josephson and Josephson, 1994). Such reasoning requires imagination (Noel, 1999). As this process develops through practice, the ability to move beyond antinomy in dynamic interaction with the environment improves.

We can see this process in action at the Toyota Motor Company. The conflict between cost and quality is an antinomy confronting all companies. One potential solution is to seek a compromise between price and quality that is acceptable to customers. At Toyota, instead of accepting the constraints as given and simply seeking an optimum solution under those conditions, they begin by questioning the constraining conditions. They question what they need to do right now to achieve their ideal level of quality and cost, and then synthesize the knowledge of all front-line workers in "*kaizen*" activities designed to make operational improvements. One result of this process was the creation of new knowledge at Toyota in the form of the now famous Toyota Production System, a new system of manufacturing that overcame paradox and enabled them to achieve both lower costs and higher quality. The company's approach to problem solving consists of the practice of asking the question "why?" five times. With the new production system this began with a situation where there was excess stock in parts, so the question was asked, "what should be done about it?," followed by the related question of "why is the stock there?" As the question "why?" is put four more times, the answer becomes increasingly focused. For example: "We produced the excess parts because we were ordered to do so, even though there was no need for it." (Why?) "Because we are still producing at the front-end, even though a problem has arisen at the back-end of the process." (Why?) "Because nobody told us they didn't need any more of these parts at the back-end process." (Why?) "Because production is based on a 'push' system, in which the front-end pushes what it produces to the back-end regardless of its needs." Toyota concluded that the solution was to build a back-end production system where the back-end orders the exact amount it needs from the front-end. By employing both vertical and horizontal reasoning in a kinetic chain of minor premises and conclusions based on specific contexts, Toyota engaged in a process of universalization that moved production from a partial to a more complete optimization.

3.3 Conclusion

In this chapter, we have explained the process of knowledge creation and how the specific components of our dynamic model of the knowledge-creating process enable a company continually to create and utilize new knowledge across the organization. Knowledge creation is not substance but process. Knowledge-based firms are conceptualized as in a state of continuous becoming through creativity and innovation. We have also discussed leadership in knowledge management and the role of Aristotle's concept of *phronesis* in knowledge management execution. *Phronesis* is the ability to make timely judgments and act on the particular "here-now" situation in the dynamic flow of moments of experience.

A company's sustainable competitive advantage ultimately depends on the kind of value it can continue to produce. Value is not created simply by combining and processing information or logically analyzing environments. Rather, it arises from the ability to subjectively interpret environments and, above all, from the practice of pursuing an absolute value determined by a company's unique vision of goodness and applying it contextually to suit the specific situation. *Phronesis* aims to establish good practice by judging the suitability of each action in each *ba* toward the highest macro good. It is knowledge that embraces idealistic pragmatism to pursue both universal value and particular reality simultaneously, and as a way of life. When one relentlessly pursues excellence as a way of life, one's knowledge becomes wisdom. The dynamic orchestration of such wisdom, or *phronesis*, is the essence of knowledge-based management.

Management of a firm is not, as Schumpeter argued, the sole domain of elite entrepreneurs, but is a distributed, *phronetic* process. The building of collective *phronesis* that synthesizes environment, organization, and the human agent is at the heart of knowledge-based management. Companies that have established organizational *phronesis* are tenacious and able to respond actively to any kind of environmental change because they are engaged in the sustainable practice of turning knowledge into wisdom, aimed at actualizing the corporate vision in real time.

We have now laid out a process theory of the knowledge-based firm and its underlying philosophy, but the most challenging part remains. That is, the crystallization of the theory in implementation. How does one sustain and increase the energy that drives knowledge-creating activities in an organization, and by what methods? We offer guidelines, but there is no manual in which the practice is standardized, because there is no single approach. Knowledge creation is a dynamic process unique to each situation and in continuous change. In the following chapters, we will try to describe this dynamic process in particular contexts, using case studies of firms that have been successful in changing themselves continuously through knowledge creation.

Notes

1. For an early application of the concept to political and military leadership, see Nonaka et al. (2005) and for strategy and management in general see Nonaka and Toyama (2005b).

2. Walton (1998, 2006) argues that since this is quite a different type of inference from deductive syllogism, it should be called practical reasoning rather than practical syllogism.

References

Badaracco, J.L. (1997). *Defining Moments: When Managers Must Choose between Right and Right*. Boston: Harvard Business School Press.
Beiner, R. (1983). *Political Judgement*. London: Methuen.
Bernstein, R.J. (1983). *Beyond Objectivism and Relativism: Science, Hermeneutics, and Praxis*. University of Pennsylvania Press.
Dobson, J. (1999). *The Art of Management and the Aesthetic Manager: The Coming Way of Business*. Westport: Quorum Books.
Dreyfus, H.L., Dreyfus, S.E., and Athanasiou, T. (1986). *Mind over Machine: The Power of Human Intuition and Expertise in the Era of the Computer*. New York: Free Press.
Drucker, P.F. (2004). *The Daily Drucker*. New York: HarperCollins.
Dunne, J. (1993). *Back to the Rough Ground*. IN: University of Notre Dame Press.
Eisner, E.W. (2002). "From episteme to phronesis to artistry in the study and improvement of teaching," *Teaching and Teacher Education*, 18, 375–85.
Flyvbjerg, B. (2006). "Making organization research matter," in S. Clegg, C. Hardy, T. Lawrence, and W. Nord (eds). *The SAGE Handbook of Organization Studies*, 2nd edn. Thousand Oaks, CA: SAGE Publications, pp. 370–87.
Gadamer, H.G. (2006). "Classical and philosophical hermeneutics," *Theory, Culture & Society*, 23 (1), 29–56.
Gladwell, M. (2000). *The Tipping Point: How Little Things Can Make a Big Difference*. Boston: Little, Brown.
Halverson, R. (2004). "Accessing, documenting and communicating practical wisdom: the *phronesis* of school leadership practice," *American Journal of Education*, 111 (1), 90–121.
Hamel, G. (2003). "The quest for resilience," *Harvard Business Review*, September.
Hayek, F.A. (1945). "The use of knowledge in society," *The American Economic Review*, 35 (4), 519–30.
Honda, S. (1996). *Ore no kangae* [My Thoughts]. Tokyo: Shincho Bunko.
Iizuka, A. (2003). "Leader no kenkyuu" [A study of the leaders], *Wedge*, 3, 68–87.
Josephson, J.R. and Josephson, S.G. (1994). *Abductive Inference: Computation, Philosophy, Technology*. Cambridge: Cambridge University Press.
MacIntyre, A. (1984). *After virtue: A Study in Moral Theory*, 2nd edn. Notre Dame: University of Notre Dame Press.
Maslow, A.H. (1970). *Motivation and Personality*. New York: Harper & Row.
Mitarai, F. and Niwa, U. (2006). *Kaisha ha dare no tameni* [Whom the Companies are for]. Tokyo: Bungeishunju.
Noel, J. (1999). "Phronesis and phantasia: teaching with wisdom and imagination," *Journal of Philosophy of Education*, 33 (2), 277–86.
Nonaka, I. and Toyama, R. (2002). "A firm as a dialectical being: towards a dynamic theory of a firm," *Industrial and Corporate Change*, 11 (5), 995–1009.
Nonaka, I. and Toyama, R. (2005a). "Phronesis toshite no senryaku" [Strategy-as-Phronesis], *Hitotsubashi Business Review*, 53 (3), 88–103.
Nonaka, I. et al. (2005). *Senryaku no honshitsu* [The Essence of Strategy]. Tokyo: Nihon Keizai Shinbumsha.

Peukert, H. (2003). "The missing chapter in Schumpeter's theory of economic development," in J. Bachaus (ed.). *Joseph Alois Schumpeter*. Norwell, MA: Kluwer Academic Publishers, pp. 221–31.

Roos, J. (2006). *Thinking from Within: A Hands-on Strategy Practice*. Basingstoke: Palgrave Macmillan.

Solomon, R. C. (2003). *Living with Nietzsche: What the great "Immoralist" has to teach us*. New York, NY: Oxford University Press.

Statler, M. and Roos. J. (2007). *Everyday Strategic Preparedness: The Role of Practical Wisdom in Organizations*. Basingstoke: Palgrave Macmillan.

Steinberger, P.J. (1993). *The Concept of Political Judgment*. Chicago: Chicago University Press.

Tagami, K. (2003). *Atarashii mono wo tsugitsugi to umidasu hiketsu* [The Secrets of Creating New Things Continuously]. Tokyo: Kanki Shuppan.

Vera, D. and M. Crossan. (2005). "Improvisation and innovative performance in teams," *Organization Science*, 16 (3), 203–24.

von Krogh, G., Ichijo, K., and Nonaka, I. (2000). *Enabling Knowledge Creation: How to Unlock the Mystery of Tacit Knowledge and Release the Power of Innovation*. New York: Oxford University Press.

Walton, D.N. (1998). *Ad Hominem Arguments*. Tuscaloosa, AL: University of Alabama Press.

Walton, D.N. (2006). *Fundamentals of Critical Argumentation*. New York: Cambridge University Press.

Watts, D.J. (2003). *Six Degrees: The Science of a Connected Age*. New York: W.W. Norton.

Weick, K.E. (1998). "Introductory essay: improvisation as a mindset for organizational analysis," *Organization Science*, 9 (5), 543–55.

4
Vision and Driving Objectives: Values for the Common Good

This chapter describes how firms create knowledge to change themselves and their environment, based on their vision and driving objectives. The vision sets the direction for the firm's strategy and its operations by drawing an image of the future that the firm wants to create. This vision motivates employees and lays the foundation for the firm's value system, based on defined relationships both inside and outside the company.

The pharmaceutical firm, Eisai Co., Ltd, considers the benefits of patients and their families to be its highest priority, and pursues research and product development with this vision in mind. The Honda Motor Co., Ltd became a global auto manufacturer by maintaining its commitment to the vision and philosophy of its founder Soichiro Honda. The experience of these two companies shows how the vision and philosophy of a firm defines its relationships with society and how its driving objectives keep it moving toward an ideal. Both companies have achieved excellence as well as profitability as a result of their relentless drive to realize ideals, rather than seeking profit as a primary purpose.

4.1 Eisai Co., Ltd

4.1.1 Company overview

Established by Toyoji Naito in 1941, Eisai Co., Ltd is a mid-sized pharmaceutical company with sales revenues in the fiscal year 2007 of 674.1 billion yen or 5.7 billion US dollars, a net income of 70.6 billion yen or 0.60 billion US dollars, and an investment in research and development of 108.3 billion yen or 0.92 billion US dollars. Although Eisai is only about half the size of Japan's largest pharmaceutical company, Takeda Pharmaceutical Co., Ltd, it is innovative and globally competitive, generating 90 percent of its revenues from products developed in-house, with such drugs as ARICEPT, now in global circulation in the treatment of Alzheimer's disease, and PARIET or ACIPHEX, used in the treatment of gastric-acid related disorders. It is aggressively expanding globally, with 56.7 percent of consolidated sales now in overseas business. Through active investment in research and development, Eisai is aiming for a consolidated sales revenue of one trillion yen or 8.35 billion US dollars in the fiscal year 2012, and an R&D investment of 200 billion yen or 1.67 billion US dollars. While many pharmaceutical companies are merging to obtain the benefits of scale that enable them to bear the burden of the high cost of product development, Eisai has maintained its independence while keeping its original focus on research and development, with strong business results. What enables Eisai to develop and market new products globally and profitably, without the scale advantages of the pharmaceutical giants, is its unique style of management based on a clear corporate philosophy and human-centered, knowledge-based management.

4.1.2 The Eisai philosophy

The company was drastically reorganized under the leadership of the founder's grandson Haruo Naito, who became the third president and CEO in 1988. In 1989, he issued a mission statement called "Commitment to Innovation." It posed the question: The world is changing; can you change along with it? This inaugurated a program to change the mindset of employees. The pharmaceutical industry was undergoing drastic change, with increasing R&D expenditure, new entrants from other industries, intensified global competition, decreasing government spending on health care, and changes in patient needs. Instead of aiming for size through mergers and acquisitions as many other pharmaceutical companies did, Eisai chose to cope with change by altering its way of doing business. They began the process by asking the fundamental question, "What kind of company do we want to be?"

The answer to that question was stated in the "Commitment to Innovation":

> We are clearly aware that patients and their families are the most important "participants" in the health-care process, and we take pride in increasing the benefit to them in the conduct of our business. The essence of Eisai is our pursuit of the "Eisai way," which is realized through the exercise of strong entrepreneurship by each employee. This means that we are continuously creating and proving our message to the world that what we should be doing as a human health care company is making a meaningful contribution to any health care system. To do that, it is most important that we know and share the feelings of patients, their joys, anger, sadness, and happiness.

This is a clear statement of the company's philosophical commitment to serve the people who need its medicinal products, and it is based on the recognition that patients and their families are the most important participants in the health care process. To serve them well, Eisai employees were required to understand that patients are not faceless targets of Eisai product marketing but living human beings with their own feelings. Thus, the important question at Eisai shifted from "What should we do to make high-quality products at low cost?" to become "For what purpose are we making medicinal products?" This led to clarification of Eisai's purpose or reason for existence, which is to ensure that all of the company's products and activities contribute to the benefit of patients and their families. Haruo Naito emphasized that profits are achieved as a result of providing such benefit and are not the purpose itself (see Figure 4.1).

The operative slogan of the new mission statement was "human health care," shortened to *hhc*, and this was communicated across the Eisai Group to become internalized as the modus operandi of every employee. It encouraged them to think continuously about how they could fulfill the goal and it gave social meaning to their work. It forced them to think about patients as individual human beings whose quality of life Eisai could help improve. The company describes its essential aim or *raison d'être* on its website as follows: "We demonstrate our obligation to society by identifying with health care recipients, developing a response to their needs, verifying the social benefits of this response, and finally, making this response available to the world before anyone else. This is what Eisai aims to realize in the slogan *hhc*."[1]

Medicine and medical supplies are generally prescribed and dispensed by doctors and pharmacists according to each country's health regulations. This system has resulted in pharmaceutical companies focusing on the

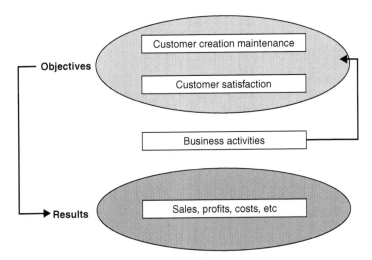

Figure 4.1 Profits as a result of providing customer benefits
Source: Eisai Co., Ltd.

needs of doctors and pharmacists as "customers," rather than on the needs of patients as "end users." Naito's "Commitment to Innovation" shifted the focus of the company to patients and their families, and mobilized the entire company to innovate to improve patients' quality of life. As he explained:

> Society expects us to be an innovator. Eisai is recognized as having a potential that other pharmaceutical companies do not, so every Eisai employee has to respond to that expectation. Before anything else, we have to identify how we can improve our products, to benefit patients, their families, and the population in general. And we have to test them, demonstrate their value, and make them available to the world. To meet this challenge, every aspect of our organization, from our employees and corporate culture to our style of doing business, must be in continual renewal. This is the meaning of Eisai Innovation.[2]

This means that every Eisai employee has to commit to the company's vision and willingly contribute to achieving it. Hence, it emphasizes the importance of each employee finding meaning in his or her own job. As the company states:

> Eisai wants to be a place for the self-realization of each employee. We want to be a company where each one of us finds work meaningful by doing something that is significant for our patients, cooperating with each other by doing our own job, and developing excellent skills in business. We strive to be considerate in communication with each other, based on the understanding that our most important resource is our people. We want to be thoughtful in encouraging each other. We want to be interested in and challenged to achieve our goal. (Eisai, 1989)

Haruo Naito said he came to understand the importance of interest and commitment on the part of employees to successful innovation during his four years as head of Eisai's Research and Development Division at Tsukuba Research Institute, a job that his father, former Eisai president and CEO Yuji Naito, had suggested he take on (Morita and Tsuyuki, 2001: 73–5). Employees in the labs had often questioned what value Haruo could contribute because he was not a professional chemist or a research scientist. Nevertheless, he developed good relationships with the research scientists based on the belief that he could understand scientists as human beings even though he might not be able to understand science. Through deep discussions with researchers, he learned that their biggest frustration was insufficient recognition of their work by the company, so he worked hard to convince them that the success of Eisai depended on their efforts. He often spent evenings at the institute talking to scientists and trying to motivate them, explaining how their work could affect the survival of Eisai in the market. He assured them that the institute was the most important part of the Eisai Group. Eventually he succeeded in changing the mindset of the scientists.

Naito also tried to create a system that would cultivate the interest of employees and nourish their sense of achievement. He introduced measures to evaluate the outcome of research by setting milestones in the R&D process, and he created a commendation system to reward achievement of the milestones. As a result of these efforts, development scientists generated a number of significant new treatments during his tenure, including ARICEPT and PARIET. There were also many product failures, but during Naito's four years at the research institute, the working environment was more vigorous than it had ever been.

Development of the drug ARICEPT, in particular, had stimulated Naito to think deeply about the nature of knowledge-creation activity and how to promote it. The lead researcher on the project, Dr Hachiro Sugimoto, had lost his mother to dementia. While nursing her he had decided to devote his life to developing a drug treatment for the disease. Despite his strong belief in the work, he had many failures and was sometimes urged to give it up. He tenaciously stayed on course, surmounting many hurdles. The new drug went on the market in 1997.[3] Observing this process left a strong impression on Naito about the force of human commitment and the sense of purpose that drives knowledge creation. Upon returning to Eisai headquarters, he began to reconsider the purpose of the company and decided that Eisai's ultimate objective was not to respond to the needs of doctors and pharmacists, but to "provide the benefit to patients and their families," which became the corporate vision and philosophy of *hhc*. He believed that once every employee understood this higher goal, they would be driven to achieve it.

4.1.3 Understanding and internalizing the *hhc* philosophy

Changing mindset through practice

Following the declaration of the "Commitment to Innovation," activities were designed to foster the sharing and internalization of the *hhc* philosophy. However, this statement of philosophy would be nothing but hollow words unless every employee committed to it and strove to realize it. First, selected managers were trained as "innovation leaders" rather than simple administrators. Over a period of approximately two years between 1992 and 1994, 103 middle managers participated in this training program. These managers then became the leaders in their workplace to change the mindset and practice of Eisai employees.

Training in an actual situation. The key to this training is in benefiting from the practical experience of working in a hospital ward. It is more difficult to "feel" the *hhc* philosophy than to understand it rationally, so training in the hospital ward was aimed at providing experiential understanding.

Employees visited hospitals and took care of patients to get a sense of their needs and medicinal requirements. The training took place at a specialized hospital for senior citizens known for its unique approach to care of the elderly. The philosophy of the hospital was to "provide relief and to brighten seniors lives," so patient autonomy was a priority, with flexible systems organized to match the individual needs of patients. By experiencing the situation of patients for themselves and observing how they were using medicines, employees could start to understand patients' points of view, their needs, and their feelings (see Figure 4.2). This made it possible for employees to gain a deeper understanding of the meaning of their own work in the pharmaceutical business. For example, after training, employees started to consider the following questions: "What is the key point of drugs for the elderly? The right form of dosage, greater efficacy, or fewer side

Figure 4.2 Empathizing with patients: Researchers indwelling with the elderly
Source: Eisai Co., Ltd.

effects even if the drug is less effective?" (Morita and Tsuyuki, 2001: 79–80). For researchers who had been pursuing development of the most effective drug treatments, this was a new viewpoint prompted by a new-found consciousness that drug treatments should be tailored to the individual patient. One employee said:

> Previously, I had only come in contact with patients and medical treatment indirectly, through the medicines we make. From the training, I realized that there are two aspects to medical treatment. One is to cure the patient, the other is care giving. After training in a hospital ward I started to think more about the role of medicines, and what kind of healthcare was appropriate at each hospital.

Another employee said:

> I had been totally focused on medicines, but at the hospital, the focus of treatment was not on medicines. I realized that drug treatments were only a tool to help people live easier even when they became old. In the lab, it is easy to mistake the development of new drugs as the ultimate goal of research. I was satisfied and felt a sense of achievement just doing that. But I realized it was not enough. Drugs are only useful in certain situations. The training gave me a new understanding of the purpose of medicines and how they should be developed.

hhc projects: putting ideas into practice

Based on the understanding and commitment they acquired through hands-on experience, Eisai employees started working in teams to discuss what they could really do to increase the benefit of their work to patients and their families. The *hhc* projects were developed along organizational lines in sales, R&D, production, and operations. Each project had a leader, and a member of each division was responsible for promoting *hhc* activities. The variety of themes ensured that every employee would belong to at least one project. In the fiscal year 2005, there were 427 projects in total, including those by foreign subsidiaries (see Table 4.1). The following are examples of business developments from *hhc* projects.

Developing the new drug ARICEPT as a social event. Dementia is regarded as a "social disease" because once the symptoms occur, every relationship is affected as family members and caregivers alike are forced to accommodate the changes in a patient's behavior. This has a major effect on the quality of life of the patient and the people around them. Thus, the effect of a drug cannot be evaluated by observing the patient alone, but has to include the relationships the patient has and how the feelings and experiences in these relationships are changed by the drug. It was Naito who decided that

Table 4.1 Number of *hhc* projects by division in 2005

Prescription drug	113
Consumer health product	16
Research & Development	102
Production	24
Global headquarters	28
Network companies – Japan	106
Network companies – US/Europe	27
Network companies – Asia	11
Total	427

Source: Eisai Co., Ltd.

"ARICEPT was not just about creation of a new drug but should trigger the creation of a society that is supportive of people with dementia."[4] With this, an R&D team began a variety of activities in preparation for the launch of ARICEPT. First, to observe the experiences and feelings of patients taking the drug, families and caregivers of the test subjects were asked to keep a diary of daily events and their feelings, which could be analyzed to identify what and how things had changed after the patients started taking the drug. Many said they felt joy and appreciation for the drug, saying it had helped them understand the patients and made them feel assured of their daily care giving activities. Through the diaries, the R&D team was able to share the experiences of the families and caregivers providing care and come up with quantitative criteria for measuring this effect, which was later transferred to marketing and sales. To trigger the creation of a supportive society, 42 regional sales managers were selected as members of a team established to educate society about dementia. At the time, many people were still unaware of the disease, and those who suffered from it were often misunderstood and sometimes neglected or abused. The team held town meetings and other similar forums to improve awareness, with dedicated sessions for doctors aimed at improving their skills of diagnosis. To sustain this support mechanism, the team helped to build hospital networks in the community and establish clinics specializing in dementia. With these activities the drug ARICEPT has become much more than just a drug, but the enabling context for a process of supporting relationships between patients, families, doctors, hospitals, and the larger community to cope better with dementia.

All the members of the ARICEPT R&D team had shared the experience of a doctor who had taken care of a patient with dementia before ARICEPT was available. The doctor, Kazuo Hasegawa, at St Marianna University School of Medicine Hospital in Kawasaki, Kanagawa, now the Chairman of the Tokyo Center for Dementia Care Training and Research, told the story of this patient, who was a priest suffering from memory loss related to Alzheimer's disease.

The patient, who used to be an enthusiastic player of music, had left scribbles on a sheet of music paper saying, "I have no memories. Will I ever get back my enthusiasm, my feelings of love?" They were cries of desperation from the depths of his soul. Dr Hasegawa said he felt powerless and incapable, knowing there was no cure for Alzheimer's disease. He told this story to the research team face to face and, through this dialogue, they came to understand in their own hearts the meaning of hhc and their shared mission to deliver ARICEPT to as many patients and their families as quickly as possible.

The training manual for caregivers: "Caring to Help Others." In aging societies around the world, the two major health care concerns are how to extend longevity and ensure quality of life, particularly for those who are ill and need medical care. To address the essential needs of patients and respond to other social needs, Eisai America and nine other health organizations in the United States, such as AARP, the National Alliance for Caregiving, and the Alzheimer's Association, cooperatively published *Caring to Help Others*, a training manual with detailed information on care giving and resources. It is distributed free by Eisai and other organizations, and is available on Eisai's website.[5]

The creators of the manual at Eisai wanted to develop a program that would improve the quality of care for seniors regardless of their level of need. They felt there was a strong need for a manual, although they were aware that it would not necessarily boost sales of Eisai products. The executive director of the Alzheimer's Association in the US at the time described the effort as follows:

> When this concept was first discussed, there was nothing like it nationally. There was no nationally developed volunteer program. There may have been select agencies that were doing training or had curricula themselves to train volunteers. But no one had looked at this at a national level until Eisai came along and created the concept for the manual.[6]

Changing the size and structure of medicines. Employees had discovered from their hhc activities as in-patient care givers that seniors were having difficulty swallowing medicine tablets because saliva secretion is reduced with age. They also noticed that some patients had medical restrictions on their liquid intake, making it even harder for them to swallow pills. Another problem was the shape and size of pills that made it difficult to distinguish one from the other. They began to wonder about the value of medicine if the patient had so much difficulty taking it. Eventually, they came up with the idea of "barrier-free medicine" and developed a variety of new products to meet this criterion, such as tablets that dissolve in about ten seconds even with just a small amount of water. There were a number of difficulties encountered in producing the tablets uniformly, but these were overcome with new equipment codeveloped with a manufacturer of food production machinery. Among other developments, medicines that had a bitter taste were modified to cover the bitterness. An adhesive patch for heart patients was reduced in size and made more comfortable for patients to wear. Barrier-free medicines were also developed for children and for general use, with significant benefit to the patient.

Such activities led to the foundation of Elmed Eisai Co., Ltd,[7] a fully owned Eisai subsidiary selling generic drugs. The pharmaceutical companies who develop their own proprietary drugs in Japan had mostly ignored the market for generic drugs, viewing it as a low-priced, secondary market that could reduce their profitability. Eisai, however, was aware that controlling medical costs was increasingly a priority with the population aging and the resulting burden on the health care system. But rather than offering just a lower priced generic alternative, the company decided it should also offer added value through such products as "barrier-free medicine" and identify new business opportunities and the potential for expanding to new markets.

Transferable labels for injections. Since liquid medicines are often colorless and difficult to distinguish, nurses must repeatedly check the labels before drawing the correct dosage into a syringe. Once they have finished extracting the medicine, they label the syringe to avoid misuse, usually writing the information directly on the syringe using a magic marker. Even with such precautions, errors can occur and the wrong medicine is administered to a patient. While the training in the hospital wards, Eisai employees noticed this danger and started working on packaging improvements to reduce accidents. Eisai could have decided that its only job was to produce medicines, and whether they were administered correctly or not was up to the doctors and nurses. However, from the standpoint of patient benefit, Eisai viewed this as a problem it should solve. In 2001 it was the first company in the health care field to create a label that could be peeled off the vial and transferred directly onto an injection syringe. Masako Kuroda, the head nurse at St Luke's International Hospital in Tokyo, commented:

> We nurses are the ones who must prepare these medicines. Eisai listened to us and immediately accepted our views. We were pleasantly surprised at their response and we appreciated how they improved the technology the way we wanted it, making it easier to use means that are safer for patients. I've always thought that it is important to listen to those who actually take care of patients every day. I was very pleased that Eisai did just that.[8]

New format for user instructions. Eisai decided that information about side effects and contraindications, which had previously been buried at the end of user instruction pamphlets, should be on the cover and front pages. This was a revolutionary change in the Japanese pharmaceutical industry. In the beginning, there was some opposition from sales people who believed that putting negative information up front would make selling more difficult. However, the final decision was based on what was more important for patients. No matter how good a drug might be, a patient's health could be damaged by side effects from inappropriate use of it. Hence, to increase the benefit to patients, such information should be easily accessible.

Customer hotline center. Eisai established the "customer hotline" product information center in 1992 for Japanese market. It is a toll-free phone-in service answering questions from users, ranging from physicians and pharmacists to patients and their families, about Eisai products and a variety of other matters, from medical science and pharmacology to everyday life. Such information services are common today, but in 1992 this was a real innovation, especially in the pharmaceutical industry, where companies considered physicians and pharmacists their customers and gave little thought to dealing with patients directly. Eisai decided that their most important activity was to enhance the benefit to patients and their families by providing the necessary information and relieving anxieties. The queries and requests that come in to the customer hotline center are fed back into company operations to develop better products. For example, B-vitamin products Chocola BB Junior and Chocola BB Syrup were created in response to inquiries about drink preparations for children.

Centralizing medical information for quick response. The responsibilities of the Medical Representative (MR) at the company changed to reflect the perspective of patients, with resulting changes in sales and the system for transferring medicinal information to doctors and pharmacists. Under the old system, medicinal information was managed by a specialized division in each regional office, which provided that information to the MR to pass onto doctors and pharmacists. Under the new system, all information on medicinal products was centralized in a computer database at headquarters, giving the MR easier access to it. The data could be quickly printed and faxed to doctors and pharmacists. This improved the speed of response to inquiries and was particularly beneficial in surgery, providing doctors with a quick reply on the possible side effects of a particular drug. The accuracy of response also improved.

The activities of the MR also changed drastically. The main task of the MR had been to provide information to doctors and pharmacists, and the job was evaluated according to an individual quota system, which was only concerned with the quantity of medicine sold and not the value provided to the patient. The quota system was replaced with a method that reflected the new approach to management based on the objectives. The MR was evaluated qualitatively as well as quantitatively according to so-called "lives activities" designed to improve the lives of patients by delivering medicinal products quickly and to as many patients as possible (Morita and Tsuyuki, 2001: 96–7). This could not be assessed on the basis of delivery to doctors or pharmacists, but only after the medicine had been consumed by patients and was working effectively. The new role of the MR was to follow up on product usage and ensure patient satisfaction had been achieved. The MR would plan monthly activities along these lines and report on results, which were shared on the company intranet. Other MRs would review the reports and award evaluation points. A superior report was selected in each region and the MR responsible would become the top regional representative. From the company's perspective, a superior MR was not only good at making quotas, but good at "lives activities." To evaluate this work more precisely, supervisors would accompany MRs in sales activities and provide instruction, sharing tacit knowledge and experiences in *ba* to impart the *hhc* philosophy and help them reach their own, tacit understanding.

4.1.4 Knowledge Creation Department: an organizational mechanism for *hhc*

Eisai had been conducting *hhc* activities since 1990, but not in a systematic fashion. The content of activity was decided by each individual department, and outcomes were not controlled or consistent across the company. There was also no mechanism for relaying results to the rest of the organization. Eisai expanded globally, establishing research centers in the US in Boston, and in London, England, and global offices and factories in various parts of the world. To link them and move them in the same direction, it had to ensure the *hhc* philosophy was tacitly understood by all employees, regardless of location or culture. The *hhc* activities had resulted in changing the mindset of individuals on the job, but this effort had to be expanded across the organization globally and the changes shared and accumulated, and reflected in new knowledge creation.

Eisai was the first company in Japan to have a "*Chisoubu*," which translates literally as a "Knowledge Creation Department." Established in April, 1997 and led by the president and CEO Haruo Naito, it had two roles. The first was to spread the *hhc* concept to Eisai group companies in Japan and overseas. The second was to cultivate knowledge creation. The Knowledge Creation Department applied the SECI model of organizational knowledge creation to change the mindset of employees and improve the quality of their performance in-line with the vision of *hhc*. A variety of *ba* was formed to activate the SECI spiral of knowledge creation, and these evolved into a layered network of *ba* both inside and outside the organization. Best practices in each division were noted and disseminated across the company. For example, the Eisai Science Prize is awarded for excellent inventions and discoveries in the research division; the Quality Performance Prize is awarded for outstanding original work in the production division; and a top prizewinner is selected from among Eisai innovation papers that describe excellent *hhc* activities: the winner is given a president's commendation. At the "*hhc* Initiative," in which examples of commendable activities in Japan and abroad are announced once a year, more than one hundred representatives of projects gather together for a lively exchange of knowledge and information. Such a system of awards and award ceremonies is considered an important way to recognize achievement and promote the sharing of knowledge company-wide.

The Knowledge Creation Department also planned and promoted *hhc* training, and acted as a liaison for global personnel exchanges and projects spanning different organizations. A Chief Knowledge Officer (CKO) was assigned to the department and 11 carefully selected veteran employees were assigned to work in the Knowledge Creation Department to ensure that the *hhc* vision was adopted in daily practice and internalized as tacit knowledge by employees. Norikatsu Yasoda was the first CKO in Japan. According to Yasoda, the mission of the Knowledge Creation Department was "to promote the creation of knowledge at all levels of the company based on the theory of knowledge creation, and to work towards the realization of global *hhc*" (Morita and Tsuyuki, 2001: 88–9). That is, to foster innovation by supporting the sharing and creation of knowledge. The Knowledge Creation Department assigns a member of staff to every department to support daily *hhc* activities and knowledge creation. These people also function as nodal points for the communication of knowledge, noting successful cases and communicating best practices to the entire company. The department is also a window of human exchange in cross-functional projects and with offices overseas, and it plans and promotes human resource development to foster the *hhc* philosophy (see Figure 4.3).

Systemizing human resource training: forming "self-in-all" in broader contexts

Human resource training at Eisai changed drastically as a result of the efforts of the Knowledge Creation Department. Previously, training was planned and designed by the human resource development department and conducted for durations of three to five years according to the rank or the position of an employee. Personnel affairs were managed separately from training. With the Knowledge Creation Department, these two functions were merged, and *hhc* activities and knowledge-creation activities were

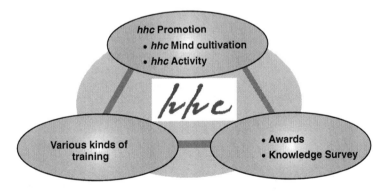

Figure 4.3 The concept of the Knowledge Creation Department
Source: Eisai Co., Ltd.

aligned. This made the objectives of human resource training clear and the program was redesigned accordingly. Furthermore, the Knowledge Creation Department discontinued the practice of training by the rank that had aimed to cultivate generalists. The new program focused on developing the creativity of employees and was matched to individual needs. It offered a variety of training courses from which employees could choose, based on their particular development needs rather than their rank.

The most typical forms of training are so-called "training by application" and the "knowledge conference." In "training by application," participants take full responsibility for their progress by applying for and buying into the program to cultivate a sense of ownership, at fees ranging from approximately 30 to 120 US dollars. Despite debate about the wisdom of collecting fees for company training, the fee requirement gave employees a greater sense of independence, responsibility, and commitment for their own education. Activities included training in hospital wards, exchanges with other industries, and exchanges with other departments. The opportunity to participate in a *ba* of knowledge exchange with people outside their department provided much needed stimulus and widened their interests to search for opportunities for career development beyond their current position.

The "knowledge conference" is aimed at training people to take action individually to actualize the *hhc* vision, and sharing the results with worldwide colleagues. This training imparts a deeper understanding of the *hhc* philosophy and of knowledge-creation theory and actual application in daily practices. The ultimate objective is to create "knowledge producers" who know the theory and methodology and can autonomously create knowledge and take practical action to support innovation.

Understanding the feelings of patients

Another form of human resource training provided by the Knowledge-Creation Department is Knowledge Leader Training aimed at cultivating the *hhc* mindset and determining what Eisai should be doing for patients. The course is open to all of about 3,000 employees in Japan and primarily imparts first-hand experience of patient needs through simulation exercises and visits to care facilities.

The simulations include the use of ear plugs to experience senior hearing loss, and the wearing of special glasses that simulate vision impairment due to cataracts and restricted field of vision. Participants also don hand and wrist weights and other devices that replicate a decline in muscle strength. This allows them to directly experience the physical and psychological feelings of old age (approximately age 75 to 80). Through such direct experience, participants learn to see things from elderly people's perspectives and understand and appreciate their feelings at a deeper level. These are some of the typical comments: "The experience was quite different from my image of elderly people." "I now have a better understanding of how the elderly feel and act." "I have developed a greater desire to help elderly people who are facing difficulties." After the simulation exercises, participants serve as assistants at care facilities to experience the reality and find they have greater empathy with patients.

Knowledge survey

The first undertaking of the new Knowledge Creation Department was a survey of all employees to determine how they dealt with their everyday duties. By analyzing work activities from the perspective of knowledge creation the survey reveals how knowledge is created, utilized, and accumulated in each part of Eisai.

The survey consists of about 200 questions, with a checklist evaluating on a five-level scale the time devoted and the importance assigned to 24 activities that represent the SECI process. The results of the survey are useful for identifying Eisai's strengths and weaknesses in terms of knowledge creation, and serve as valuable data from which subsequent knowledge-creation activities can begin. The first survey in 1997 revealed the "internalization" score to be very high at Eisai regardless of age or rank, while the scores for socialization, externalization, and combination are average (see Figure 4.4). This suggests that although the acquisition and utilization of knowledge on

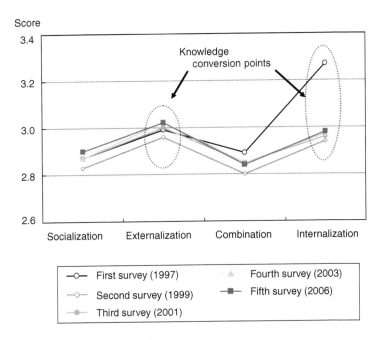

Figure 4.4 Results of the Knowledge Survey
Source: Eisai Co., Ltd.

an individual level was high, that knowledge was not effectively shared to create new knowledge organizationally. The speed of progress in medicine and pharmacology demands that personnel in the pharmaceutical industry, especially MRs, spend a great deal of time acquiring new knowledge. The survey revealed that employees were too busy acquiring and digesting new knowledge and information and not spending enough time creating their own knowledge.

A Knowledge Survey was carried out for each of approximately 600 organizational units and the results were fed back to the entire organization. In particular, personnel from the Knowledge Creation Department visited the Sales Department and other organizational branches in the company to provide direct feedback on their particular characteristics and problems, while giving briefings on specific knowledge-creation activities. A comparison was made between the best organization and others, which revealed that vigorous knowledge-creation activity is associated with good performance. The results showed that organizations with good business performance rank high in socialization, externalization, and combination, and also have high ability in combining leadership and knowledge. By analyzing and modeling the organizational processes of the best-performing unit, it was possible to show each unit what they could do to stimulate and enliven their knowledge-creation activities. Also, each unit ascertained its own strengths and weaknesses from the survey results, thoroughly discussing how to become a best-performing organization and drawing up an individual plan of action.

The follow-up surveys in 1999 and 2001 showed significant changes in knowledge-creating activities had taken place after feedback, training, and various *hhc*-related programs offered by the Knowledge Creation Department. Instead of internalization, Eisai employees were spending more time in externalization to create concepts and other explicit knowledge from their accumulated tacit knowledge. The latest survey in 2006 suggests that knowledge creation has become a part of the creative routines at Eisai.

Following application in Japan, Knowledge Survey was also conducted in the United States, Asia, and Europe, and the Knowledge Creation Department provided direct feedback on the results, which was made available for the formulation of plans of action using the same methods as those used in Japan.

4.1.5 The global spread of *hhc* activities

The *hhc* mission at Eisai puts priority on developing medicines for unmet medical needs to increase the benefit to patients. To gain a better awareness of these needs, *hhc* activities increase interaction with patients, their families, and health care providers by bringing in health care workers to speak to employees, and by visiting hospitals and engaging in volunteerism, not only in Japan, but worldwide. The following are examples of global *hhc* activities.

The Eisai Research Institute of Boston, Inc.

Staff at the Eisai Research Institute of Boston, Inc. – ERI, in the USA – originated the Eisai volunteer program called the "Road to Recovery" with the American Cancer Society (ACS) in which volunteers provide rides to cancer patients to and from medical treatment facilities. The program serves to enhance employees' understanding of patients' experiences. While providing much-needed transportation, employees also listen to patients' concerns and offer friendship and support. Through volunteerism, ERI employees gain knowledge about patients' needs and their feelings and acquire a greater sense of urgency and purpose about drug research and development, as well as experiencing the rewarding feeling of contributing time and effort to helping others in need in the community.

Eisai (Thailand) Marketing Co., Ltd

Eisai Thailand Marketing Co., Ltd (ETM) has found that patients seeking treatment in hospitals in Thailand have great difficulty obtaining the health care information they need. "Patients in Thailand face extremely long waits to see a physician, and when they do see a doctor the visit is typically limited to about three minutes," says an associate in the Knowledge Creation Department. "This is an insufficient amount of time for patients to fully explain their symptoms or receive adequate feedback to understand how to manage their medical conditions."[9]

In response to this need, ETM arranged a series of "Eisai Days" at hospitals in four cities in Thailand for patients and caregivers. Seminars were presented by doctors on such topics as Alzheimer's Disease and GERD (gastro esophageal reflux disease), followed by question-and-answer sessions. This provided a large number of patients with valuable health care information all at once, maximizing the time contributed by participating physicians. Eisai medical sales representatives in Thailand also participated, assisting with event coordination, registration, and distribution of health care materials. More than 3,000 people have benefited from these events and provided positive feedback and letters of appreciation. This *hhc* initiative has been commended as a best practice.

Eisai Korea Inc.

Eisai Korea Inc. (EKI) has identified a need for education about Alzheimer's disease in a society where it is only beginning to be recognized and diagnosed. Through the "Eisai Loveshare Campaign" they provided workshops for patients and caregivers with presentations from physicians and opportunities to interact with them. EKI employees played a key role in running the workshops and presenting information. More than 40 workshops have been held since the campaign was initiated in 2006.

4.1.6 Realizing the *hhc* concept in daily operations

Eisai states its operational objectives as follows: "to satisfy unmet medical needs, provide a stable supply of quality products, and deliver information on safety and efficacy." These objectives are pursued while keeping in mind the value of the total supply chain and the ideals of the company. Ideas and action are synthesized based on the corporate philosophy of *hhc* and practiced in a way that is appropriate to each particular situation and across the whole Eisai group. The operative phrase in Eisai's organizational process is the "seamless value chain," which aims to actualize effectiveness in operations and safety and reliability of their products across the value chain from R&D, production, and sales, to the delivery of medical information and quality control supervision. For example, to change the shapes of medicinal tablets, production processes were reorganized into a cell system managed by multiskilled workers. The aim was to expand the perspectives of employees by increasing individual knowledge of the entire process to maximize productivity.[10] Such changes were introduced based on the belief that "every single tablet, capsule and tube we produce is connected to the life of a patient," as the Eisai quality control policy states.

As a result of these activities, Eisai employees now think about their objectives in terms of the philosophy of *hhc* and consider their social meaning, and then determine the most desirable direction for planning business activities to realize their objectives. Naito asserts that the one and only objective of Eisai is to achieve patient satisfaction, and then be rewarded with good sales and profits. This is even stated in the articles of incorporation. In June, 2005, Eisai modified its articles of incorporation to include the *hhc* vision to "give first thought to patients and their families, and to increase the benefits that health care provides" as its corporate concept. It states that Eisai's mission is "the enhancement of patient satisfaction" and says the company "believes that revenues and earnings will be generated as a consequence of the fulfillment of the mission. The Company places importance on this positive sequence of the mission and the ensuing results." This article of incorporation also states that "the Company's principal stakeholders are patients, customers, shareholders and employees. The Company seeks to foster a good relationship with stakeholders and to enhance their value."[11] Naito says at Eisai they strive to share the corporate philosophy of *hhc* so that every single employee strives to realize it by continuously creating knowledge in his or her own job.

4.2 Honda Motor Co., Ltd

4.2.1 Companey overview

The Honda Motor Co., Ltd was founded by Soichiro Honda in 1948 in the provincial city of Hamamatsu in Shizuoka Prefecture, a distance of about

200 km from Tokyo. Following the principles of its founders the company has grown from a small town factory into a global competitor in the automobile industry with a unique business strategy and technological development process.

Honda's core business is the production and sale of automobiles, motorbikes, and power products, such as outboard engines, tillers, and power generators. They also produce solar batteries, humanoid robots, and jet engines. At the end of March, 2008, it had worldwide unit sales of 3.93 million four-wheeled vehicles, 9.32 million motor bikes, and 6.06 million power products, with profit generated mainly from North America. Total market capitalization in Japan was about 86 billion yen or 735 million US dollars, with unconsolidated net sales of approximately 4.1 trillion yen or 389 billion US dollars, and about 26,700 employees. On a consolidated basis, worldwide sales income for the same period totaled 10,028 billion yen or 95.5 billion US dollars with 167,200 employees. Recent trends in sales and profits on a consolidated basis are shown in Figure 4.5 and 4.6.

4.2.2 Corporate philosophy

Honda says its corporate philosophy is the basis of daily business activities and judgments made at all companies and associated companies in the Honda Group,[12] and this is the most valuable legacy of Honda's founders, Soichiro Honda and Takeo Fujisawa, whose leadership shaped the company.

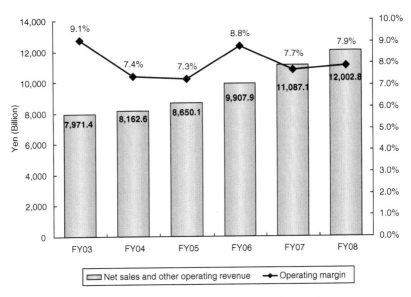

Figure 4.5 Honda's net sales and other operating revenue/operating margins

Source: Hondo Motor Co., Ltd, "Financial Highlights," http://world.honda.com/investors/highlight/

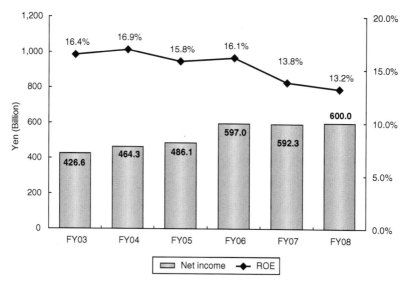

Figure 4.6 Honda's income/return on equity (ROE)
Source: Hondo Motor Co., Ltd, "Financial Highlights," http://world.honda.com/investors/highlight/

Soichiro Honda, founding president from 1948 to 1973, a genius engineer who took the lead in technology development at Honda, often talked about the importance of philosophy. He said, "more than technologies, it is human philosophy that we really have to value most. Technology has no meaning if at its base it does not consider people" (Honda, 1996: 61). He also said, "each individual, acting appropriately in his or her role, must translate the philosophy into action."[13] Takeo Fujisawa, vice president from 1964 to 1973, and was responsible for the management side and laid the foundation for Honda as a business organization, said, "what sustains and prospers is a way of thinking and the values in the minds of people in the organization" (Yamamoto, 1996: 331).

Philosophical foundation of Honda management design

Respect for the individual. Honda's corporate philosophy is based on two fundamental dictums: "Respect for the Individual" and "The Three Joys." As described in the *Honda Philosophy* handbook, distributed to all Honda employees, Respect for the Individual means that "the human being is born as a free and unique individual with the capacity to think, reason and create – and the ability to dream,"[14] so each individual should be given opportunities to develop their unique capabilities without inhibition. Soichiro Honda expected every employee to take an active role in an area where they could perform well and make a contribution to the company and society. He also believed that a supervisor had to be able to perceive people's capabilities and develop them based on the recognition that each person has his or her own, unique character and strengths and weaknesses. Therefore, he believed that no human being was expendable. Even while Honda was still a small company, Soichiro gave employees responsibility and autonomy in their work and deliberately put them into situations where they would grow through struggle.

The philosophy of Respect for the Individual is supported by the three basic values of initiative, equality, and trust. Initiative emphasizes that one should "not be bound by preconceived ideas but think creatively and act on one's own initiative and judgment, while understanding that you must take responsibility for the results of your actions."[15] Soichiro often said that people should not feel bound by or buried under an organization. Rather, they should make full use of their capabilities toward a higher goal, and act independently. Equality demands that people "recognize and respect individual differences in one another and treat each other fairly."[16] Trust emphasizes the building of relationships based on mutual trust "by recognizing each other as individuals, helping out where others are deficient, accepting help where we are deficient, sharing our knowledge, and making a sincere effort to fulfill our responsibilities."[17] Speaking at Honda's 50th anniversary party, Nobuhiko Kawamoto, president from 1990 to 1998, characterized life at Honda as "beyond business and beyond national borders, where people strive to understand each other and experience happiness. This is our philosophy, our uniqueness that hasn't been changed since the time of [our] foundation, and what the Old Man (Soichiro Honda) called *Respect for the Individual.*"[18]

In product development, Respect for the Individual is based on the understanding that a vehicle is entrusted with the care of human lives, so passenger safety and comfort must be considered at all times. Soichiro believed that the purpose of technology was to serve humanity. In a lecture he gave at the University of Michigan in 1974 he said: "Technologies are simply tools to serve human beings... No matter how much science and technology or social structures develop and advance, it will always be human beings who operate them. We must not forget this. However, just one human being cannot make things happen. We can use machinery and social structures more effectively if we foster the sense of connectedness, heart-to-heart, between us" (Harada, 1977: 198–202). Honda's process and way of thinking in product development reflects these views, as captured in the slogans "Utility Minimum," which aims to minimize the use of space for the engine to enhance space efficiency in the whole car, and "Man Maximum Machine Minimum," aimed at maximizing passenger comfort in the cabin while minimizing the machine for the sake of economy and efficiency.

Respect for the Individual also means that at Honda the bottom line is not about money, but about developing the individual so he or she can contribute to his or her world. Profit was not the primary objective of

Soichiro Honda in founding the company, but Honda as a corporate entity needed to make a profit. Honda urged employees not to become attached to short-term profit and to set goals from a broader point of view. Even when the company was just a small local factory in Hamamatsu, Soichiro insisted in making the point that the firm exists for the sake of human beings and society, so employees should think about how the company can make a social contribution.

The development of the CVCC engine shows how Honda's pursuit of a social goal has been put into practice. When the 1970 Muskie Act in the United States tightened fuel emission controls, the level of technology at the time seemed inadequate to enable compliance, so the US Big Three automobile manufacturers strongly opposed it. Seeing this as an opportunity for Honda to overcome its disadvantages as a latecomer to the auto industry and become a major competitor, Soichiro decided that Honda would build a new engine that could comply with the new standards. Honda engineers, however, were driven more by their concern about the environment than the desire to beat the competition. They told Soichiro that they were developing the engine for the future of their children, not because they wanted to beat competitors. This was the higher goal. Soichiro later recounted this story, saying it made him realize that he was getting old and that it was time for him to retire (Honda 2001: 253).[19]

On October 1972, Honda introduced the CVCC engine, the world's first engine of its kind to comply with the environmental standards dictated by the Muskie Act. The technology had a global impact and Honda announced that it would make it widely available, licensing it later to Toyota, Ford, Chrysler, and Isuzu.

The Three Joys: buying, selling, and creating. The Three Joys first appeared in the *Honda Monthly* magazine in December, 1951[20] in a statement by Soichiro Honda, giving a more active focus to the company value of Respect for the Individual. At Honda, joy is a deeper concept that stresses that the company should strive not only to eliminate unsatisfactory conditions, but also give and share happiness and surprises with employees, stakeholders, and customers, by exceeding their expectations. The first joy is the Joy of Buying, which is "achieved by providing products and services that exceed the needs and expectations of each customer."[21] Honda considers the Joy of Buying "the fairest determiner of the product's value. It is neither the manufacturer nor the dealer that best knows the value of the product and passes final judgment on it. Rather, it is none other than the purchaser who uses the product in his daily life. There is happiness in thinking, 'Oh, I'm so glad I bought this.'"[22] The Joy of Selling expresses the pleasure experienced by Honda employees, dealers, and distributors "who are engaged in selling and servicing Honda products that help develop relationships with a customer based on mutual trust,"[23] which then results in profit "as well as pride and happiness in handling those items. A manufacturer of products that do not bring this joy to people who sell those products is disqualified from being a manufacturer worthy of the name" says the company literature.[24] The third Joy of Creating "occurs when Honda associates and suppliers involved in the design, development, engineering and manufacturing of Honda products notice the sense of joy in customers and dealers."[25] Having the means to create an excellent product that is appreciated by society is the chief motivator for a Honda engineer, and brings honor to the person and the company. As Soichiro Honda expressed it: "When that product is of superior quality so that society welcomes it, the engineer's joy is absolutely not to be surpassed. As an engineer myself, I am constantly working in the hope of making this kind of product."[26]

The Three Joys define the absolute value that Honda employees should pursue in every aspect of their daily activities. They are encouraged to create and sell products that are their pride and joy because such products give customers value that exceeds their expectations, giving them joy as well. This absolute value also prevents Honda from pursuing relative values that merely imitate another company's success. By pursuing The Three Joys, Honda aims to build mutual relationships of sharing, in joy and trust, between employees, distributors, and customers. This is stressed in the corporate credo of 1956: "Expansion of our company is not only meant to contribute to the happiness of employees and stockholders. The purpose of our existence is to make customers happy by supplying them with good products, to help our associate companies develop, to raise the technological level of Japanese industry, and to contribute to the welfare of society." This contribution to society guarantees Honda's survival in return. In the *Honda Philosophy* handbook it states: "We believe that sincerely responding to the changing demands of the world through The Three Joys will provide joy to society and make Honda a company that society recognizes and wants to exist."[27]

4.2.3 Company principle: global vision

Honda's company principle is the statement of its ultimate goal and its reason for engaging in business. It was first written down in 1956 showing that the company already had a global vision, even though it was young and just a small town factory: "Maintaining an international viewpoint, the company is dedicated to manufacturing products excellent in performance yet at an inexpensive price in response to the needs of the customers."

Hideo Sugiura joined the company in 1953 and became Honda chairman in 1982. He said "I think that the passage about taking an 'international viewpoint' might have been somewhat of an overstatement, considering Honda's position at that time." He continued:

> However, that was really how the top management thought, and they were seriously attempting to put it into action. When young people like

me watched our seniors acting that way and listened to them talking that way, we would get caught up in it and start doing it ourselves. The Old Man [Soichiro Honda] said what he thought from the bottom of his being and with everything he had. We were just young kids, and when he talked like that, we tended to pick it up from him and go along.[28]

The current statement of the company principle is as follows: "Maintaining a global viewpoint, we are dedicated to supplying products of the highest quality yet at a reasonable price for worldwide customer satisfaction."[29] The phrase, "international viewpoint" was changed to "global viewpoint" to emphasize the possible negative impact of Honda on the global environment and the importance of striving to contribute to sustainable development in society. The term "we" replaced "company" to emphasize the importance of each employee's contribution to the company. It is meant to express "the idea of individuals working together to realize a common purpose and at the same time, the pursuit of an understanding of the work at hand."[30] Honda says the word "dedicate" is used because it "recognizes that true joy comes from doing something worthwhile – something to which a person can be dedicated,"[31] such as, "supplying products of the highest quality yet at a reasonable price for worldwide customer satisfaction."[32] It says that "customer satisfaction" goes beyond just meeting specific customer needs and desires and aims to "satisfy – and even exceed – each and every customer's expectations all over the world."[33] To do this, Honda employees must "anticipate social and cultural changes, as well as customers' changing lifestyles."[34] While the simultaneous pursuit of "the highest quality" and "a reasonable price" often conflicts, Honda recognizes that knowledge is created in the synthesis of contradiction. As stated in the company handbook: "It is imperative that both of these goals be achieved. Real progress comes from finding new ways to meet both goals simultaneously."[35]

4.2.4 Management policies

Based on its Corporate Philosophy and Company Principle, Honda has set management policies to guide employees in their daily activities. Managers are required to create a working environment in which these policies can be pursued in practice. The policies are:[36]

- Proceed always with ambition and youthfulness;
- Respect sound theory, develop fresh ideas and make the most effective use of time;
- Enjoy your work, and encourage open communication;
- Strive constantly for a harmonious flow of work;
- Be ever mindful of the value of research and endeavor.

Proceed always with ambition and youthfulness

Honda aims to remain at the leading edge of industrial development. It takes risks and challenges conventional wisdom in order to be first and be the best, and this requires ambition and youthful energy.

The word "ambition" is translated from the Japanese word *"yume,"* which means "dream." Honda sees itself as a company driven by the power of dreams. "When every employee has a dream and pursues it in the company, they bring their individual ability into full play and are motivated to contribute to the welfare of society," said Hiroyuki Yoshino, the fifth president of Honda from 1998 to 2003. "That is why Honda as a company places special emphasis on individual dreams."[37] As noted in the Honda literature, dreams empower people, sparking their passions and giving life deeper meaning.[38] This encourages them to seek out challenges and to be unafraid of failure in the pursuit of those challenges.[39] By striving to realize the future they dream of, Honda employees have sometimes achieved the seemingly impossible. As noted in the literature, this is because "the power borne of a dream is a creative force, capable of producing revolutionary ideas."[40] Soichiro valued challenges that demand creativity to face the future. He disliked imitation in technological development and often set goals that seemed too high, but he always took on a challenge with the absolute belief that the company would succeed. There were many failures, but he trained people to examine the reasons for failure and to apply their understanding to the next task. He said failures offered important tips and if people stayed motivated and kept trying they would succeed. This became the Honda mindset. As Kiyoshi Kawashima, the second president of Honda from 1973 to 1983, is quoted as saying: "What he [Soichiro Honda] said was about making tomorrow's products for the customer, but we would often carry things too far, deviating from the Company Principle and that was the problem." He also said:

> Mr Kihachiro Kawashima [vice president in charge of sales from 1974 to 1978] and his colleagues would say to me, "This is awful, we can't sell this. The customers haven't advanced that far yet." However, if we hadn't experienced that bold failure, and if we had only been building that day's products, I think Honda would have been a shrimpy little company that probably would have disappeared. If the Old Man's [Soichiro Honda's] objective had been to be Number One in Japan, and he had taken a Japanese perspective, I have no doubt that today's Honda would not exist.[41]

Honda has always been guided by a dream, creating its own challenges and facing them with well-planned goals. In 1954, just six years after the company started, Soichiro declared that they would enter and win the world famous Isle of Man Tourist Trophy Motorbike Race. This challenge was considered impossible at first, but it drove strong technological development at the company, making Honda a leading motorcycle manufacturer in a very short period of time. In the same way, management decided that they should enter a Formula One race in 1964, shortly after Honda had started producing automobiles. The objective was not only to introduce Honda to the world but to raise its level of technology by subjecting its engineers to the challenge of tough, competitive racing as well as to the pleasures of winning after trying their best. With the potential for a win that would clearly demonstrate Honda's technological strengths, and with little time to prepare, the race was the ideal venue for conveying the feel of Honda to the world. It was an exercise in the Honda process of setting a goal and focusing time-use and capabilities to achieve it. As former Honda president Nobuhiko Kawamoto, the forth Honda president from 1986 to 1998 said, "For brainstorming, the F1 race was the prime venue. It's okay to fail. We wanted them to feel challenged, like they were climbing a cliff vertically from the start. Then they would pass on this Hondaism to the next generation" (Katayama, 1999: 19).

The project to develop the walking, humanoid robot ASIMO provides another example of the Honda process. The chief engineer for Asimo Project at Honda R&D Co., Ltd at the time, Toru Takenaka, said the robot would not be profitable in the short term but would push Honda far into the future and challenge employees to create more innovative technologies. "Honda loves a challenge," said Takenaka. "What is great about Honda is that the structure for this is established and it has become the corporate culture. As long as you like the work, you can stay motivated. That is one essential factor in creativity" (Katayama, 2002: 53). Takenaka also emphasized the importance of people inspiring each other in lively and thorough discussion of dissenting views, even to the point of fighting. It could be said that innovation at Honda is a strategic process of externalizing a difficult R&D theme, supported by the passion and interest of engineers working to actualize that theme.

Honda also values youthfulness in creating and meeting challenges. Soichiro defined youthfulness as the will to face obstacles and the wisdom to create new values without being constrained by existing frameworks. It is "the wholehearted commitment to ideals" and "the fresh, open-minded passion for learning."[42]

Respect sound theory, develop fresh ideas, and make effective use of time

Known as a company that values the tacit knowledge gained at *"genba"* or the frontline of business, Honda also values theory. It emphasizes the importance of sound theory in the creation and efficient implementation of new ideas so it can continue to be an innovative company. This does not necessarily mean that one should follow accepted theory or the standard way of doing things. Honda encourages employees to "look behind the habit [daily routine] to understand the theory on which it has been based" and to "challenge or change the habit with fresh ideas."[43] Honda continues to innovate by constantly pursuing an understanding of the essence of reality and seeking a better way of doing things. It also pursues more efficient and effective use of time, emphasizing simplicity, concentration, and speed.[44] Simplicity directs one to grasp the essence of what one has to do, requiring a focus on critical issues. Concentration is aimed at focusing resources and thinking where they are most needed to reach essential goals. Speed refers to fast implementation. Effective use of time also means being ready on time. The importance of timing in everything is well understood at Honda and being on time and being well-prepared is viewed as critical. Employees know they are expected to come up with original ideas with limited time and resources in order for Honda to survive, and the timing of decision-making is also of critical importance.

Enjoy your work, and encourage open communication

Honda believes that it has to create an environment in which employees can feel a sense of joy and pride in their work, which comes with the spirit of a challenge and using their own creativity and intellect to the fullest. Believing that employees at the frontline have the best understanding of the reality of the workplace, Honda encourages them to take the initiative to make improvements in operations daily and expects supervisors to support such efforts so the combined and cumulative efforts bring about a better working environment, more employee satisfaction, and more competitiveness.

Honda also emphasizes good relations in teamwork, believing that this can make work more enjoyable. Everyone on the team has to understand the goals and their individual role in order to make a contribution. When a problem occurs, rather than thinking, "that's not my responsibility," all members of the team are expected to take the initiative to work together and resolve it. And communication is critical to effective teamwork. Honda encourages discussion, feedback, and information sharing at every level of the company.

Strive constantly for a harmonious flow of work

The harmonious flow of work promotes efficiency and effectiveness. To achieve a harmonious flow, individual employees have to understand their own work as a part of the larger task, and organize their work to have a natural and consistent flow that can be easily understood.

Be ever mindful of the value of research and endeavor

As a company that values innovation, Honda is never satisfied with what is, but always in search of what can and will be. What has distinguished Honda from other automobile companies is the fact that all of its top managers, following Soichiro, have been relatively young and have had a deep understanding of technologies. Honda management has always viewed technological development as the foundation of the company and its primary business. Vice president Fujisawa who retired in 1983 disapproved of the pursuit of profit through speculation. He warned managers not to dabble outside of their primary business. As testament to Fujisawa's lasting influence, Honda did not speculate in stocks or property during the bubble years of the Japanese economy in the late 1980s. Fujisawa's guiding principle was "the business that makes us proud" (Fujisawa, 1998: 69) and he fought to preserve the identity of Honda as a manufacturer.

Therefore, Honda values research and never-ending endeavor. Even if research doesn't bear fruit in the short term, the company believes that the knowledge and experience gained from long-term effort and the resulting satisfaction is what prepares employees for the future. Supervisors are expected to be patient and to put their trust in the team. When there is no progress for a long period of time and motivation starts to decline, the supervisor has to be able to assess the situation at the frontline, give appropriate advice, and take action if necessary to maintain enthusiasm and motivation.

For example, Honda's first passenger car, the H1300, was a market failure even though it was equipped with an innovative air-cooling system for dissipating heat. However, the experience gained in developing it brought about a turning point at Honda that helped them build a much more successful car, the Civic, launched in 1972. The efficiency of fuel consumption in the Civic made a name for Honda overseas, resulting in strong exports, signaling the end of their image as just a motorcycle manufacturer. With the Civic, Honda raised the level and number of technologies used in small cars and was better able to meet customer needs. More importantly, development of the Civic effected a drastic reorganization of product development processes at the company.

Evidently, the corporate culture at Honda is such that it accepts failure and learns from it, utilizing those lessons in the next task. Everyone works to the limit of their capabilities and, if the project fails, the effort will be analyzed thoroughly to determine the reasons, and no one individual will be held responsible. This is established practice at Honda, and young employees in particular are encouraged to take up the challenge of breaking a new path without fear of failure.

Research at Honda is guided by the Three Reality (*gen*) Principle, or the three Gs: *Genba*, the actual place; *Genbutsu*, the actual thing or situation; and *Genjitsu-teki*, being realistic. The Three Realities Principle is derived from the belief that direct experience provides employees with valuable knowledge to solve problems and innovate. The principle of *Genba* emphasizes the value of going to the actual place to see what is going on, such as the shop floor in production or the frontline in retail sales. In a practice that started with Soichiro, top managers frequently visit, or "dwell," at the frontline to see what is happening at the place where the company's real value is being created. *Genbutsu* emphasizes the importance of knowing the actual situation by being in physical contact with the elements of that situation, including human contact. Knowledge acquired from direct experience is of far greater value at Honda than knowledge from reading books or reports. The principle of *Genjitsu-teki* urges employees to be realistic in their assessments based on knowledge of the actual situation. As a company in pursuit of dreams and ideals, Honda is also realistic about their methods of achieving such ideals.

We can see how the Three Realities Principle was applied in the process of developing the minivan Odyssey and the compact car Fit/Jazz. The development teams started out by observing how and when vehicles of these types were used in their target markets. In developing the Fit, the team went to Europe, its initial target market, to see and feel the market themselves. They did not rely on the information received from their European subsidiaries because they valued knowledge acquired from direct experience and without any preconceptions. They also examined assembly-line methods to see how they could be built. The teams worked together for long periods of time and discussed issues exhaustively in open communication that built a shared experience and understanding of the goals and how to achieve them.

Team leader for the development of the first generation Civic introduced in the 1970s, Shinya Iwakura, described the importance of feeling customer needs directly: "You need a balance of 'marketing in' user needs and 'product out' to create something that captures the flavor of the times, as well as having absolute value and practical use" (Iwanaga et al., 2001: 48). Since it takes three or four years to get a product to market, product designers have to be able to take the measure of future consumer needs.

4.2.5 Organization and activities

Soichiro and Fujisawa tried to create an open-minded atmosphere in the organization, enabling free expression of ideas and acceptance of difference, based on the philosophy of Respect for the Individual and the belief that all human beings are equal and should be allowed to utilize their individual potential to the maximum. As a result, hierarchy is minimized to allow for open debate regardless of one's position or specialty, contributing to the environment of creativity at Honda. Moreover, they tried to eliminate factionalism in order to maintain a dynamic organization. Rules of protocol forbade the routine employment of the children of company officials. They also prohibited the traditional practice of a superior acting as a go-between for a subordinate, and the formation of groups based on the universities employees had graduated from. The rejection of these customs, once typical of many large Japanese organizations, has helped to maintain the vitality of Honda and its corporate culture.

Fujisawa made conscious efforts to build an organization that could survive even after the departure of the charismatic and genius leader, Soichiro

Honda. Fujisawa had his own unique process-based view expressed as the law of *"banbutsu ruten"* or "all things flow." He said: "The reason why Honda could grow so much is because we follow the rules of 'all the things flow.'" However, he also said: "But it is also [by] the rule of 'all the things flow' that Honda would be defeated by newcomers someday. So, we have to think how we can avoid the rule then." He added: "Soichiro Honda is a special person. It would be impossible to nurture a person like him. Then, we have to build a system in which several people can work together to exceed Soichiro Honda" (Fujisawa, 1998: 104). With this in mind, Fujisawa established the core of the current organization of Honda as he deeply understood from experience that human beings perform best not in isolation from each other but in relationships. He said, "everyone needs to be part of the network," and he aimed to establish an organization of people in human relationships that are transparent and frank. His ideals were passed on and sustained by later presidents and became one of the foundations of Honda's organizational culture.

Research and development autonomy

The organizational uniqueness of Honda lies in the independence of its research and development division. In 1957, Honda split off the design department from its Saitama factory and in 1960 incorporated it into a new entity called Honda R&D Co., Ltd. Honda's management of research and design laboratories embodies the company values of equality, independence, and the spirit of challenge. The organizational structure is flat and all employees are considered equal except for the president, who reserves the right to make final development decisions. In the labs, subordinates and their supervisors are encouraged to express their opinions and debate freely, based on the motto, "all engineers are equal before the technology." Original ideas are valued more than seniority and position of authority. Even a person whose behavior seems beyond the pale is still valued for their abilities and given equal opportunity to exercise them (see Figure 4.7).

The phrase "minimum rule" is often heard at Honda. It describes the tacit understanding that each and every employee has creative abilities. In product development, individual autonomy and creative freedom is respected and encouraged, based on the belief that freedom enhances creativity. New employees with insufficient knowledge of design are frequently assigned to draw plans for important parts. Honda employs this method of assignment to enhance the process of learning from others while encouraging the individual to make full use of his or her existing capabilities. Novices are expected to complete the design on their own, but in order to do this they have to tap the knowledge of more experienced colleagues. Therefore, they are required to build relationships with various people in the organization, rather than working alone or just with their supervisors.

100 *Managing Flow*

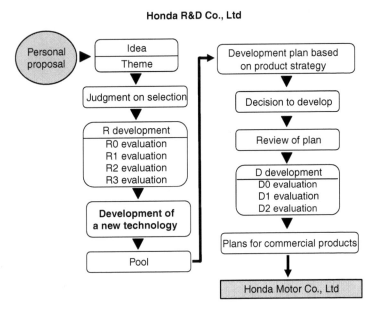

Figure 4.7 R&D system in Honda R&D Co., Ltd
Source: http://www.Honda.co.jp/RandD/system/index.html.

Organization and evaluation of R&D

The organization and evaluation of R&D at Honda is a main pillar of its organizational structure, supporting competitive advantage. This structure reflects the company's emphasis on autonomy and creative freedom beyond fixed organizational boundaries, enabling the pursuit of essence in innovation and product development. Evaluation meetings take place at Honda R&D Co., Ltd. at every stage of development, but a more significant evaluation meeting is a gathering of managers of the Honda group called the "evaluation council." At this council, members of the project team exchange opinions with management as equals, sharing their views about the product thoroughly and candidly, unencumbered by the vague and indirect language associated with deference to authority in Japan. The preservation of creative freedom in research and development has strengthened at Honda as the company has grown. Among the organizational systems that are characteristic of Honda are its Sales, Engineering, and Development model (SED), and the Large Project Leader (LPL).

SED: integrating multiple perspectives. The strategy of integrating sales, engineering, and development began at Honda in 1986 with the formation of ad hoc cross-functional project teams aimed at improving cooperation among these functions. The so-called SED teams consisted of individuals working in each of the three areas in the Honda group and Honda R&D. The teams cut across six regional head offices and four departments to effectively synthesize a strategy for product planning, implementation, and evaluation. SED team leaders were called large project leaders or LPLs. Once a team achieved its goal, it was disbanded. The personal networks that developed in the synthesis of functions on SED teams continued to operate as informal routes of information sharing.

LPL: stressing the human element in team leadership. One of the systems for developing leadership capabilities at Honda is the LPL, which provides real-time opportunities for individuals to experience the demands of leadership, not only in product development, but also in other functions such as marketing. When project teams are set up, an LPL is assigned to lead it, along with two acting LPLs. The LPL is responsible for coordinating the activities of the team and overseeing the progress of the whole project. The acting LPLs oversee costs and engineering respectively. Project managers, or PLs, report to the LPLs and are experts in each of the categories of sales, engineering, and development, respectively. Their role is to supervise the team in their area of expertise. An LPL is selected from among those who have been PLs on past projects. These roles provide the on-the-job training necessary for cultivating experienced leadership (see Figure 4.8).

Each project team sets a concrete goal and strives to achieve it by periodically evaluating their progress. If evaluations reveal little possibility of success, the team will halt the project and divert their efforts into another to maintain efficiency in the development process.

The number of people who have the capability to become an LPL may number only one or two in a thousand. Acting LPLs are chosen on the basis of whether they have the potential to become an LPL. The position not only requires management skill, but imagination and a sense of appropriate action beyond one's particular field of expertise. It calls for artistic sensitivity and insight. "An accomplished engineer must be not only an excellent engineer but also a preeminent artist," said Soichiro Honda. "That person should have both the knowledge of a scientist and the feeling of an artist" (Honda, 2001: 218).

It is interesting to note that the LPL does not have power over personnel, meaning they cannot influence the potential promotion or salary level of project members or even choose the individual members of the project. This is meant to avoid the yes-man syndrome, where a project goes off the rails because no one is willing to criticize the boss. An LPL leads a team not by power legitimated by organizational hierarchy, but by their personal magnetism and power to attract people to their vision, commitment, integrity, energy, and expertise. An LPL gains such power by earning the respect of individual team members arising from relationships of mutual trust, which is built through relentless dialogue among team members in *ba*. The most important

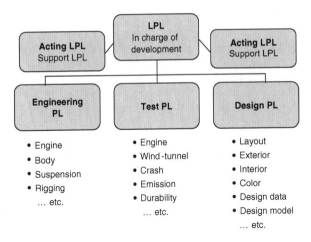

Figure 4.8 LPL system to distribute practical wisdom (*phronesis*)
Source: Author amendment to Honda Motor Co., Ltd internal material.

role of the LPL is to create the variety of *ba* that will encourage members to collaborate independently to achieve the goal. In the process, each member of the team experiences and learns about the capabilities required of a leader, looking to their LPLs and PLs as exemplars. This process is central to Honda management focused on human development.

4.2.6 Maintaining vitality

The automobile industry has survived recent global restructuring, and in Japan only Toyota and Honda have remained independent. Honda is still only half the size of Toyota in sales and has not yet made it into the so-called "4 million club," the number of units a company is expected to produce annually to remain competitive. The biggest challenge for Honda, however, is maintaining the vitality needed for continuous innovation. In the days when the company was still small, many employees learned their jobs directly from colleagues and from interacting with Soichiro. Those who had worked closely with him ensured the succession of his ideas, which they had come to understand through direct, tacit experience on the job. Soichiro transferred his tacit knowledge through shared experiences in actual situations, cultivating exemplars to support the future growth of the company. Most of the direct successors of Soichiro are now retired, as Honda has grown from a small, family-like company to a large global corporation. There are now more than 10,000 employees at Honda R&D alone.

Taking a hard look at the future, Honda is choosing to maintain its independence as a corporate entity. Respect for individual autonomy in the creative process remains a pillar of the company philosophy inherited from

Soichiro. At the same time, significant changes have been made to respond to changing times in an evolving management style that pursues efficiency in flexibility. The key to success in this evolution is continuous creation of knowledge at every level of the organization, and activities to foster the next generation of leaders to lead the knowledge-creating process. Echoing Fujisawa, Takeo Fukui, who took over the presidency in June 2003 as sixth president, has said, "Honda is not a company in which only top management plays an important role. Everyone at the frontline is very important. Every worker should be Soichiro Honda. It is important to create many Soichiro Hondas" (Akai, 2006: 217). Honda's sustainability, achieved by formulating new management methods and maintaining organizational creativity, continues to depend on its ability to deal with the reality that "all things flow" as it develops the next generation of creative leaders at the company.

4.3 Implications

In this chapter, we have presented two companies that are driven by their respective visions and ideals. In a dynamic, ever-changing business environment, these companies relentlessly pursue ideals to create unique values beyond mere profitability. Both have built systems and routines to realize their visions, with the clear understanding that they have to mobilize the entire organization to do so.

The uniqueness of Eisai is in their way of transforming their entire organization based on the vision of *hhc*. Faced with the need for change to survive in an increasingly tough business environment, they started the process of change with the question, "what kind of company do we want to be?" The answer they came up with was a *human health care (hhc)* company. This means that Eisai aims to be a company that can contribute to society by increasing the health care benefit to patients and their families. The *hhc* vision defines the company's *raison d'être* and the kind of future that everyone at Eisai should strive for. It also defines the value system that is the basis on which Eisai employees make decisions and take actions. With the *hhc* vision, the answer to the question "what is good medicine?" changes, because it changes employees' perceptions, from one that sees medical drugs merely as substances to be marketed, to a perception of the process and relationships a particular drug defines with patients and their families aimed at increasing their health care benefit. The *hhc* vision also helps employees see patients and their families not as faceless targets of Eisai products, but as human beings with their own needs, dreams, and emotions. For Eisai, a good medicine is something beyond efficacy that can only be measured scientifically; a good medicine should not only improve the symptoms of the patients but the situations of the patients and their families. To actualize such good medicine, employees have to have a wider perspective and relationship with patients, their families, caregivers, and the community and society that surround them. Instead of just catering to the doctors and hospitals that are Eisai's direct customers, employees have to think deeply about how they can increase the health care benefit to patients while they are developing, producing, and marketing drugs. Eisai has formed various *ba* where employees can interact in actual situations with patients and their families and experience actual clinical services. This enables them to establish a process for applying *hhc* themes and activities and feed these direct experiences back into product development and sales and marketing. It means Eisai is paying attention to every process of how and where their drugs are developed and used, while relentlessly reflecting on what a good medicine should be. All the activities at Eisai are focused primarily on realizing the *hhc* vision rather than on increasing sales, market share, or profit. As stated in Eisai's articles of incorporation, profit is not the goal but the result of the process of contributing to the patients' benefit.

In the second case, Honda, we are looking at a different industry, but there is commonality between the companies because both base their entire systems and operations on vision and ideals. Honda's vision of its future as a global company, even when it was just a small town factory, continued to drive the company to realize its dream. Such a future was realized not by the charismatic leadership of Soichiro Honda alone, but by knowledge-creation activity at every level of the organization among individual employees driven by ideals, dreams, and high-quality experiences. What drives them relentlessly to pursue their ideals is the Honda philosophy that is shared by every employee, which provides the common basis for, and direction of, the knowledge-creating processes. Respect for the Individual, one of the two fundamentals of the Honda philosophy, defines the process and relations that Honda employees should have with each other and with the world. The other fundamental belief, The Three Joys, defines the Honda value system for judging "goodness" in thinking and for assessing the value that Honda creates. Like Eisai's philosophy of *hhc*, at the center of both visions is the view of the human being as a unique individual, each with his or her own thoughts, dreams, emotions, and capacity to create. Honda's value is created by and for such human beings. As Soichiro Honda said, Honda is not a place of research on technologies, but a place of research on human beings. Honda's management policies, organizational systems, and routines are built on such beliefs aimed at creating value for customers and society.

In summary, these two cases illustrate how knowledge-based management pursues a vision for the future based on ideals that consider the relationships of people in society. When a company pursues the common good, good business results follow and are sustainable.

Notes

1. Eisai Co., Ltd website *"hhc & Compliance*: What is *hhc?,"* http://www.eisai.co.jp/ecompany/ehhc1/html
2. Extract from "Eisai Innovation Declaration."
3. Eisai discovered the possible candidate for the chemical compound in 1985. ARICEPT was put to clinical test in 1989, approved by the FDA in 1996, and introduced to the market in January 1997.
4. Interview with Chihiro Takayama, the Chief Knowledge Officer of Eisai, August, 2007.
5. http://www.caringtohelpothers.com
6. Eisai Co., Ltd (2004).
7. Elmed is coined from "elderly medicine."
8. Eisai Co., Ltd (2004).
9. Interview with Norihito Watanabe of the Knowledge Creation Department at Eisai, August, 2007.
10. Aitsugu seizou bunsha tokusakuka [Spinning out the production lines: good for the company?]. *Nikkei Sangyo Shinbun*. (October 6, 2004), p. 22.
11. http://www.eisai.co.jp/ecompany/ecgguideline.html
12. From the preface of the *Honda Philosophy* handbook, written by Nobuhiko Kawamoto, then the President and CEO of the Honda Motor Co.
13. The *Honda Philosophy* handbook, p. 15.
14. Ibid., p. 13.
15. Ibid., p. 14.
16. Ibid.
17. Ibid., p. 15.
18. http://www.mobilityland.co.jp/english/motegi
19. At his retirement speech in August, 1983.
20. Although it was "the joy of producing, selling, and buying" in 1951, it was revised to "the joy of buying, selling, and producing" in 1955 to emphasize the idea that the customer should come first. This was later revised to "the joy of buying, selling, and creating."
21. *Honda Philosophy* handbook, p. 17.
22. http://world.honda.com/history/limitlessdreams/satisfaction/text/03.html
23. *Honda Philosophy* handbook, p. 19.
24. http://world.honda.com/history/limitlessdreams/satisfaction/text/03.html
25. *Honda Philosophy* handbook, p. 19.
26. http://world.honda.com/history/limitlessdreams/satisfaction/text/03.html
27. *Honda Philosophy* handbook, p. 21.
28. http://world.honda.com/history/limitlessdreams/satisfaction/text/01.html
29. http://world.honda.com/profile/philosophy/
30. *Honda Philosophy* handbook, p. 31.
31. Ibid.
32. Ibid., p. 29.
33. Ibid.
34. Ibid.
35. Ibid., p. 31.
36. Ibid., p. 33.
37. Excerpted from a speech given by Hiroyuki Yoshino, president of Honda at the time, at the "Marunouchi knowledge forum" on December 10, 2001.

38. http://world.honda.com/ThePowerofDreams/
39. *Honda Philosophy* handbook, p. 35.
40. Ibid.
41. http://world.honda.com/history/limitlessdreams/satisfaction/text/01.html
42. *Honda Philosophy* handbook, p. 37.
43. Ibid., p. 39.
44. Ibid.

References

Akai, K. (2006). *"Tsuyoi kaisha" wo tsukuru: Honda renpo kyouwa koku no himitsu* [Establishing a "Strong company": Secrets of Honda Federal Republic Corporation]. Tokyo: Bunshun Bunko.

Eisai Co., Ltd. (1989). *Eisai Commitment to Innovation.* Unpublished manuscript.

Eisai Co., Ltd. (2004). *Eisai Experience.* Tokyo: Eisai Co., Ltd. [Company introduction video.]

Fujisawa, T. (1998). *Keiei ni owari ha nai* [No Ending to Managing a Company]. Tokyo: Bunshun Bunko.

Harada, K. (1977). *Honda Soichiro: Jonetsu to namida* [Soichiro Honda: His Passion and Tears]. Tokyo: Gomashobo.

Honda Motor Co., Ltd. (n.d.). *Honda Philosophy.* Unpublished handbook. Shizuoka: Honda Motor Co., Ltd.

Honda, S. (1996). *Ore no kangae* [My Thoughts]. Tokyo: Shincho Bunko.

Honda, S. (2001). *Honda Soichiro: Yume wo chikara ni* [Soichiro Honda: Power of Dreams]. Tokyo: Nikkei Business Bunko.

Iwakura, S., Nagasawa, S., and Iwaya, M. (2001). *Honda no design senryaku: Civic, 2daime Prelude, Odyssey wo chushin ni* [Design Strategy of Honda: With Focus on Civic, Second Generation Prelude and Odyssey]. *Ritsumeikan Keieigaku* [Ritsumeikan Business Journal], 40 (1): 31–51.

Katayama, O. (1999). *Honda no heiho* [Tactics of Honda]. Tokyo: Shogakukan Bunko.

Katayama, O. (2002). *Honda Soichiro to sono shirarezaru deshitachi* [Soichito Honda and his Unknown Apprentices]. Tokyo: Kodansha.

Morita, H. and Tsuyuki, E. (2001). "Case study: Eisai Corporation," in D. Senoo, S. Akutsu, and I. Nonaka (eds). *Chishiki Keiei Jissennron.* [On Practice: Knowledge Creation and Utilization]. Tokyo: Hakuto Shobo, pp. 69–102.

Morita, H., Tsuyuki, E., and Nonaka, I. (2001). "Case study: Eisai Corporation." Unpublished manuscript.

Nonaka, I. and Peltokorpi, V. (2006). "Visionary knowledge management: The case of Eisai transformation," *International Journal of Learning and Intellectual Capital,* 3 (2), 109–209.

Tanaka, S. (2007). *Honda no kachikan: Genten kara mamori tsudukeru DNA* [The Honda Value: DNA Maintained from the Origin]. Tokyo: Kadokawa Shoten.

Yamamoto, O. (1996). *Honda no genten* [The origin of Honda]. Tokyo: Narumi Bunko.

5
Ba

In this chapter we elaborate on the concept of *ba*, the enabling context for knowledge creation and innovation. Applying the theory of organizational knowledge creation to the case of the Mayekawa Manufacturing Co., Ltd, we illustrate the importance of co-creating a shared context or *ba* in the firm's relationships with customers that enables continuous, joint creation of knowledge to achieve sustainable competitive advantage. Mayekawa has been creating new knowledge and new businesses by building and connecting *ba* both within and across organizational boundaries, providing the most vivid example of *ba*-centered management in a business ecosystem.

The KUMON Institute of Education Co., Ltd is in the education business with operations in 45 countries. Their education method and system of organization are unique as an illustration of the feedback loop of knowledge creation in multilayered *ba*, a process that accelerates improvement and enables continuous expansion. Moreover, the company's philosophy is to develop intimate relationships with the aim of making a social contribution as they expand internationally.

5.1 Mayekawa Manufacturing Co., Ltd

5.1.1 Company overview

Mayekawa Manufacturing Co., Ltd.[1] began producing industrial freezers and associated systems in 1924 and is now one of the world's leading companies in industrial refrigeration. In 2007, Mayekawa was ranked the second manufacture in the industrial refrigeration market, and the firm continues to play an important role in the fields of food refrigeration and thermal control technology. Mayekawa is a privately held company with the consolidated sales of 126 billion yen or about 1.23 billion US dollars. The company employs 3,180 people (2,130 in Japan and 1,050 overseas) as of 2007 had 60 affiliate offices overseas in 20 countries. Throughout its 70-year history it has expanded the spectrum of its activities in services and technology in the energy sector, in food processing, and in the provision of extremely low temperature environments. In step with the times, Mayekawa has developed from a small, refrigerator manufacturer into a full-service organization with a wide range of capabilities (see Figure 5.1). Sales of refrigerators and food processing machines now represent only one-third of gross income. The remaining two-thirds come from services such as engineering and maintenance. Mayekawa's business concept is "total heat engineering," meaning it supplies total solutions through plant engineering using thermal control technologies. Mayekawa not only sells refrigerators and compressors but designs, installs, and maintains systems such as production lines and utilities. It has even expanded to energy consulting and food processing machinery.

The company vision at Mayekawa is based on the two concepts of *"kyousei"* (co-existence) and *"total system."* For Mayekawa, *"kyousei"* means the building of a new relationship with its customers, and the concept of "total system" functions to change the relationship from a simple buyer–seller arrangement to a business partnership that continuously creates new businesses that start as a *total system* project. Underlying this idea is the understanding that the era of mass production, when manufacturers simply produced goods for sale, is over. This means that the market should no longer be viewed "objectively" from the outside but from the inside in *ba*, as an amalgamation of people in relationships.

Mayekawa understands that it is no longer sufficient to just produce and sell industrial parts. By shifting its emphasis to sharing context and jointly creating new knowledge with clients, it has combined its product offerings with knowledge of processes offered as consulting advice in a more comprehensive service. In this way, Mayekawa has transformed itself from a simple supplier of physical products and parts to a provider of total solutions. The difference is that these solutions are not predefined processes and manufacturing models. They are innovations created jointly with the customers.

Throughout its history, Mayekawa has grown by building deep relationships with its customers to find and cultivate niche markets. Such relationships make it possible for the company to keep innovating in products and services that have value for specific customers, and this is the source of its sustainable competitive advantage. This approach has enabled them to avoid cut-throat competition and create a new space in the market "untainted by competition" (Kim and Mauborgne, 2004: 77). It is a philosophy expressed at Mayekawa in the phrase *"mu-kyouso,"* meaning "no competition," and is conveyed in internal publications, such as *From Competition to Co-creation* (Shimizu and Mayekawa, 1998). Mayekawa considers it more important that a firm find its own path, regardless of the competition. Its methods render the competition irrelevant, demonstrating

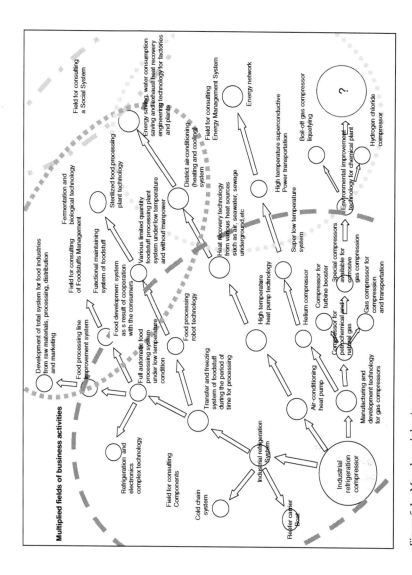

Figure 5.1 Mayekawa's business areas
Source: Based on company information.

5.1.2 Organizing the companies: *doppos* as dynamic autonomous entities

To realize its vision of co-creation, Mayekawa has a unique project-based *"doppo"* organization, which is a collective of many, small independent companies. Short for *"dokuritsu hojin,"* *"doppo"* literally means "independent legal entity." Each *doppo* or company employs from 10 to 15 people and serves a particular region or focuses on a specific market, like food, industrial freezers, or energy related services. Mayekawa has about 80 such corporations in Japan and about 40 overseas. In a sense, they are small, independent venture businesses constituting the Mayekawa company network.

The objective of this organization is to locate decision-making where the relevant knowledge and information resides, and to increase environmental sensitivity, entrepreneurial action, and innovation by creating an organization that leverages the knowledge and ideas of all employees. Since Mayekawa products and services are customized and the company expands business by cultivating niche markets one by one, it is critical that they be able to identify and accommodate the specific needs of existing and potential customers quickly. The *doppo* organization was developed to give Mayekawa the flexibility and speed it needed to quickly transform customer needs into new businesses. The *doppo* concept is based on the notion of self-organization, so the individual units are relatively free to organize themselves according to their environmental stimuli. Each company is responsible for its own business and is self-sufficient, containing all necessary functions such as design, installation, sales, marketing, maintenance, accounting, and personnel, and producing its own financial statements. Each *doppo* draws up its own strategy and investment plan, develops its own products, markets them, and manages its own human resources.

While the *doppos* are autonomous and self-sufficient, they are not isolated from each other. Some even share the same office space, and members of different *doppos* often spend time together in informal relationships. Sometimes a new project and even a new *doppo* is created out of such a relationship. While individual employees identify themselves with their *doppo*, they share similar corporate values, visions, and beliefs across the network. In this sense, Mayekawa as a collective of *doppos* is a collaborative community (cf. Heckscher and Adler, 2006).

The *doppos* often work together and several working together form a block, categorized by industry or by region. *Doppos* in a block share information and technologies, supplementing each others' work on a project that is too large for a single *doppo*, while allowing each *doppo* to retain its uniqueness. Cooperation can also take place across blocks. In principle, all of the entities can draw on each other's resources according to their market needs. Yoshio Iwasaki, the president of Mayekawa Research Lab., describes the importance of the relationship among *doppos* as follows:

> A *doppo* is designed to be a self-sufficient organization. But when members of a *doppo* think deeply about how they can exist as a *doppo*, they come to understand what they lack. Then, they start thinking about how they should work together with other *doppos* or groups. Of course, each *doppo* has to make a profit. However, regardless of how much money a *doppo* makes, we have to keep a close eye on its relationships or lack thereof with other *doppos*. If we are unable to see what a particular *doppo* is doing, it means there is something wrong with it.[2]

In the end, Mayekawa is a coherent organization with its various parts interacting organically. Figure 5.2 shows the organic configuration of *doppos* and blocks.

5.1.3 *Kigyouka Keikaku*: strategic planning for co-creating the future

Each *doppo* devises strategy to develop its own niche businesses, and this strategic process is described by Mayekawa as "*kigyouka keikaku*," which literally means "enterprise planning to make a corporation." This approach stands in contrast to conventional analytical strategy-making The term "*kigyouka keikaku*" derives from the belief at Mayekawa that everyone should be an independent decision-maker and should participate in fashioning their own company into what they desire it to be.

Kigyouka keikaku is a four-part strategic process that consists of: (i) understanding the environment and one's own position in it; (ii) visualizing *kigyouka* or imagining the company they want to create; (iii) understanding the

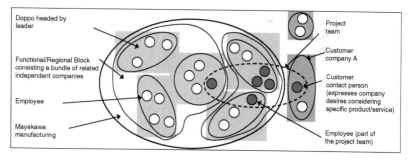

Figure 5.2 Mayekawa as an organic configuration of doppos and blocks
Source: Based on Peltokorpi and Tsuyuki (2006: 41).

direction of *kigyouka* or the company they want to create; and (iv) articulating an action plan and important issues. During these stages of the process, *doppo* members go out into the field to get close to the customer and sense and experience the market and the environment on the spot in order to understand it and anticipate change. They synthesize this knowledge in dialectical interaction with existing viewpoints, which are grounded in historical experience and the culture of the company. All members of a *doppo* participate in the discussion of *kigyouka keikaku*. Final agreement is recorded on one sheet of A3-size paper as a commitment made by all members of the organization and serving as the guide or strategic map for carrying out the plan. Through the process of imagining and drawing in *kigyouka keikaku*, each individual comes to commit to the goal and the plan of their *doppo* and understand what he or she should do to realize it.

Understanding one's position as part of the environment

The understanding of one's position as a part of the environment emerges from the process of defining the relationship between the *doppo* and the environment. This may look like a typical process of strategic planning based on analysis of the environment and the firm's internal resources. However, "environment" here is not simply the market and objective analysis of it, but the whole, living, changing world in which the *doppo* exists. According to Iwasaki, this means the market and the world we live in, including the local community. "We view ourselves as a part of the world and express our position in relation to the world as a whole. At the basis of this process is the idea of *kyousou* (joint creation, or co-creation). That is, we are created in the relationship with the environment, rather than existing as an independent, isolated entity."[3]

During this process, it is important that all *doppo* members express what they "feel" in their daily operational environment, rather than logically reiterating what they have gleaned from newspaper and magazine accounts of the environment. "You should behave in accordance with what you feel, not what you think," says Masao Mayekawa, the honorary chairman of Mayekawa. Doppo members are expected to feel the environment by transcending the boundary between the organization and the market and indwelling with customers. Employees are encouraged to spend time out of the office and on the client's factory floor. Even a very junior member of a *doppo* can visit a client without submitting paperwork for internal approval, no matter how far away the client is. Mayekawa thinks it is important to "get out into the actual world" to achieve a seamless, direct experience with the client. By indwelling, engineers are able to grasp the needs of clients more precisely. They do this by observing the client's production line alongside the client, fostering a relationship of trust more so than those engineers who focus only on technical specifications. Customer needs and solutions to their problems often are only tacitly understood and difficult to articulate. One acquires that tacit knowledge and solves problems effectively only by experiencing what the customer experiences. As Masao Mayekawa describes it, indwelling with the client achieves a merging of subject and object to perceive the client's essential needs.[4] He calls this "letting the customer grumble." However, just experiencing the customer's world does not lead one to innovation. It is important to be able to separate the customer's essential needs and wants from their grumbling. This requires an understanding of the importance of timing and an ability to act in a timely fashion, because a customer's grumbling has a "here-now" quality that can quickly be lost. A former manager of the Total Service Food Department explains:

> Often, customers themselves don't know what they want. Even though they can't articulate it, they are saying something, like they want to change something, cut the cost more, or have better quality. At the beginning, we don't know what to do because we can't understand them. Only after we talk with them many times or dwell in and around their shop floor do we come to understand them. (Tsuyuki, 2006: 61)

The subjective "feeling" of each *doppo* member about customer needs is objectified through dialogue with other *doppo* members. And it is not only engineers who dwell in the customer's space, but other Mayekawa employees, in functions ranging from sales and design to maintenance. All of them examine the customer's problems and needs from their different perspectives and discuss and synthesize their views to arrive at an understanding of the customer's true needs. This multiperspective approach is termed "*sei-han-gi ittai*," which literally translates as "production, sales, and technology integrated." Thus, *kigyouka keikaku* is a mechanism for cultivating dialogue to create new business plans that incorporate diverse viewpoints and knowledge from different backgrounds. In the process, *doppo* members delve deeply into themselves and the customer to position the *doppo* in the environment as a whole. To do that, they have to look not only at their technologies and resources, but at their organizational culture, traditions, vision, and mission.

The image of Kigyouka: *visualizing the company one wants to create*

In the imaging process, members of the *doppo* express how they want their *doppo* to be. While understanding the environment and one's position in it, it is a process of looking at the past and present of the *doppo* and the world in which it lives. Visualizing the company that one wants to create is a process of looking into the *doppo*'s future, as Iwasaki explains:

> In this process, it is important to leap to an image of how we want ourselves to be in the future. To leap means to be free of the conventional way of seeing and thinking and the existing way of the organization, its

system and rules. To leap, you need intuition. It is the active and creative ability to see the environment and ourselves intuitively. We try to grasp the messages of change and the changing environment using our five senses. We know that our organizational intuition is working when we are able to use it to think about how we can go beyond our present situation. (Iwasaki, 1995)

The image of the company has to be stated in simple words. These words represent the essence of *doppo* members' collective thoughts, dreams, and emotions. The image doesn't have to be a concrete one, but it has to trigger in *doppo* members the vision of the future. Iwasaki says it is not an image based on the present state of things but an image of the future pulling the present forward.

In this process, *doppo* members determine what they will do to realize the image of *kiguouka*, based on their understanding of the environment. In the previous stage, goals have been set to achieve the image. In that stage it is more important to lay out general principles and ways of thinking rather than draw up a concrete plan. According to Iwasaki, the mountain to be climbed is determined by the process of imagining *kigyouka*, while the route of the climb is determined by understanding the direction of *kigyouka*.

The most important question asked in this process is: How should we change the relationship with others to actualize the image of *kigyouka*? The direction of *kigyouka* articulates how the *doppo* can build and change its relationships with other *doppos* and blocks or other firms. In other words, it defines what kind of *ba* the *doppo* must build to realize their vision of the future.

The plan of action: creating narrative

In this process, *doppo* members draw a concrete plan of action for realizing the image of *kigyouka*, including a schedule, an investment plan, and sales and profit projections. The action plan can be flexible and change as the project progresses and unforeseen situations unfold.

In summary, *kigyouka keikaku* is a process in which *doppo* members create their future based on their understanding of their past and present in terms of their relationships with others. This method should not be mistaken as conventional, analytical planning. Rather, it is a co-creative process that pursues visionary innovation, starting with imagination and the development of ideas based on feelings, experience, and the exploration of hunches. It requires an entrepreneurial spirit and aims to instill such spirit in *doppo* members, as well as a feeling for decision-making and responsibility. *Kigyouka keikaku* is future-oriented planning based on tacit knowledge acquired by asking existential questions, in contrast to formal, analytic planning based on explicit knowledge of facts and statistical data. In the process, *doppo* members share and synthesize their contexts and perspectives to create *ba*. In such *ba*, knowledge emerges not only in the form of an action plan but also in the form of a unique culture of seeing things in relations with others.

Mayekawa sees *kigyouka keikaku* as a process of creating and handing down the culture of the company. The unique character of the process is its perspective of seeing the present from the future, the inside from the outside, and the micro from the macro. *Doppo* members view themselves and their relationship with the environment in terms of their vision of who they are and how they want to be in the future. Such a perspective enables them to see what they must do to realize the desired future, rather than seeing the future as an extension of the present. They also must see themselves and the environment from the outside and from the top down, although *kigyouka keikaku* is very much a bottom-up process at the start. In *kigyouka keikaku*, *doppo* members bring together their tacit knowledge about the market or the environment based on their "feeling" about daily operations. This is not simply the sum of bottom-up knowledge. *Doppo* members must see the environment and themselves from the macroperspective in order to grasp the essence of what they feel. After deep, self-examination there may be times when a *doppo* or even Mayekawa as a whole must question and rethink its position and its entire method of doing business.

Figure 5.3 is a simplified model of *kigyouka keikaku* as envisioned by the company. Starting with an undetermined condition, it moves to broader and

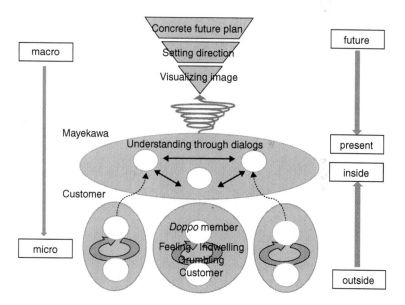

Figure 5.3 Simplified model *of kigyouka keikaku*

deeper sharing of tacit knowledge in *ba*, while distilling the accumulation of knowledge into more explicit language and images for broader distribution, toward creation of the new. Note that this is not a singular, linear process but a recurring, expanding spiral process.

The co-creative development of new businesses to leverage creative synergies occurs not only at the *doppo* level, but in overall corporate planning. After completion of the *kigyouka keikaku* process at each *doppo*, leaders and subleaders engage in the same process again with the block to which they belong, sometimes joined by leaders from other blocks and even senior management. Representatives of the block then meet with the general research institute where all information is shared and ideas and problems discussed. Eventually, a new overall business plan is summarized in a pamphlet, which is then circulated to all *doppos*.

5.1.4 Knowledge co-creation with customers: the case of the bread factory kaizen

A process similar to *kigyouka keikaku* can be found in the co-creation relationship with customers. Mayekawa's Bread Factory Kaizen (improvement) Project began in 1997 and is a vivid example of co-creation.[5] The client, Takaki Bakery, was a long-established and renowned maker of European-style bread in Japan, and Mayekawa, among others, had provided almost all of Takaki's original cooling and freezing systems in a business relationship dating back to the 1960s. When Mayekawa was asked to take part in the upgrade of these systems, they knew they would have to acquire a more detailed understanding of the bread-making process and the bread market in order to adequately serve the client's needs. Years earlier, concerns had arisen at Mayekawa about the traditional approach of generalizing the food industry in a way that did not recognize the reality of its diverse products and services. Customer needs in the food processing sector had become more and more complex, requiring suppliers to provide more customized and flexible solutions. It was no longer enough to simply sell and install equipment and parts to compete successfully in a cost-driven market.

To be able to respond flexibly to individual client needs, Mayekawa's food products block had been restructured to create four different *doppos* in accordance with industry type and market. Sensing a crisis in the industry, Mayekawa wanted to be able to offer their long-established clients newer, more comprehensive solutions. In 1997, they initiated the Bread Factory Kaizen Project at Takaki. As a supplier of freezers, Mayekawa already had knowledge of the dough-freezing process, but felt that it needed to understand the entire bread-making process to serve Takaki better. The kaizen project members asked Takaki to teach them the entire process. Takaki agreed, and the four *doppos* in Mayekawa's food products block joined forces to cooperate with each other and Takaki, dispatching engineers to Takaki's factory to learn how to make bread.

At the outset, the project was mainly concerned with improving Takaki's wholesale factory, which produced for mass market retailers such as supermarkets and convenience store chains. When Mayekawa came on the scene, Takaki had already commissioned a proposal for improving productivity from an outside consulting firm, but they were still unsure. Mayekawa also had no ready-made solutions to the problems at Takaki, so they began with classic kaizen measures and were able to deliver good results in utility improvements on the production line, leading to energy savings and higher efficiency. However, it soon became apparent that these improvements were not sufficient. There was a need to address the root cause of inefficiencies at Takaki that could inhibit sustainable, long-term competitive advantage and profit.

By "indwelling" at Takaki's factory, Mayekawa's cross-functional teams found the root cause of manufacturing inefficiencies in the complicated process of sales and shipping to customers, which were creating complications on the bread production line. The bread making industry in Japan had recently undergone a dramatic change due to the so-called "freshly baked bread wars" in which retailers had committed themselves to "freshness" and "variety." This demanded production of many different types of bread products in lower volumes and more frequent delivery to ensure freshness. Production shifted away from items with a daily volume of 1,000 in favor of items with a daily volume of 100, and the bread had to be baked two to three times each day to ensure fresh delivery, leading to increased costs and a decrease in manufacturing efficiency.

Based on this finding, Mayekawa's team proposed two solutions. The first was to simplify the bread production process to meet the fluctuating demands of shipping. The second was to simplify the shipping process, which meant sales and distribution had to be restructured. Inevitably the project led to a review of Takaki's entire wholesale business. To identify the essential problem and its solution Mayekawa and Takaki had to engage in deep discussion about the essential role and function of the wholesale business and what they thought it should be in the larger context. Mayekawa brought the *kigyouka keikaku* process to the discussion and managers in sales and planning at Takaki, who normally were not included in factory improvement projects, joined in.

The following questions were asked during the *kigyouka keikaku* process at Takaki:

- What are the existing and future characteristics of the market that Takaki is currently serving?
- Which market is Takaki targeting?
- What does Takaki value?
- What kind of relationship does Takaki want to build with the market?
- What is unique about Takaki?

- How are relationships within the division?
- How are relationships among divisions?
- What is Takaki's culture?
- What is Takaki's history?

Based on these questions, everyone freely discussed their thoughts and feelings. It became clear that the essence of Takaki's problem was in the discrepancy of its role as a wholesaler and its vision of providing excellent, high-quality, European-style bread products to the Japanese consumer. The high-quality ideal didn't match Takaki's wholesale objective to supply the mass-produced, American-style, white-bread product the mass market preferred. Takaki had a long-standing reputation in Japan as a leading producer of European-style bread and bread culture. This had been its mission, tradition, pride, and core competence. On the other hand, the wholesale business demanded a different level of quality to satisfy the mass market. In the process of *kigyouka keikaku* it became apparent that the problems would not be overcome by improvements inside the factory alone. At this point, the project team had to ask the fundamental question, "what does Takaki want to be as a company?" They proposed a rethinking of all major processes, from purchasing to sales, and a rethinking of the essential role of the wholesaler from the point of view of the retail customer.

Since Takaki's tradition and strengths were in its ability to promote bread culture, it was determined that as a wholesaler it should be able to recommend better ways to sell bread in accordance with the unique situation of each retailer, rather than just passively filling retail orders. It followed from this strategic approach that the factory should be multifunctional to respond flexibly to variations in demand. Discussion then focused on the factory and what functions it needed to implement the strategy.

Takaki had both a wholesale and a retail business and a separate factory for each, located about 60 km apart. The wholesale factory produced dough and baked it into bread, while the retail factory produced frozen dough that had to be shipped to Takaki's retail stores. If the two factories worked together, allowing the wholesale factory to use the retail factory's frozen dough, it would give the company more flexibility to produce a greater variety of products more efficiently. Mayekawa ran a simulation to see if this was feasible. It showed promise and Mayekawa started developing the necessary technology and systems for a smooth integration of the two factories. In the end, the project team not only improved the bread-making process and achieved a better taste through kaizen, they also improved many other processes at the factory, including bulk production for wholesale distribution and coping with more variable demand. All of these efforts eventually led to a better quality product at a lower production cost.

The bread factory case shows how Mayekawa established a joint *ba* with the client for the co-creation of knowledge and value through interrelatedness.

Mayekawa leveraged its customer-oriented *doppo* system of distributed, autonomous leadership to work closely with Takaki to co-innovate a problem and a solution. With the emphasis on co-creation of knowledge and innovation, Mayekawa applied the concept of *sei-han-gi ittai* to integrate the customer's knowledge assets in production, sales, and technology through dialogue and questioning to reach understanding on an essential level. The entire process was fostered by relationships of trust and reliance or interdependence, and a shared mindset cultivated by indwelling in Takaki's world and sharing their tacit knowledge and feelings. Commitment on the part of the team members is a *sine qua non* for successful sharing and co-creation in *ba*. In the business ecosystem that Mayekawa is a part of, the customer is the most important entity. Note that this is not just the immediate customer, but also the customer's customer or the final consumer of the bread product.

In co-creation, building relationship based on openness is crucial. Masao Mayekawa describes the shared context of *ba* as "a world that appears when the relevant people open themselves to each other to deepen their relationship.... To open one's self means to lose oneself, and the more you do so the more you will be able to grasp *ba*." He says this is possible and necessary not only for the individual but for the group and the organization as a whole: "Through losing ourselves by putting ourselves in the position of the client and functioning from their viewpoint, the *ba* evolved very naturally into a cluster of relationships, and Mayekawa was able to actualize itself in the *ba*" (Mayekawa, 2004: 179–183). This philosophical notion of losing the self to find the self is not simply the shedding of preconceptions and biases to perceive present reality. It means individuals and companies must overcome their self-centered worldview and see themselves and others within and through their relationships. At *ba*, individuals, the organization, and the environment interpenetrate each other as the relationships among them keep changing. Hence, Mayekawa employees must be open and transcend themselves in order to see themselves in terms of their relations with others, particularly the client, and the client's customers. Through deep interaction in *ba*, Mayekawa employees are able to grasp the customer's latent needs and wants, thereby realizing what they want to accomplish themselves. Masao Mayekawa says their approach is not to ponder a problem intensely before acting, but to act immediately and naturally to "feel" their way through trial-and-error, reducing the sense of "misplacement" to reach that moment "in between" subject and object where co-creation of knowledge is possible. He says the answers to questions and problems may pass in front of one's eyes over and over again in *ba* but are difficult to grasp. Practice as routine is essential to learn to differentiate and discern appropriate answers from the blurred and complex reality, and to allow the gradual emergence of abstraction from within local experience (Bakken and Hernes, 2006).

Co-creation of *ba* with customers is not limited to Mayekawa Japan. The company applies these same principles with customers overseas. An example of a recent success is the co-development with a US customer of a humidifying cooling system that freezes freshly baked bread for transport and distribution without damage to the bread's consistency or flavor. Mayekawa developed the technology in the US in close cooperation with the customer. The system was then exported to Japan and Europe. The creation of *ba* with customers in Europe and North America worked well, although it took slightly longer to establish these relationships due to language barriers.

5.2 KUMON Institute of Education Co., Ltd

5.2.1 Company overview

Established by Toru Kumon in 1955, the KUMON Institute of Education Co., Ltd is one of the largest, privately held educational institutions in the world, serving 4 million students in 45 countries (as of July 2007). Its core business is educational services based on its unique method of learning, the KUMON method. The method was originally devised to teach mathematics, but has been expanded to Japanese, English and other languages.

KUMON insists that the KUMON method is not about teaching the child but about discovering their autonomy and hidden potential so they will be motivated to learn by themselves. The ultimate goal of the method is to nurture the person's ability to contribute to society, as articulated in the KUMON mission statement:

> By discovering the potential of each individual
> and developing his or her ability to the maximum,
> we aim to foster sound, capable people
> and thus contribute to the global community.
> (KUMON, "Company Profile 2006–2007")

KUMON states that its vision is to contribute to world peace through education. This means that it aims to motivate people to participate actively in society and with a greater sense of humanity and harmony by fulfilling their need to learn and fully develop their capabilities.

5.2.2 Why and how the KUMON method started

Young people in Japan have to pass difficult examinations to gain entry to high school and university and, in some cases, even junior high school. As a result, a small industry in so-called "cram schools" has developed around the periphery of the education system to help students pass these exams. KUMON also began as one of these privately run schools, but its aim is not the passing of exams. Instead, it focuses on autonomous learning tailored to each individual. As a result, its curriculum does not conform to education system guidelines, especially at the level of elementary and junior high school, although it does offer courses up to completion of senior high school.[6] The KUMON method is generally perceived as a way to enhance ability and achievement, but its real aim is to develop students' confidence and nurture their sense of humanity. Its creator, Toru Kumon, was originally a high school mathematics teacher. After long experience and close attention to student behavior he began to devise ways of learning tailored to individual students. The seeds of the KUMON method were planted in 1954 when he created a special program for learning mathematics for his son Takeshi. He had been tutoring his son using an exercise book that conformed to government guidelines for elementary school texts, but had found that the structure was inappropriate to his son's learning process. He decided to design a self-study workbook so his son could teach himself. Each worksheet in the workbook was geared toward understanding one, overall point. This became the basis of the KUMON method.

The KUMON method was a well-planned system of self-learning. It started with a learning goal and then followed the steps to reach it. Toru Kumon's aim was to design a process that would be less burdensome for children and help them reach the goal by the shortest route and in the shortest time possible. While the cram schools focused on improving exam scores by helping children understand elementary and junior high school textbooks, Toru Kumon bypassed those texts and set his sights on incremental achievement towards a senior high school level of mathematics capability for each student. This shifted the focus from the short-term goal of passing exams to the far-reaching goal of senior high school level comprehension, and this greatly influenced later refinement of the KUMON method.[7]

Toru Kumon started the business of teaching with his method in 1957, but he soon realized that the high cost of renting space for the classes was an unrealistic burden on operations, so he began to recruit well-educated housewives to become KUMON franchisees who could teach at home or at nearby facilities using the KUMON workbooks and instruction methods.

In 1962, Kumon reorganized his company[8] under the name of the KUMON Method. The publication in 1974 of KUMON's book *The Secret of the KUMON Method in Mathematics* (*Kumonshiki sansu no himitsu*) triggered a massive increase in enrolments in KUMON correspondence courses and the addition of more classes. One year later there were 110,000 students and 1,960 classes in Japan (see Figure 5.4).

5.2.3 Learning system centered on students

It is difficult to explain the merits of the KUMON method precisely. Media reports focusing on the self-study nature of the system have erroneously described KUMON as a method of learning from printed materials. The basic elements of the system, derived from the mission principles, are: its philosophical approach to teaching; the instructors' background and teaching methods; its administrative support; and the workbooks, which

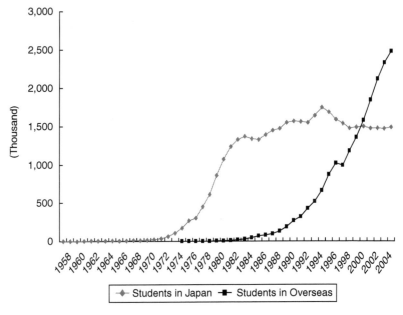

Figure 5.4 Enrollment trends in the KUMON Centers
Note: Accumulated number of students in each subject.
Source: KUMON internal records.

are continuously modified. To see the merits of the system it is important to Understand how these elements function as an organic whole.

Basic philosophy

The philosophical aim of the KUMON method is to raise the human being to a higher level of awareness by identifying his or her potential and developing it. In the KUMON Centers, which are classes run by the franchise KUMON instructors in local communities, one often hears the saying, "help each child by fostering their will to live and their spirit for challenge." This assumes that each child is different and has a way of learning suited to that difference. Toru Kumon called it "learning at the 'just right' level." He meant that learning has to be tailored to the particular situation of each student, rather than universally following the same process for everyone.

All students start at their own level and proceed at their own pace, moving forward only when they are ready. Recognizing that there is variation in human ability, the KUMON method aims to encourage and enhance individual ability and the willingness to learn, and the materials and instruction guidelines are not the essence of the method, but merely the tools for achieving this. This does not mean that students work entirely on their own. Instructors in class must motivate each student and provide the support they need. Toru Kumon believed that every child had the potential to improve, and that it was not the child's fault if he or she could not make progress. "If children do not progress smoothly, there is a problem with the education and instruction methods" (Kumon, 1991: 251). "The mainstream of education in the twenty-first century will be 'individualized, just-right' education represented by the Kumon Method," he said (Kumon, 2007: Preface).

Materials and methods

The KUMON method and materials are unique in their systematic structuring of content according to level of ability, with each level further broken down into achievable steps. Students proceed to the next step only after they have understood the prior step. In mathematics there are ten worksheets in each step, and 20 steps or 200 worksheets in each level, with some exceptions. Each step has an average time for completion as a guideline for measuring the skills and progress of the learner. Results will indicate if review is necessary and the learner will continue to review until the material is fully understood. On completion of a step, the instructor marks the sheet with a large circle indicating 100 percent completion. This gives the student a sense of achievement and satisfaction. Students are only in class twice a week, but it is important that they study the workbook every day. Instructors collect the workbooks each time the students come to class and mark them, giving students something to reflect on to confirm their level of understanding (see Figure 5.5). The advantage of the KUMON method is that students set their own targets and pace under the watchful eye of instructors who confirm their progress at each level.

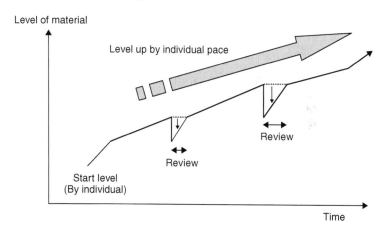

Figure 5.5 Self-learning system of the KUMON method
Source: Author's summary based on interviews.

To get started in a KUMON class, students take an exam to evaluate their level of understanding, and they begin with study materials that are easy enough to ensure they get 100 percent without any difficulty. The student's level is determined not only by the difficulty of the questions and the student's precision in answering them, but also in their speed to completion. Students are tested at the end of each level to evaluate how much they have mastered. Class instructors adjust a student's course of study according to their progress, and offer advice. They also praise students to encourage them to study. Instructors determine the workload of each student depending on their level of motivation and their school workload overall (see Figure 5.6).

The KUMON method is vastly different from the conventional method of learning mathematics in school, which starts with the teacher explaining concepts and principles and then giving students problems to solve that are at the average level and speed of learning for the class. In contrast, the KUMON method encourages "tacit understanding through multiple experiences." Students learn principles and concepts spontaneously, in repetitive exercises involving multiple calculations. They learn by doing and, at the more critical stages, they are given an example of how to solve a problem. The more difficult problems are broken down into several steps using different kinds of questions and more exercises. Even difficult, abstract concepts are grasped spontaneously through repeated exercise. This is a key element of the method. The combination of these factors helps students gain a tacit understanding of the subject matter. The learning structure is illustrated in figure 5.5 in a graph resembling the teeth of a saw, with the speed of progress varying with each student.

The essence of KUMON method is its emphasis on human relationships. It is possible to see the individual pace and learning style of each student and watch them improve. Instructors sense the actual progress of each student and reflect this in the materials and instructions. KUMON instructors become linchpins in their communities as they interact closely with children and their parents to build human relationships that increase the effectiveness of the learning process. Unlike conventional distance learning through correspondence, interactions between instructors and students in the KUMON method are actual and contextual and result in improved processes.

The material that is currently in use is an enriched version of the original developed by Toru Kumon. As Toru Kumon often said, "There is no more improvement at the moment when we think 'this is good enough.' There must always be something better." "Realizing that you are 'unfinished' and having the attitude of striving to improve are the priceless assets of a Kumon instructor." The fundamental rule in developing teaching materials is to understand the actual situation at each KUMON center, based on direct

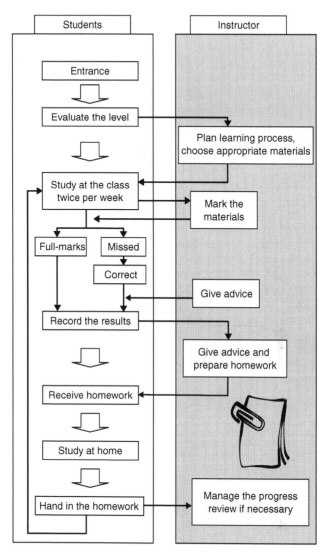

Figure 5.6 The process of learning in the KUMON method
Source: Authors' summary based on interviews.

observation and feedback from instructors. The KUMON method places students at the center of the process and "learns from the children" whether the materials are appropriate or need updating. "If some worksheets require more time for many of the children, we will extend the time limit slightly or make the questions a little easier," said Toru Kumon. "We always watch the children closely and update our materials according to their behavior."[9] He was emphatic that changes in content reflect feedback from the classes. Instructors are continuously improving the method with more refined instructions to students while providing feedback to headquarters for improvements in the materials. This upward spiral of interaction between instructors, students, and headquarters accelerates the identification of issues and improvements in process.

Instructors exercising practical wisdom

The instructors are the most important asset in the KUMON franchise. Unlike in other cram schools, students at KUMON study independently and spontaneously and rely on instructors who can effectively observe study habits and intervene in a timely manner. Instead of a teaching manual, instructors are given a guide titled *Points to Note for Instruction*,[10] which accompanies each teaching module. The guide offers basic rules while leaving ample flexibility for instructors to exercise their own judgment in response to the unique character of each student and the particular situation in class. These guidelines are updated according to feedback from instructors, and changes in content and the reasoning behind them are communicated through training sessions conducted by KUMON head office. KUMON instructors not only manage the KUMON Centers but are the channel of communication with students. "We must be able to instantly judge the situation of each child by the look on their face as they come into class," said one experienced KUMON instructor.[11] Instructors often hire assistants to mark worksheets to free themselves up for observation and counseling. For students to progress in self-study, the role of the instructor is vital in creating an environment that motivates them. The student's initial effort to understand the materials must be praised, regardless of mistakes or the need for review, because the key objective is to motivate the student to want to proceed to the next step. Instructors have to cultivate a high level of sensitivity to each child, while observing their behavior and progress. While the attitude of the student is very important, their progress is greater when parents and instructors share the goals and are able to give the necessary support at the right time. Instructors pay close attention to eye movement, general attitudes and behavior, how the children use their pencils, their physical health, mental states, and family environment. Instructors' reactions to the children must be flexible and based on hypotheses developed from keen observation honed through an accumulation of teaching experiences that cultivate knowledge and wise judgment.

In short, the success of the KUMON method is highly dependent on the instructors' abilities to observe and make comprehensive judgments to provide unique learning experiences tailored to individual students. Situations vary with each student in terms of how much they should review and how much work they should take home. Instructors judge the "here-now" situation of each student they encounter at the KUMON Center, using accumulated past experiences to inform their judgments and providing flexible and appropriate support in a *ba* with individual students. In the process they are continually learning what works for different students and adjusting the materials and methods accordingly, creating knowledge in the course of daily routines and sharing that knowledge in the greater *ba* of the KUMON Center.

5.2.4 Regenerating KUMON

With large-scale expansion of the KUMON franchise, effective sharing of the KUMON vision was becoming more difficult, eventually resulting in dilution of the company philosophy. The focus had switched from process to the materials themselves, and the ultimate goal articulated in the KUMON vision was displaced by a focus on increasing the number of franchises. Toru Kumon passed away in 1995 and his son Takeshi, who succeeded him, was not in good health. It was time for a change at the KUMON group. Yasuo Annaka, former CEO of Sanyo Security, was invited by Takeshi to join the company. Annaka carefully studied the KUMON method and concluded that the original philosophy and vision were the company's most valuable assets. In 1997 Annaka[12] became KUMON CEO. He took the lead in reaffirming the vision and philosophy, putting priority on improving human resources so the vision could be realized under any and all circumstances.

Common good and rebuilding social ba

Annaka reformed the company by restoring the emphasis on human resources and philosophy in the following three ways: sharing values, communicating real intentions, and creating *ba*. He believed that shared philosophy and values were essential to an organization, and vitality could only be maintained through the active exchange of knowledge and real communication of intensions in a culture of generosity and openness. To revitalize KUMON, Annaka visited the work sites all over Japan to build active and positive communication with all employees, including part-time staff, and he flattened the organizational structure to enable more agile decision-making. He also organized situational training sessions. His reforms drastically changed relationships in the KUMON group, particularly those between franchise instructors and staff at headquarters. Interaction to share information increased and deepened, and the role of headquarters expanded from developer and distributor of the materials to a facilitator of the relationship between learner, instructor, and the local community, capturing the essence of the learning process. Headquarters continuously reflected feedback from stakeholders in improvements to the materials and instruction guidelines. The KUMON Centers were treated as the cornerstone of all KUMON operations, and the organization was restructured to support them.

Annaka accelerated decision-making by creating a variety of opportunities for communication and sharing of objectives in *ba*, promoting greater knowledge sharing throughout the organization and empowering operations at the frontline.

Annaka's biggest contribution was to help employees become aware of the meaning of their work and their *raison d'etre*, fostering their own potential for leadership. Annaka articulated the three basic values of the company as follows: KUMON Center development equals contribution to society; every employee is the leader in every activity; contribute to regional communities (KUMON Institute, 2001). These values clearly emphasized meaningful social relations over profit, though profit was also considered essential to sustain the company. Annaka's philosophy was "morality first, profit next." He thought it was important to consider right action first, believing that profits would follow if the company pursued firm values in the right direction. He put priority on sharing those values so all employees would understood the direction. He believed that people in an organization grow when they recognize their own *raison d'être*. "Employees will drastically change their mindset when they experience success and empowerment, even through small, but visible results," he said.[13] This way of thinking was consistent with the original KUMON philosophy.

Contribution to regional communities

At a meeting of KUMON group employees in July, 2006, the company issued a directive to build community relationships in the regions, expressed in the slogan, "Now the creation of new regional communities." The company expanded its activities in Japan from offering classes to elementary and junior high school students to assisting in the care of infants and toddlers[14] (see Figure 5.7). It also introduced the KUMON method to the public education system called Task 21[15] and began applying it to the prevention and treatment of dementia in the elderly, with special classes for senior citizens in regional communities. KUMON aimed to help slow the progress of dementia among the elderly with learning activities designed to stimulate the prefrontal cortex, offered at homes for the elderly. The company also designed these activities to increase and enrich social interaction between the elderly and others in the community.

In 2007, KUMON started to expand childcare support at all KUMON Centers in Japan, which until then was primarily a voluntary activity in many parts of the country. Childcare support at KUMON offers a place for novice mothers to share their troubles and questions in the care of infants and toddlers. It is a place for learning and obtaining sound, practical advice. The decision to offer the service was triggered by the apparent weakening in traditional community relationships that had once provided young mothers with occasions to learn about child rearing. Mothers were having more difficulty with this role and worried about it. KUMON instructors provide

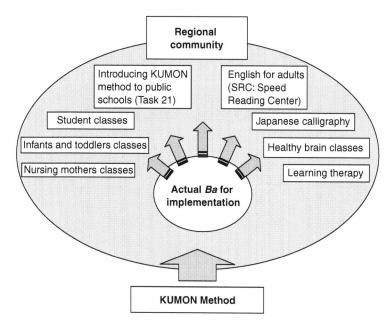

Figure 5.7 Expansion of KUMON activities

mothers with tools such as picture books and educational toys and assist them in various methods of communicating with their children. The instructors operate from the perspective that it is the mothers who are in charge of raising their children, and instructors are there only to offer support. A *ba* develops among the participants as mothers share information and activities, such as singing and reading books together with the children. KUMON instructors act as coordinators, utilizing their experience in the regular KUMON classes. At the start, instructors lead most of the activities, but, as the mothers become acquainted with each other and start to feel their progress, they gradually self-organize in *ba*.

The activity does not contribute directly to KUMON business. Rather, instructors maintain the discipline of not trying to persuade mothers to make their child attend to the KUMON Center. Under the slogan of "Moving Towards Community-based Child-raising", the idea of providing childcare support at KUMON emerged from the social perspective that helping mothers might also help revitalize the community by encouraging an increase in the number of births. Instructors aim to transfer their tacit knowledge of childcare to other mothers, expanding their relationships in the community beyond the teaching of children at the KUMON Center. This gives the KUMON Center the role of stimulating the emergence of new *ba* for the cultivation of desirable relationships in the community.

5.2.5 Globalization and the KUMON philosophy

As the KUMON name penetrated the Japanese market, interest grew among Japanese living outside the country, and offices were established overseas to serve them, eventually expanding to serve the local populations in those countries as well. There is a need in every country in the world to improve the general level of education and KUMON's method of "self-learning," where each child studies at their own pace, has attracted considerable attention.

Toru Kumon had said from the beginning that his dream was to expand the KUMON method worldwide, and he believed this was possible because of the universal language of mathematics (Kumon, 1991). But expansion of the KUMON Centers was organic rather than strategic, occurring naturally in response to demand, first from Japanese living abroad and then from indigenous populations. The New York KUMON Center opened in 1974, followed by the Taipei branch in 1975 to host only the Japanese children in these cities but gradually started to accept local children. Expansion was faster or slower depending on educational system regulations in each country. Meanwhile, the reputation of the method continued to spread by word-of-mouth.

In the U.S. and Europe, KUMON Centers expanded when states sought educational reform and there was greater social interest in educational efficacy. In the U.S., the Reagan Administration had issued in 1983 the report, *A Nation at Risk*, and called for educational renewal (Kinoshita, 2006). That same year the first KUMON Center opened for the children living in the U.S. In Germany, the first KUMON Center opened in 1986. The Programme for International Student Assessment (PISA) of the Organisation for Economic Co-operation and Development (OECD) ranked Germany 20th in mathematics and scientific literacy, generating a sense of crisis among parents concerned about their children's education. The KUMON method was one option in the search for better educational methods, and this resulted in a proliferation of KUMON Centers there (Fuches, 2004).

In developing countries, the situation was a little different. The KUMON method was employed to boost local economies through education. In the Philippines, the first KUMON Center had opened in 1982 for the children of Japanese working there, but it expanded to serve the local population in various ways, with centers tailored to the intellectual class facilitating introductions to private schools and to local educational organizations asking for KUMON support in educating the children of the poor. The primary goal of KUMON instructors in the Philippines is to contribute to community development by improving the educational level of the local population. Teresa V. Santos runs a KUMON Center in the city of Valenzuela. She says the advantage of the KUMON method is that it improves knowledge and skills by motivating children to learn, and it is this element that has the potential to get the country and the region moving in a more positive direction.[16]

While globalization of the KUMON method proceeds for different reasons in different countries and regions, one reason remains the same, and that is the common desire of parents to improve their children's access to quality education to ensure they have a viable future. Another commonality has been the universal language of mathematics from which the KUMON method originated.

Universality is the strength of the KUMON method, crossing borders to build learning capabilities that can be effectively tracked and evaluated. In most educational systems it is difficult to quantify the immediate effects of study in terms of actual learning capability. With the KUMON method, students and parents can actually feel and see both incremental and long-term progress. This is common to every KUMON Center regardless of country or region. An instructor of North America said "I define an 'excellent' as a click or 'aha moment' when the 'light bulb' came on during which a student discovers how to become 'unstuck' on a new concept." "The importance of learning from excellent students does not lie in trying to apply the observed excellent moments' to other students. It lies in helping us focus our attention on the importance of close observation of all students' learning activities, to identify each student's excellent moments in learning, and to use that information to modify our planning and guidance of their progress. When we are able to truly individualize the KUMON program for each student and facilitate independent learning of advanced material, then we are becoming excellent coaches."[17]

Since there is no operational manual for the KUMON method, the details of how it functions vary from country to country, but the exchange of knowledge among instructors is relatively seamless because they share the philosophy and values embedded in the materials and the KUMON practice. Instructors from North America and Asia regularly meet at KUMON's World Instructors Forum to discuss the status of current instruction materials and other issues, and differences in culture and customs are not at issue.[18]

5.2.6 The characteristics of the KUMON method

KUMON has proved to be a precedent-setting model in the education industry, expanding rapidly around the globe from its humble origin in Japan in just half a century. Clearly there is no ultimate educational method that suits everybody, including the KUMON method, and there are criticisms that the KUMON method only emphasizes calculation speed in mathematics, and concern about the potential harmful effects of early childhood education. But the widespread acceptance of KUMON around the world suggests it does address a deficiency in conventional approaches to education that is universally experienced.[19]

The inherent strengths of the KUMON method are in three areas. The first is the system of developing materials for self-learning that can be tailored to each individual and to practice on the ground, which is easily convertible to language learning for use in other countries and cultures. The universality of the KUMON system and its methods is evident in the global *ba* of information sharing among instructors, where KUMON concepts and terms have become a common language for communicating ideas and practice. The second is the cultivation of instructors who care about each individual student in the context of their larger social relations. In the education business, the quality of service provided is intangible and depends on the quality of the persons providing it. The ability of the instructor to make timely and appropriate judgments according to the particular situation is essential, and such abilities and the shared experiences of KUMON instructors are the most important knowledge assets, and the source of competitive advantage for the company. The third is the existence of *ba* that enable the deep communication necessary for continuous improvement of the service. These *ba* exist in the form of training and study groups for the exchange of knowledge between instructors and head office. Through such *ba*, the hands-on experience of instructors is communicated to head offices and reflected in content for continuous improvement in teaching. Its *ba* also extends into local communities as it aims to support young mothers and the elderly and strengthen social relationships through education. The aim of this expansion is not only to enhance the functions of the KUMON Center but to establish an organic network of *ba* among KUMON Centers globally, and this is driven by the KUMON ideal to create a better future through education based on a spiral of knowledge creation and practice within the larger society. The effectiveness of the KUMON method emerges in the interconnection of its three strengths, driven by a shared aim to foster human capability.

One KUMON employee working overseas has noted that people cannot understand the KUMON method from verbal explanations alone, but have to experience it first hand in the KUMON Center. "We explain the method in detail and ask them to attend classes so they can actually feel how the students change...Developing human resources will be the key to KUMON becoming a global company. It will be important to develop people who can act globally, regardless of nationality, by giving them chances to take an active role in global events."[20] In other words, the value of the KUMON method is not apparent in explicit descriptions of it, but becomes visible in the virtuous circle of continuously expanding knowledge creation processes in the KUMON Centers. These are processes of continuous interaction, between the learning experiences of learners and the instructing experiences of instructors in multiple *ba*, for the continuous improvement of instruction methods and materials, guided by the KUMON philosophy.

5.3 Implications

In this chapter, we analyzed the concept of creating the right context or *ba* as an essential enabling condition for deep business relationships and co-creation of knowledge and value, both within the organization and between firms. The two cases are the examples of the companies which create unique value through interconnectedness and relationships among people and the organization developed in *ba*.

Ba is the continuum in which knowledge emerges in the process of interacting within and between firms in the business ecosystem. Instead of treating a firm as an isolated entity, the *ba*-centered approach to management facilitates co-creation of knowledge and value with a variety of players in the business ecosystem, particularly with the customer in Mayekawa's case and with students and local communities in KUMON's case. Unlike structure that reflects a fixed image of relationships among individuals as agents, the organization, and the environment, at one particular point in time, *ba* makes it possible to see the process of changing relationships. Thus, *ba*-centered management enables managers and firms to see the business ecosystem as a whole and to act in a timely fashion to the benefit of all players rather than just their own.

Mayekawa, with its multifunctional engineering teams and *doppos* building social networks of knowledge-creating capability, is a particularly good example of multilayered *ba*, which extend to other entities in the business ecosystem, such as suppliers, customers, and competitors. Mayekawa establishes intimate and "here-now" relationships in *ba* by indwelling with customers to understand their essential needs for improvement and reform. Their establishment of trusted relationships enables exchange of knowledge on a tacit level for intuitive understanding of hidden customer needs and subsequent provision of customized technological and organizational solutions that are difficult for competitors to duplicate. Masao Mayekawa speaks of "*ba*-centered" or "*ba*-based" corporate activities that continuously enlarge the span of knowledge in each *ba*, in areas of production, sales and technology. In becoming one, the greater *ba* is revealed and with this, all the things that could not be seen up to then become actual and realizable (Mayekawa, 2004). Through the relationships with such various players, both the individual and the firm evolve from self-centeredness to *ba*-centeredness. In such a sense, *ba* is both an enabling condition for and a result of co-creation.

The co-creation of *ba* usually starts with very weak incoming signals from the customer, who is often not fully aware of their own needs or able to express them explicitly. These vague clues are then discussed within a *ba* that is internal to Mayekawa. Through continuous meetings with the customer a *ba* develops in which more and more information is exchanged, and the co-creation of knowledge begins. When the tacit knowledge

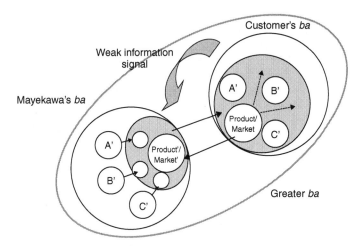

Figure 5.8 Co-creation of *ba* between Mayekawa and a customer
Source: Based on Mayekawa (2004: 201).

accumulated at *ba* with customers is externalized, the Mayekawa process of *kigyouka keikaku*, in which employees feel the environment, place themselves in the environment, and imagine what they want to achieve, is particularly relevant here. Over time a greater *ba* emerges that spans both Mayekawa's internal *ba* and the *ba* with the customer (see Figure 5.8).

Indwelling is particularly important for sharing tacit knowledge and concept creation, and the prerequisite is a high level of care in organizational relationships (von Krogh, Ichijo, and Nonaka, 2000: 57–58). This understanding can be achieved only by working closely with the customer in *ba* to achieve joint creation of knowledge and "co-innovation" through effective communication and sharing of tacit knowledge. The direct interactions with customers and the development of trust are essential to the creation and nurturing of *ba*. Rich communication – called "context communication" at Mayekawa – leads to the creation of superior knowledge and value for all parties through deep understanding developed in long-term relationships characterized by empathy and mutual concern. As Mayekawa builds and sustains relationships long-term rather than for short-term financial gain, the shared context with customers grows. This collaboration creates superior service and innovation while building knowledge assets that are refined with use over time. The evolving relationship comes to be based on a communal destiny in a network economy, rather than a simple trade between buyer and seller (Mayekawa, 2004). In this way, Mayekawa has evolved from being a simple manufacturer to become the company of integrated solutions that it is today.

The educational services company KUMON has devised the KUMON method to orient teaching to the needs of the individual, with instruction geared to the level and pace of the individual learner. Their overarching objective is to contribute to the well-being of society by enhancing the capability of individuals to contribute to society. Teaching is developed in multilayered *ba*, starting with the student–teacher relationship and expanding to the local community and globally through knowledge sharing among instructors at KUMON Centers worldwide. The key to the KUMON method is the ability of instructors to build trusting relationships in *ba* that help them to identify learning issues for the individual and the community and initiate appropriate adjustments in KUMON materials and services to reflect those needs. Instructor's ability to see each student's situation and give them appropriate help is also developed in such *ba*. The exchange of knowledge with students and members of the community in *ba* becomes a feedback loop of knowledge creation for continuous customization and improvement of their service. The KUMON Center builds *ba* to motivate individuals to understand and pursue KUMON's philosophy, that is, to raise the human being to a higher level of awareness by identifying their potential and developing it. For KUMON, profit is not the primary motivation but a result of their activities to contribute to the common good of the community.

These two companies and their operational activities illustrate the limitations of a static analysis of organizational structure, internal resources, and strategic positioning in explaining a company's successful growth and international expansion. An organization is made up of people, and knowledge emerges from the creative interactions of those people in the invisible timespace of *ba*, where the key factor for success is the relentless pursuit of relationships acting for the realization of a better future.

Notes

1. The official English name is MAYEKAWA MFG. CO., LTD.
2. Interview with Yoshio Iwasaki, August 2, 2007.
3. Ibid.
4. Mayekawa's activities and initiatives to build relationships and co-create knowledge with customers should not be mistaken as a market research method for eliciting tacit knowledge and tapping sources of innovation like von Hippel's (2006) lead user method or Zaltman's (2003) metaphor elicitation technique. The purpose at Mayekawa is to establish long-term business relationships and to co-create innovations through natural interaction on-the-job. It is about co-creating value and innovation rather than merely gathering information through techniques of inquiry.
5. This project was first described and discussed by Tsuyuki (2001, 2006) and we have built on her work with additional interviews.
6. At present, a "research course" at university level is available in Japan.
7. Handwritten class materials by Toru Kumon are displayed at the Toru Kumon Memorial Museum.

8. The organization's name was changed several times. In 1962, the name was the Osaka Institute of Mathematics. In 1972, the offices in Osaka and Tokyo were named the Osaka and the Tokyo Institute of Mathematics, respectively. In 1981, the two offices became corporations, and in 1982 they were merged to become the KUMON Institute of Mathematics. In 1983, the name was changed to the KUMON Institute of Education.
9. "Jyuku: Sangyo tenkai no kiseki (9)" ["Cram schools: Tracking industry developments, vol. 9"]. *Nikkei Sangyo Shimbun*, 20 September 1990.
10. A booklet that summarizes the principles and points to note for giving instructions; this booklet is distributed to every class instructor.
11. Interview with Hiroko Kuramoto, a KUMON instructor in Tokyo. December 3, 2005.
12. CEO in 1997–2005 and consultant in 2005–07. Annaka had been a colleague of Takeshi Kumon when they were at Nomura Securities. He was the youngest managing director at Nomura, then moved to Sanyo Securities before joining KUMON.
13. Interview with Yasuo Annaka, January 30, 2006.
14. Activities to provide a place to share information and knowledge on how to raise a child and obtain support for child rearing.
15. Activities to support introduction of the KUMON method to public elementary and junior high schools aimed at increasing student autonomy and concentration and improving levels of capability.
16. Interview with Teresa V. Santos, an instructor at Valenzuela, Philippines, December 9, 2006.
17. The 29th KUMON International Instructor's Conference Research Papers.
18. At the World Instructors Forum, instructors gather from all over the world and actively discuss and exchange information.
19. Annaka says the "market decides whether it is good or not."
20. Interview with a KUMON employee, 16 April 2006.

References

Fuchs, M. (2004). *Nihon no Kumon, German no kyouiku ni deau* [Japanese Kumon Meets German Education]. Tokyo: Chikuma Shobo.

Heckscher, C. and Adler, P.S. (eds). (2006). *The Firm as a Collaborative Community: The Reconstruction of Trust in the Knowledge Economy*. New York: Oxford University Press.

Iwasaki, Y. (1995). *Kigyouka keikaku tokucho no memo* [A Memorandum on Characteristics of *kigyouka keikaku*]. Unpublished manuscript.

Kim, W.C. and Mauborgne, R. (2004). "Blue ocean strategy," *Harvard Business Review*, 82(10), 76–84.

Kinoshita, R. (2006). *Terakoya globalization* [Globalize a Small School]. Tokyo: Iwanami Shoten.

KUMON Institute of Education. (2001). *Shinsei Kumon no kiseki* [The Miracle of the New Kumon].

KUMON Institute of Education. (2007). *Company Profile 2006–2007*.

KUMON Institute of Education. (2007). *The 29th KUMON International Instructor's Conference: Research Papers English*. Kobe, Japan.

Kumon, T. (1991). *Yatte miyo* [Let's Do It]. "Kumon Shuppan. Juku sangyo tenkai no kiseki (3)" ["Cramming School: Tracking the industry development (3)"]. *Nihon Keizai Shimbun*, 12 September 1990, p. 32.

Mayekawa, M. (2004). *Monozukuri no gokui, hitozukuri no tetsugaku* [The Secret of Manufacturing, the Philosophy of Forming People]. Tokyo: Diamond.
Peltokorpi, V. and Tsuyuki, E. (2006). "Knowledge governance in a Japanese project-based organization," *Knowledge Management Research & Practice*, 4(1), 36–45.
Shimizu, H. and Mayekawa, M. (1998). *Kyoso kara kyoso he* [From Competition to Co-creation]. Tokyo: Iwanamishoten.
Tsuyuki, E. (2001). "Mayekawa seisakusho 'kokyaku to no kyoso no bazukuri'" ["Mayekawa manufacturing 'co-creation of *ba* with customers'"]. in D. Senoo, S. Akutsu, and I. Nonaka (eds). *Chishiki keiei jissenron* [On Practice: Knowledge Creation and Utilization]. Tokyo: Hakuto Shobo, pp. 275–320.
Tsuyuki, E. (2006). "Jusoteki 'ba' no keisei to chishikisozo – Mayekawa Seisakusho" ["Formation of multilayered '*ba*' and knowledge creation in Mayekawa Seisakusho"]. in I. Nonaka and R. Toyama (eds). *Chishikisozokeiei to Innovation* [Knowledge-creating Management and Innovation]. Tokyo: Maruzen, pp. 50–75.
von Hippel, E. (2006). *Democratizing Innovation*. Cambridge: The MIT Press.
von Krogh, G., Ichijo, K., and Nonaka, I. (2000). *Enabling Knowledge Creation, How to Unlock the Mystery of Tacit Knowledge and Release the Power of Innovation*. New York: Oxford University Press.
Zaltman, G. (2003). *How Customers Think: Essential Insights into the Mind of the Market*. Boston: Harvard Business School Press.

6
Dialogue and Practice: Leveraging Organizational Dialectics

Breakthrough occurs in knowledge creation not only in the form of radical innovation in a product or service, but also in the form of gradual innovation through everyday practice. In this chapter, we shall examine the operations of the retail companies Seven-Eleven Japan Co., Ltd and Ryohin Keikaku Co., Ltd, where dialogue and practice driven by a shared objective and corporate philosophy have resulted in superb operations that differentiate these companies from their competitors.

6.1 Seven-Eleven Japan Co., Ltd

6.1.1 Company overview

In 1973, The Southland Corporation (USA) licensed Ito-Yokado Co., Ltd the rights to develop the Seven-Eleven convenience store concept in Japan. The concept, the gross profit sharing arrangement, and the trade mark were all inherited from the original US franchiser and applied to Japanese operations. Southland's operations manual for running the stores, however, was completely out of touch with the reality of the Japanese market. Seven-Eleven Japan Co., Ltd (SEJ) had to improvise, using trial and error to alter store operational methods to fit the local environment. In the process, it created a unique style of convenience store management that breathed new life into what had become a moribund business model.

Since opening the first store in Tokyo in 1974, SEJ has been one of the most profitable retail store companies in Japan. The ratio of profit-to-sales was about 32 percent in 2007, while that of its main competitors in Japan, Lawson and Family Mart, was about 17 percent and 14 percent, respectively (see Table 6.1). The number of Seven-Eleven stores in Japan had expanded to 12,004 by February 28, 2008, representing the largest number of stores held by one retail store company in a single country anywhere in the world. Total sales of Seven-Eleven stores were 2,574 billion yen or about 24.6 billion US dollars in the same period. In 1991, SEJ acquired a major interest in the bankrupt Southland (then 7-Eleven Inc.), turning the company around in just three years; and in 2005, SEJ made 7-Eleven Inc. in the U.S an unlisted subsidiary with the aim of quickly introducing the SEJ management system there. As of March 31, 2008, Seven-Eleven had an overall network of 34,147 stores in 15 countries including Japan.

SEJ's expansion in Japan and its success in turning around Southland has made it famous as a management case study at the Harvard Business School and other university business schools, although the analysis has tended to focus on SEJ's highly developed management systems, such as its point-of-sale (POS) information system and its method of *item by item management* or *tanpin kanri* in Japanese. In fact, it is not these systems alone that enable high profitability at SEJ stores, but an approach to management that focuses on the quality of human interaction in the gathering of data that feeds these systems. This focus on the human factor is the basis of SEJ's competitive advantage. It starts with alert, daily observation of customer behavior and trial-and-error analysis of it, which is then connected to new marketing ideas to accommodate ever-changing customer needs. This results in the creation of new knowledge in products and service, and ultimately the creation of

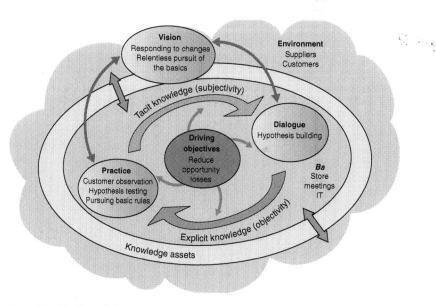

Figure 6.1 The knowledge-creating process of Seven-Eleven Japan

Table 6.1 Sales and profits of major convenience store franchisers in Japan

		Fiscal year	Seven-Eleven Japan	Lawson	Family Mart	Circle K Sunkus	Mini Stop
Results (un-consolidated)	Total store sales (B Yen)	2005	2,498.8	1,360.5	1,031.7	898.7	260.2
		2006	2,533.5	1,377.8	1,068.8	872.8	268.2
		2007	2,574.3	1,402.8	1,121.8	860.0	282.2
	Sales revenue (B Yen)	2005	492.8	248.0	184.1	180.6	56.5
		2006	517.0	256.0	194.1	183.5	57.9
		2007	527.7	269.6	210.4	189.2	61.0
	Profit from operations (B Yen)	2005	177.4	43.8	29.8	25.7	7.5
		2006	172.8	44.4	27.5	22.9	7.3
		2007	168.1	45.3	28.6	21.5	7.6
Growth from previous year	Total store sales growth (%)	2005	2.4	2.4	3.3	0.8	5.9
		2006	1.4	1.3	3.6	-2.9	3.1
		2007	1.6	1.8	5.0	-1.5	5.2
	Sales revenue growth (%)	2005	5.5	3.6	6.2	33.9	5.2
		2006	4.9	3.2	5.4	1.6	2.5
		2007	2.1	3.2	5.4	1.6	5.4
	Profit from operations growth (%)	2005	1.7	3.8	4.0	36.5	-4.6
		2006	-2.6	1.4	-7.7	-10.9	-2.7
		2007	-2.7	2.0	4.0	-6.1	4.1
Operation Profit to Sales Ratio (%)		2005	36.0	17.7	16.2	14.2	13.3
		2006	33.4	17.3	14.2	12.5	12.6
		2007	31.9	16.8	13.6	11.4	12.5

Notes: Fiscal year ends at February of each year. "Total store sales" includes sales of both direct and franchisee stores. "Total store sales", "Sales revenue" and "Profit from operations" are for the individual company. Circle K Sunkus was established in 2005 by the merger of Circle K and Sunkus and Associates. Their growth in 2006 is driven by the merger of regional chains in 2005 and 2006. Total store sales of SEJ is only for Japanese market.

Source: Authors summary based on publicly available financial data of each convenience store chains.

profit (see Figure 6.1). In Japan, this method is supported by a strong tradition of employee participation and an emphasis on human relationships, but recent successful application in other countries as well suggests it has the potential for global application as a preferred approach to retail management in the knowledge era. Asked whether this management system could work globally, the Chairman and CEO of SEJ Toshifumi Suzuki says retailing anywhere is geared to a highly localized pattern of consumption, and the more sophisticated the level of consumption, the more localized it is.

If we create a convenience store retail model that enables an operator to match the goods supplied to changes in demand over time and to the overall level of consumer sophistication in a country, then that model will be sustainable anywhere. Once the basics are established, all you have to do is tailor them to the country (Nikkei Business, 2006: 46).

6.1.2 Management philosophy: "Keep changing!"

The two philosophical principles that drive SEJ practice are *Adaptation to Change and Getting the Basics Right*. The principle of Adaptation to Change is meant to encourage response to a changing environment and changing customer behavior based on an understanding of the essential meaning behind that change. The principle of Getting the Basics Right seems on the surface to be contradictory with the first principle, but without a clear understanding of the basics of "cleanliness, friendly service, and product freshness", the principle of Adaptation to Change also will not be realized. Thus, it is not about Getting the Basics Right and continuously duplicating that same basic conduct, but about learning to recognize what's going on at a fundamental level in each particular situation in daily store operations, and maintaining that practice of heightened awareness. This requires employees to think hard about the essential meaning of the phenomena they observe. These principles are continuously communicated throughout the organization on every occasion possible, and in different ways that ring true to the experience of each and every employee.

In the convenience store business, winning the loyalty of customers who visit the store every day is crucial to success. The general rule is to satisfy the customer today, not think about how you could have satisfied him or her yesterday (Katsumi, 2002). In today's world of diverse and rapidly changing customer needs, Suzuki says there can be no permanently fixed way of doing business. In other words, everything is in flux. Hence, SEJ does not have a long-term plan, nor does it plan to create one. He says there is no sense in trying to follow a long-term plan under conditions of constant change in customer needs and wants. Instead, he emphasizes flexible thinking, and he warns store-staff[1] not to be blinded by past success because they may miss business opportunities that can only be perceived by looking at things in a way that is different from past practice. This does not mean that one should ignore past experience, but rather make experience the raw material for generating new hypotheses that suit the present situation. At SEJ, past experience is integrated with "here-now" experience in the practice of hypothesis building to create a future, that is, a better store. And this practice is shared throughout the organization in direct interaction and dialogue. Thus, strategy at SEJ lies in a distributed leadership, emerging as the initiative of the many store-staff who create knowledge in their daily work.

6.1.3 The daily practice of hypothesizing, testing, and verification

The average SEJ store in Japan is only about 1,200 square feet, half the size of an average Seven-Eleven store in the U.S. Given this limitation, the typical SEJ store carries only 3,000 units of stock at any one time. Hence, it is important that each store sells exactly what customers want, and does not try to sell what they don't want. Timing is of the essence. This makes inventory management, down to the level of a single item, crucial. Each store relies on effective hypothesis building and testing by every store-staff to identify so-called "dead items" and replace them with hot-selling items. Due to this policy of *item by item management*, about 70 percent of the goods typically sold at SEJ stores are discontinued after one year. More importantly, *item by item management* is aimed at identifying "live items" that are likely to sell well tomorrow and in the foreseeable future. To grasp the changing needs and psychology of tomorrow's customer, SEJ store-staff engage in a cycle of hypothesizing, testing in practice, and verification. This is practiced by every store-staff, including part-time workers. As Suzuki points out, change is not achieved by one charismatic leader, but through a collective knowledge-creating process, where leadership is distributed. "I only have two eyes," he says. "There are several tens of thousands of part-time workers at Seven-Eleven Japan stores. If everyone can make judgments on their own, we will have quite a few pairs of eyes" (Ogata, 2005: 185).

What drives the never-ending cycle of hypothesizing, testing and verification at every level of SEJ is the firm's objective to *reduce opportunity losses*. These are potential sales lost because customers couldn't find what they wanted when they wanted it, meaning the store was unable to provide the right product or service at the right place and time. For example, if customers don't find their favorite boxed lunch when they come into the store at lunch time, they would leave without buying anything. It is not just the boxed lunch that becomes a lost sales opportunity, but all the other items, such as drinks, that the potential customer would have bought along with it. The relentless drive at SEJ to cut opportunity losses has led to daily sales per store that are much higher than competitors, leading to higher profits. Unlike the visible costs of overstocking inventory, opportunity lost from unrealized sales is invisible and, therefore, a difficult concept to grasp because it is buried in the tacit insights gained by each store-staff in the particular context of each store, based on face-to-face interaction with the customer. SEJ empowers individual store-staff, including part-time workers, with the responsibility for ordering specific categories of items to be stocked in their store, which requires them to build their own hypotheses about the sale of particular items. Since local store-staff are also members of the local community, they know their customers better than anyone else does, including staff at SEJ headquarters.

It is frequently argued that SEJ's strength lies in *item by item management* based on its POS data system. This assumes that the POS data system itself is the mechanism for determining which products to sell and which to terminate, when in fact it is the human process of hypothesizing, testing, and verification that enables the system to function. As Suzuki points out: "A POS system can be set up at any company, but it can only tell you about the past, it cannot tell you how to act in the future. In order to stay profitable and competitive you have to figure out what will sell tomorrow and what products to develop for the future" (Suzuki, 2006: 126). When a store storestaff changes a pattern of ordering to test a hypothesis, the POS system can provide immediate feedback that may help to validate the hypothesis, but it won't help the store-staff to foresee a future opportunity. In that sense, the POS system only plays a supporting role, says Suzuki. What is more important is the human ability to continue to create hypotheses based on an ability to understand the essential meaning of consumer behavior and the phenomena affecting it, and data and past experience in the market can help in making such judgments or hypotheses (Katsumi, 2002). Thus, information systems do not provide the whole truth, and hypotheses are only a basis for further reflection, testing, and validation. While accumulated data may reveal patterns of change from past to present, determining what will sell in the future depends largely on intuitive understanding of the market, based on accumulated tacit knowledge.

To build a hypothesis about how well an item will sell tomorrow, one has to try to understand the essential nature of the particular situation in which it sells or doesn't sell. Even if the item sold well today, there is no guarantee that it will sell well tomorrow, because customers and situations change quickly and are affected by factors such as weather and other events. The SEJ store-staff doesn't just order soft drinks, but the specific brand and size of soft drinks that customers at that store prefer. *Item by item management* ensures that supply meets the specific, contextual demand of each store. That demand can vary significantly, even between stores in the same neighborhood. Hence, every store-staff at every store is required to be able to make decisions and act according to the particular situation he or she faces. For the same reason, there is no universal model for franchise management and no written manual to guide store-staff. Rather, each store-staff is required to think and act based on his or her own, subjective insights about the local market, accumulated through daily interaction with customers. These subjective insights are verified objectively through hypothesis building and testing.

To build effective hypotheses that can accommodate customers' ever-changing needs, store-staff at Seven-Eleven stores are encouraged to think *as* customers, instead of thinking *for* customers, first from the perspective of an average customer, then from the perspective of an average family, and finally from the perspective of a close friend. This forces them to suspend judgment based on preconceptions and past experiences in order to see things directly from the customer's viewpoint. By thinking about products and services from different standpoints, employees become attuned to particular contexts while developing a broader hypothesis that can be universalized through group validation.

While thinking as a customer, store-staff are also encouraged to relentlessly question their observations and the underlying assumptions and contexts of their interpretations. In the course of daily activities, hypotheses are developed only after continuous rethinking and investigation through dialogue with other store-staff and with operation field counselors (OFCs) who visit stores regularly to give advice. The hypothesis is then put to the test by ordering goods, and the order is verified against data in the company's POS system in a continuing spiral of hypothesis, testing, and verification.

The particular situation that each Seven-Eleven store-staff faces differs not only by place (store), but also in time. Suzuki tells store-staff to "cast off past experience" when building hypotheses and not accept raw data at face value, but look beyond the surface of data and experience to find essential meaning in consumer behavior. He says one cannot equate the circumstances of the present with those of yesterday and tomorrow. "What is needed in the present is a product that satisfies tomorrow's customers, because satisfying yesterday's customers may not be enough," he said (Katsumi, 2002: 46). Even the customer who visits the store every day may be in a different psychological or economic state at different times, making him or her a completely new customer each time. For Suzuki, yesterday's success doesn't guarantee success in the future, and he warns store-staff not to be blindsided by past successes. He emphasizes that human beings are as changeable as the weather. Store-staff must be able to read changing conditions in detail on the shop floor and in the context of larger contexts, and adjust merchandise accordingly through a continuing cycle of hypothesis, testing, and verification. For example, if the temperature outside yesterday was only 20 degrees and today it is 25 degrees we will think today is warm, but if yesterday's temperature was 30 degrees, we will think today is cool. In the former case, ice cream sales might be good although they wouldn't be in the latter case even though the temperature outside is the same.

Suzuki emphasizes the importance of imagination and deeper thinking to create a hypothesis that fits a particular situation. He says creating a hypothesis is a process of creating the story that you want to communicate to your customers, and if they agree with your hypothesis then they will make the purchase you expect them to make. He offers the example of a store near a marina that hypothesizes what its customers, the people who come to the marina to go fishing, might want for lunch. Since they probably eat while fishing, they want something that is easy to handle, like a sandwich or rice balls. If it's a hot day, rice balls stuffed with pickled plum are good because pickled plum prevents food from spoiling. "A rice ball is a simple 'thing' when you order it without any hypothesis-making," says Suzuki. "However, when you add a meaning to the thing, it changes into an 'event,' that is, 'a rice ball that customers who are out fishing can eat safely on a hot day'" (Suzuki, 2008: 119).

Daily practice of the knowledge creation spiral through hypothesizing, testing, and verification engages common sense and objective data as well as human feelings and psychology. Through continuous practice, Seven-Eleven store-staff can improve their understanding and expertise while creating valuable knowledge. In this process, it is important to remain flexible in one's reasoning and to make decisions based on an understanding of the *essence* of particular objects and situations. Too much focus on the shop floor alone can also prevent one from seeing reality, because other potential customers are at least as important as existing customers. It is vital that an operator focuses not only on his or her particular store but on the wider commercial area as a whole. Population statistics and consumption survey data can also be helpful in analyzing consumer behavior from a different perspective.

Case 1: hypothesizing, testing, and verification in salad sales

The hypothesizing on salad sales is an example of the effective use of careful market observation and objective data to accommodate the latent needs of customers. Staff at a Seven-Eleven store located in a central business district in Japan had observed the striking frequency of female white-collar workers buying salads at lunch time and confirmed this against information about customers and purchase times in the POS data system. However, the store-staff at the store who were responsible for ordering this item saw something more in the POS data and were able to capitalize on that to increase sales further. The store had been selling salads on the supposition that they were only consumed for lunch, and was ordering a large number for the lunch period and less at dinner time, assuming female office workers didn't work overtime and wouldn't be buying salads for dinner. However, the POS data also showed a small amount of sales at night, with more in the morning. The store-staff responsible for ordering the item thought they could increase sales by ordering the previous night to supply the morning demand. They tested this hypothesis, changing the order and the delivery pattern, and they placed the salads prominently in the store with special advertising. As a result, salad sales soared, particularly in the morning as customers sought to avoid buying during the congested lunch period. The hypothesis was validated by the increase in sales, proving that deeper analysis of objective data can reveal unforeseen customer demand and sales opportunities.

Case 2: hypothesizing, testing, and verification in 7-Navi

To continuously create knowledge to adapt to change, it is important to accept the need for an immediate change in strategy if a hypothesis proves wrong. Even when hypotheses are proven wrong, the process alone and the experience is vital for fostering wise judgment or *phronesis* in each employee so they can build better hypotheses in the future. In 2002, SEJ discontinued a service called 7-Navi, a multimedia information terminal for electronic trading that had been set up in metropolitan stores jointly with the company's online shopping firm 7dream.com. 7-Navi was introduced in October, 2000 and had been installed in 1,200 stores by spring 2001, with a plan to introduce the system throughout Japan. However, SEJ abruptly terminated the service in October, 2002 because of under use. Parts of the original service, such as ticket sales for events, were incorporated into existing, multifunction copy machines in stores. At the time, SEJ was also installing automatic teller machines (ATMs) in stores and needed the space, so it made even more sense to get rid of the 7-Navi machines quickly. The move to terminate 7-Navi was in keeping with the SEJ philosophy of adapting quickly to change, despite the costs incurred in the original investment. The hypothesis of 7-Navi was put into practice and proved wrong, making immediate change necessary to cut further losses.

6.1.4   Direct dialogue in *ba*

To foster continuous knowledge creation in daily practice at SEJ stories, the company encourages direct communication through dialogue, so the knowledge of all store-staff is mobilized and synthesized. Dialogue also helps store-staff clarify their understanding of the company's business policies as well as changes in customer needs. Suzuki's way of thinking and the information he wants distributed throughout the organization is shared through direct dialogue in *ba*, which also becomes a mechanism for reinforcement through repetition. The venues of *ba* include the managers meeting, the business reform meeting, and the field counselors (FCs) meeting, as well as FCs' visits to stores and meetings among store-staff. Managers from headquarters are also in close contact with store-staff to connect them to this process and offer advice. SEJ is organized into 15 zones in Japan. Each zone is supervised by a zone manager and divided into several districts, each supervised by a District Manager. Operation Field Counselors (OFCs) play an important role in the districts, connecting franchise stores to the head office and giving advice on merchandising and store operations suitable to each region.

Managers meetings and operational innovation

All managers, including all District Managers, meet bi-weekly at 9 a.m. on Mondays. This is followed by the Business Reform Meeting at 3 p.m. Everyone at head office above the rank of manager attends both meetings. Managers who directly support franchisees present their issues and questions. The basic rule of thumb at the managers meeting is to come up with a solution to a problem on the spot and implement it, even if the relevant person in charge has to step out of the meeting to do this. This practice ensures timely decision-making and action.

Field counselors meeting

The Field Counselors (FCs) meeting is held on Tuesdays and is attended by 1,600 people. It includes OFCs, Recruitment Field Counselors (RFCs) who are responsible for franchise development, Zone Managers, District Managers, and all Merchandisers at head office. The meeting starts at 9 a.m. and lasts the whole day. The OFCs return to their regions in the evening and adjust their activities based on decisions made at the meeting. This pattern has continued for more than 35 years, since SEJ was founded.

The FC meeting is regarded as the most important place for sharing knowledge and information and achieving mutual understanding on a company-wide basis. The agenda includes any issues raised in the previous day's managers meeting, and information about merchandising, sales campaigns, and success stories. Knowledge of successful store practices can also be shared. Either the chairman or the president will deliver a speech that articulates the company's fundamental *way of thinking* on a number of company-wide topics. This is an opportunity to demonstrate the application of company mottos, such as: "Think as a customer"; "Forget past success"; "Hypothesis, testing in practice, verification." The FC meeting enables top management to talk directly with employees to ensure they understand the importance of the company's fundamental values and principles.

SEJ spends about 3 billion yen annually just to gather employees from across the country for the FC meeting. This illustrates the importance placed on sharing time, place, and context in face-to-face communication for tacit knowledge sharing between top management and employees. As Suzuki says, up-to-date information is the key in the convenience store industry. "That is why I stick to direct communication. By attending the meetings and having direct contact with the managers who are important sources of information, employees can absorb that information and expand on it themselves, and when they return to their workplace they communicate it directly to the franchise owners" (Katsumi, 2002: 164).

By meeting face-to-face, employees not only benefit from direct, verbal exchange but learn to absorb information on a more tacit level in *ba*, a shared space of meaning and physical interaction. With depth of understanding they are able to communicate more fully with fellow employees back in their regions, and with franchise owners. The objectives of the FC meeting are precision and speed in the transfer of knowledge and information. With everyone at the same place, listening to the same information at the same time, the message is less likely to become distorted as it does in more indirect, hierarchical communication.

Employees working in information technology also attend the meeting so they can respond immediately to issues that may require modification of information systems. These systems are effectively utilized at SEJ because IT staff participate in meetings and understand the requirements of end users in the field. Back in the regions, OFCs utilize the zone meeting to consult and exchange detailed information, and transmit the contents of the FC meeting to the furthest points of the organization. In all of these meetings, face-to-face communication is fundamental.

Ba, *connecting franchise stores and head office*

OFCs play the most important role in SEJ's franchise system. A *ba* for direct communication between employees and managers in the form of the FC meeting is meaningless if it does not close the gap in communication between head office and the stores.

OFCs give the franchise stores managerial guidance and are an important link with headquarters. Each OFC is assigned eight to ten stores and visits each store twice weekly. During these visits they provide information about ordering, company policies, sales campaigns, and new products. They introduce best practices by communicating success stories and experiences from other stores, teach effective sales techniques, and provide overall support for store management. Suzuki warns: "An OFC should spend time on the shop floor and not waste time in the office" (Suzuki, 2003: 185).

In addition to OFCs, the "Owner Consultation Department" is another venue linking headquarters to the franchises. This was established in 1979 as a department linked directly to the president of SEJ and is comprised of selected experienced employees from diverse backgrounds whose average age is 50. Members of the department visit all Seven-Eleven stores once or twice a year, holding intimate face-to-face meetings with the franchise owners. Consultations vary from complaints and concerns related to business operations to franchise owners' personal problems. After the consultation, department members write up a report for each store which will be presented to the president of SEJ. The reports are written with an open and frank attitude and include any criticisms about the company and top management. The president reads every report and will immediately refer any problems he recognizes to the FC meeting. He also circulates the reports to the divisions concerned for quick follow-up action.

The role of the Owners Consultation Department (OCD) is different from that of an OFC. They focus on qualitative issues while OFCs focus on the quantitative and operational aspects of franchise management. The OCD supports OFCs by building relationships with the franchisees while monitoring OFC guiding activities.

In-line with the SEJ philosophy of Adaptation to Change and Getting the Basics Right, OFCs recommend stores pursue the following four, basic rules:

- Offer the freshest products (Freshness Management);
- Never run out of stock (Assortment);
- Provide friendly service;
- Keep stores clean and bright.

These rules may seem like common sense in retailing, but achieving them everyday at every franchise in the system is a difficult task. Rather than using an area franchise system, SEJ relies on direct interaction between OFCs and the individual franchises to inculcate the values of the company.

6.1.5 Support systems

To achieve its driving objective to *reduce opportunity losses*, SEJ has to be able to offer its customers what they want when they want it. This means directing the entire operation toward understanding customer needs, offering products that satisfy them, and delivering them at the right time. To build an efficient and flexible organization that can respond quickly and appropriately to changes in the environment, SEJ cooperates with various external partners to synthesize their knowledge of customers with its own.

SEJ believes that it is more difficult to share information, develop a common attitude, and adapt to change in a growing organization. The company avoids organizational complexity by keeping employee numbers down and by extensive outsourcing of operations. In February 2008, the total number of employees was 5,294. Of the thousands of delivery trucks advertising the Seven-Eleven logo throughout Japan daily, SEJ owns none. Furthermore, while SEJ's information systems are highly sophisticated, its IT department functions only to convey the needs of frontline users to outside specialists who develop the systems.

Gathering and maintenance of information

SEJ combines the subjective insights accumulated by individual store-staff with the objective data accumulated in its state-of-the-art POS information system. For example, store-staff can hypothesize that consumption of beer and fast food will increase on the day of a local festival. Before ordering they can check the accuracy of the hypothesis against consumption patterns during previous festivals. As the order is placed, sales data from the POS system verify whether the hypothesis is accurate and this information is stored for use the next time the store places an order.

SEJ has completely revamped its information system six times. At a cost of 50 billion yen or 480 million US dollars to develop, the current sixth-generation system, introduced in May 2006, is the largest of its kind, connecting convenience stores, distribution centers, manufacturers, headquarters, Field Counselors, and offices by satellite and an integrated digital network. The main feature of the sixth-generation system is its optical fiber network connecting all Seven & *i* group companies, SEJ headquarters, regional offices and Seven-Eleven stores, with high-speed,reliable communication to match widespread broadband use. SEJ says the system is "seamless" in linking a variety of information for convenient use by all to enhance back-office support to the store operations. The system improved efficiency in *item by item management* by connecting store computers and Graphic Order Terminals (GOT) with the wireless LAN, so that each GOT displays the various indicators such as weather, events, commercial messages, and campaigns needed for making decisions about ordering. Store-staff are able to make prompt and timely decisions based on improved hypothesis testing with the support of this effective and efficient information system. The stores are provided with information in multimedia format, from numerical data, text, and audio, to still and moving pictures. The system allows store-staff to see the latest product information and product display methods, the weather and public events listings, and the company's current television commercials. It provides information about past order entries, sales records, sold-out stock, sales trends, and new products. Seven-Eleven stores are now equipped with POS registers that accept smart cards including "nanaco" issued by Seven & *i*., and others, offering further convenience to customers. Moreover, the new system enables each store to create its own database of sales performance figures. Moreover, the new system enables each store to create its own database of sales performance figures.

POS data is accumulated from customer transactions. Store-staff scan the purchased item by bar-code reader, and enter information about the type of customer. The data including gender and estimated age of the customer is collected and analyzed at SEJ headquarters. The POS system collects more than one year's worth of sales data per item and supports refined, objective analysis for sales forecasting. This detailed information on how many goods were sold to what kind of customers is also used in future product development.

Store-staff test their hypotheses about their local market every day using POS data and analysis. New knowledge created and compiled in this manner is validated against real purchasing behavior. If a gap is found to exist between the newly acquired knowledge and the reality, a new spiral of knowledge creation is triggered. Meanwhile, Field Counselors continuously refine their way of using the POS data based on their interactions with frontline employees. This cycle is repeated every day in a never-ending process of hypothesis building and testing that makes SEJ capable of constant change and self-reinvention.

In addition to POS data, SEJ collects information on consumer and business trends, market movements and strategies, information on product life cycles, regional differences in population, school events, and the weather. Weather forecasts are particularly useful in Japan, where temperatures in towns only 40 kilometers apart can vary by as much as 5 degrees Celsius. Every day, five reports arrive electronically from hundreds of weather centers, each report covering a radius of 20 kilometers.

Information on sales trends is used to decide whether to keep or drop an item. Typically, a new product reaches its sales peak within a week or two and begins to decline several weeks later. Once sales drop to a certain level at each store, the product is deleted from the recommendation list. The lifespan of most products shrinks over time, and new products are being introduced and older products dropped at a faster rate. Sales trends data can also guide adjustments in store layout several times each day. For example, a store may detect a sales pattern in the amount of premium brand ice cream sold at different hours of the day. Using the data and their tacit intuition, store-staff can rearrange the display of the ice cream so it is easier for customers to pick out their favorites when they come into the store. During one winter influenza season, yogurt was highlighted on the order screen because the head of dairy products at SEJ headquarters had analyzed several years of data and found a relationship between influenza and yogurt sales. Yogurt sales doubled following the screen alert.

6.1.6 Product development

SEJ puts a lot of effort into developing new products to meet quickly changing customer needs and desires, paying particular attention to regional variations in demand. About 100 new items appear in each store every week, and the company is putting more emphasis on developing its own, original products. Merchandisers from headquarters spend about 60 percent of their time on new product development. These products are not only a private brand (PB) of SEJ but also are developed with national brand (NB) manufacturers for sale only at SEJ stores. SEJ does not have the capacity to manufacture products itself, so it engages in so-called team merchandising (MD). In team MD, SEJ works together with manufacturers and wholesale vendors in a system of intensive cooperation to develop a shared understanding of the customer's perspective. Under the conventional structure, manufacturers had to gather their own information before beginning product development, and vendors were only engaged to facilitate distribution. This separation of roles prevented effective sharing of knowledge to create products that truly met customer needs. Team MD brings the different entities together as though they were part of a single company. They exchange knowledge, skills, and information as partners with a common goal and develop better products as a result. Product development teams create value-added products at lower cost by combining SEJ's knowledge of customers and sales data with manufacturers' expertise in production and vendors' knowledge of distribution. Team merchandising is a systematic process, starting with determination of market needs and the formulation of hypotheses on the type of product to introduce. Identification of market need is based on POS data, surveys, and knowledge from direct interface with customers. The constant interplay of knowledge from various sources makes it possible to break with conventional assumptions. For example, an analysis of POS data revealed that premium ice cream sells well not only in the summer but throughout the year. SEJ was the first in the industry to offer oven-fresh bread, filling in the gap they perceived between consumer preferences and the products supplied by national brand bread makers (see Case 3: SEJ's original bread).

SEJ approaches manufacturers with product ideas and gets their feedback on feasibility and production costs. The manufacturers outline costs, breaking down the components of the product into raw materials, and they emphasize product quality as the best way to attract customers. To create its premium brand ice cream, SEJ had approached five major manufacturers. Morinaga Milk and Akagi Milk agreed to jointly develop the product. The new ice cream sold an average of two to six times more than other ice cream brands.

Team merchandising is based on the concept of openness in knowledge sharing. SEJ starts by sharing the POS data that is considered the retailer's most valuable asset. This helps build a shared understanding of the target customer for the new product. The most intense knowledge sharing occurs at meetings in which manufacturers try to improve on products by sharing product samples, recipes, and other related know-how. Information about projected costs and sales is also shared. Under the conventional system, distribution worked as a kind of mutual aid arrangement between the manufacturer, wholesaler, and retailer in which unsold goods could be returned or retailers were given financial incentives to sell excess production. In team MD the parties plan production jointly, combining their different perspectives to reduce the risk of cost and production overruns in advance to prevent losses. The manufacturer is obliged to produce only the planned amount, and SEJ takes full responsibility for selling it. The synergy achieved from the combined knowledge of production, distribution, and marketing increases the potential for producing a higher value product with greater sales potential.

It takes some time and quite a number of meetings before a product concept is approved for production. It took one and a half years to develop the right taste for a popular fried rice product. Production starts after the board gives final approval. SEJ's ultimate aim is to systematize the process using "dream teams." For example, a recent project to create a noodle product brought together five well-known noodle manufacturers with three soup companies, five ingredients manufacturers, two packaging companies, and six noodle restaurants.

The work of product development is not limited to SEJ's product development department but includes board members, who taste and evaluate prototypes. Top managers, including board members, do not rely on the presentations of project managers to find out what's going on in the company. Rather, they engage directly in operations at the frontline to see, feel, and taste their products and experience the business first hand.

In addition to team MD, SEJ engages in Group MD. Group MD is joint product development among several companies in the Seven & *i* group, such as Ito-Yokado and Yoku Benimaru.

Case 3: SEJ's Original Bread (Direct from the Oven)

Even though rice is the traditional Japanese staple, bread has become one of the main items for sale at convenience stores. But sales at SEJ had been stagnant since the start of the 1990s, demanding counteraction. Japanese consumers have high expectations for freshness in food products. With this in mind, SEJ teamed up with a bread manufacturer in 1992 to offer freshly baked bread delivered direct from the oven. Given the short shelf life of bread it made no sense to have it mass produced at a bread factory and then delivered to stores. SEJ wanted to offer bread soon after baking, so it came up with the idea of working with bread factories near the stores and having them bake bread made from frozen dough, then deliver it immediately after baking. However, Japan's main bread maker was reluctant to do a special production run for SEJ alone. They also pointed out that bread made from frozen dough spoils quickly, so the SEJ team went looking for a company with the technology to improve the quality of frozen dough. Eventually, they found two companies, Francois Co., Ltd in Kyushu, which had the technology to freeze dough without spoiling the taste, and Robapan Co., Ltd in Hokkaido, one of Japan's traditional bread makers. The trading company ITOCHU Corporation coordinated the effort, and Ajinomoto Co., Inc. took responsibility for adapting the freezing technology. To maintain the freshness of just-baked bread, the team decided they would need certain conditions. The "best before" date would have to be 30 hours from the time of baking to match the lifestyle of their target customer. This was shorter than the expiry date on national brands but longer than the town bakery. The baking factory would have to be near the dominant stores to match delivery to fluctuations in demand during the day (Yoshioka, 2007).

A market test was conducted in Hokkaido with five stores in the Robapan sales channel, and the first baking factory opened in 1993. By 2002 SEJ had baking factories nationwide. Its brand, "Direct from the Oven" (*Yakitate Chokuso Bin*), has become a major item in SEJ stores, with sales of more than one million units every day. Suzuki says the lesson is that even when common sense tells you it's impossible to make a certain product, it is important to try to bridge the gap between the seller's circumstances and the customer's requirements.

6.1.7 The distribution system

Distribution is a vital component in supplying customers with what they want, when they want it. Customers can't buy boxed lunches if they are not delivered to the store until after lunchtime. SEJ works closely with manufacturers and wholesale vendors to maintain an effective distribution network. It has reduced daily deliveries to each store from 70 vehicles per day to nine. This not only reduces logistics costs but also helps stores manage freshness and respond more efficiently to changes in consumer demand.

SEJ stores are connected by an online information system to almost 300 distribution centers, categorized by climate. These centers connect to about 300 production plants within easy reach of the stores for convenient delivery. Trucks at the distribution centers are controlled by GPS, with a sensor installed in each truck. High turnover items, such as boxed lunches and rice balls, are delivered three times a day. Slower moving items, such as frozen products, are delivered three to seven times per week. Separate distribution centers deliver books and magazines every day.

Since the distribution centers and delivery trucks are owned and operated by other vendors and manufacturers, frequent, personal interaction with them is central to SEJ's improved distribution system. SEJ holds regular meetings with the heads of the distribution centers to improve efficiency, and distribution officers from headquarters pay regular visits to the centers to address potential problems. Knowledge sharing enables both sides to identify new areas for improvement at the distribution centers and in the information system.

This integrated supply chain enables quick processing of data in the information system. Orders sent by 10 a.m. for delivery after 4 p.m. are processed electronically in less than seven minutes. Innovations in 2002 that reduce delivery time have allowed SEJ to eliminate the use of food preservatives and artificial coloring in most fast-food items. Moreover, there is no loss due to excess production and no need to carry large inventories thanks to system integration.

6.1.8 Globalizing know-how

Plans to expand the Japanese-style franchise system in the US have already begun with the assembly of land and store space, but there are still many issues to resolve in implementing SEJ management style. These concern the conversion of distribution from a system of manufacturers' sales routes to a collaborative system, and application of *item by item management* and *fresh food management*. This is not a simple matter of system organization and logistics, but of ensuring that U.S. store owners and their store-staff truly understand the fundamentals of the SEJ management style and the thinking behind it.

The biggest challenge in turning around The Southland Corporation was figuring out how to transfer SEJ know-how to US employees. The company understood the sensitivity of retailing to local conditions and knew they could not simply uproot the Japanese model and replant it, exactly as it is, in the US. One of the causes of Southland's bankruptcy was its expansion into unrelated businesses such as real estate, finance, and oil refining, but the company's core, convenience store business had also lost competitiveness. The stores were dimly lit and female customers were reluctant to shop in them. In addition, merchandise management was ineffective, sales of food and daily items were low, and discounting was routine, putting pressure on gross profit. Once SEJ assumed control, a core management team was recruited in the US and it met every two months in Japan and the US by turns. The meetings were meant to help US managers understand the essence of the convenience store business and to show them how to build and utilize competitive advantages in the business.

From August, 1991, 50 stores in Austin, Texas were reorganized for test marketing. To make the stores more attractive to women and children, the lighting was changed from 500 lux of intensity to 900, and the exterior walls were changed to glass. Store layout and signs were unified in a new look. Nylon stockings were placed near the entrance and adult magazines were eliminated from the magazine shelf. Excessive discounting was stopped and product sizes and packaging were shrunk for quicker consumption. Food items such as sandwiches, which previously had been made in each store, were supplied centrally to improve and stabilize quality.

The changes quickly bore fruit, with sales revenues rising an average of 17 percent. The better sales results encouraged US employees, changing their mindset and making further reforms easier to implement. OFCs were retrained, and *item by item management* was introduced. SEJ intentionally delayed introduction of the POS system to allow store-staff more time to experience *item by item management*. Store-staff manually prepared a list of merchandise morning and night, checking sales volume to determine if an item was selling or not. This helped them to acquire a sense of how to control merchandise. The objective of *item by item management* is not only to get a feel for the sales situation at each store, but to understand the essence of supply chain management as a whole. Classes on merchandising were held every week to help employees deepen their understanding of the process. After this was accomplished, the POS system was introduced in 1997.

Adopting the SEJ delivery system has proved more difficult. In the US, companies such as Coca Cola have their own sales route system, offering discount pricing with volume purchases and accepting returns for resale. With the globalization of Seven-Eleven it remains to be seen whether the efficiencies of the Japanese operations can be implemented effectively in the US with its different language, customs, and demography. The customer-focused philosophy and management system is becoming accepted practice in US operations, thanks to concrete evidence of its value in improved business results. The methods used to improve bread and boxed lunch sales in Japan are now applied to sandwiches in US stores, guided by the company's underlying values of *Adaptation to Change and Getting the Basics Right*. Seven-Eleven is also starting Team MD product development in US operations. Competitors in the convenience store market could introduce similar POS information and distribution systems, but the SEJ philosophy remains the decisive difference, with its emphasis on people, their tacit knowledge and experience, and the system that effectively mobilizes and synthesizes that knowledge for innovation. A customer-focused mindset and the relentless practice of knowledge creation are essential to the successful globalization of the SEJ method.

6.2 Ryohin Keikaku Co., Ltd – Muji

6.2.1 Company overview

Muji is a growing international retail brand. It began as the private label of the Japanese supermarket chain Seiyu and has since been developed and adapted to changing markets in Japan and overseas. It is an example of a successful conversion of a private label into a mass market brand, and one that synthesizes the paradox of brand as non-brand in the ever-changing business environment of fashion and household products. The company that developed and markets Muji-branded products is Ryohin Keikaku Co., Ltd. It has grown by coordinating the technologies and know-how of its stakeholders – customers and manufacturers – to develop the unique Muji brand. The key to the company's success has been its ability to sustain and evolve the original Muji brand concepts of quality and ecology and adapt organizational structures in accordance with changes in the market environment. This ability is based on an understanding of the dynamics of knowledge sharing through dialogue in *ba* to accelerate the exchange of knowledge both inside the company and with external partners. The strength of the Muji brand is not only in the functionality of its products, but in the invisible values they represent.

Muji was the brainchild of Seiji Tsutsumi, founder of the Japanese retailing giant, the Saison Group, and a keen observer of changing consumer trends. Originally a private label launched in 1980 at Saison's Seiyu supermarket chain, the original concept was to provide quality goods at a price

25 percent to 30 percent lower than that of other national brands, by eliminating waste in manufacturing and unnecessary packaging. The original product line was limited to daily food items and detergents.

The name "Muji" is short for the Japanese "*Mujirushi Ryohin*," meaning "no brand name [but] good quality." The company chose the name in just 30 minutes during a meeting on branding. Saison copywriter, Shinzo Higurashi, casually murmured the word "*mujirushi*," meaning "non-brand," and art director Ikko Tanaka quickly added the phrase "*ryohin*," meaning "good quality products" (Iwanaga, 2002). Together they became the brand symbol for a product concept focused on functionality and simplicity, and this has remained the core concept of product development ever since.

By the early 1980s, Japan's rapid, post-war economic development had fully provided for the basic needs of Japanese consumers, and consumer trends had begun to diversify according to individual tastes. Consumers began to choose products based on personal values, selective consumption habits, and increased knowledge about products, and showed a willingness to take part in marketing research for product planning. There was a clear preference for products that were simple and functional, without elaborate packaging, and people also tended to purchase goods that matched their values regardless of the price. Every retail company in Japan was sensitive to these changes and began reviewing product planning policies. During this time, the supermarket chains came out with their own private labels, one after another.

The direction Seiyu had set for itself was to develop "simple, good quality products" without extraneous features. The supermarket company had reviewed its supply chain, from purchasing materials to manufacturing and packaging, and decided it should be offering a unique product at a lower price but at a level of quality similar to existing national brands.

6.2.2 The expansion of Muji

Ryohin Keikaku was founded on June 30, 1989, to take over product development, sales, and marketing of all Muji brand products. All trademark rights and responsibility for Muji store operations were transferred to the new company in March, 1990 and it began operating as a wholly owned subsidiary,[2] while Seiyu concentrated on its own general merchandising. Ryohin Keikaku became the wholesaler of the Muji brand and also directly managed the Muji brand stores, bypassing Seiyu's established system of operations.[3]

Thus, development of the Muji brand and Ryohin Keikaku progressed in four stages. First, from 1980 to 1988 Muji was a private label at supermarkets, department stores, and other shops; second, from 1989 to 1995 it was sold in Muji stores; third, from 1995 to 2000 the stores were expanded in the larger cities; and fourth, after 2000 the company underwent a strategic restructuring of operations.

Expansion in Japan

The opening of the first Muji store in Japan was a significant step for a brand that had originated in a supermarket chain. The store opened in 1983 in the fashionable district of Aoyama, where it could establish a strong image and be the antennae for sensing new consumer trends. Sales were good and the store attracted media attention, which expanded awareness of the brand exponentially. Rhohin Keikaku now sells Muji products through three channels: directly at its own stores; as a wholesaler to licensed stores[4] and convenience stores; and on the Internet. In May, 2000, Muji.net Corporation (Muji.net) was founded to oversee Internet shopping on the Muji website (www.muji.net) and to support the company's foray into housing construction.[5] Muji.net is continually expanding its product range and looking to diversify business online. The portal is instantly recognizable by the dark red color of the Muji brand. The site consists of the net store, which sells the usual Muji products, and the Muji.net community, which sells the bigger items not sold in the stores.

Expansion overseas

The first international stores opened in London in July, 1991 and in Hong Kong in November, 1991. A global development strategy was put in place targeting Europe, where consumption was fully matured, and Asia, where it was still developing.

In Europe, Ryohin Keikaku planned to open 50 stores, expecting them to turn profitable by February, 2003. When the company recognized that this would not happen it was forced to re-examine its development plan. Economic decline had forced a withdrawal from Asia in 1999, and in 2001 three unprofitable stores in France and one in Belgium were also closed down. In a bold move Muji had closed its Paris flagship store in the Louvre Museum after only one year from its opening in 2000.

Customers in Europe had given Muji full marks for design and concepts, but profitability remained low. The failure in Europe was attributed to the imbalance customers perceived between the Muji theme of "creativity and elegance within a certain price range" and the high prices being charged,[6] especially in France. Rents for favorably located stores were also high. The stores in Europe that were closed had been in good locations and paying rents that might be affordable for a boutique with a high gross margin, but not for a stationery and general merchandise store like Muji.[7] The company had erred in giving priority to opening more stores in the chain without considering costs in rent and human resources. It had also been costly to establish logistics and management for the expansion.

Ryohin Keikaku learned from this experience and reviewed its international strategy, later improving profitability by tightening up inventory control and operations, and by matching goods to local needs. In Europe,

Ryohin Keikaku opened stores in Italy, Germany, Sweden and other countries, and in 2007 established its European headquarters, Muji Europe Holdings Limited, in London, England. By February, 2007 it had opened 43 stores in Europe. In Asia, the Hong Kong store was reopened in 2001, and in Singapore in 2003, followed by stores in Korea, Taiwan, and China.

6.2.3 Principles of product development

In the early stages, Muji's concept was to provide simple, good quality products at lower prices; the goods were "lower priced for a reason." A review of materials, manufacturing processes, and packaging had revealed numerous ways to cut costs and pass them on to the consumer. The marketing strategy was not to sell brand-name products, ironically providing Muji with its own brand identity. While there was no precedent for the private brand of a supermarket going independent, Muji's concept of simple, elegant, and intelligent design and use of natural materials quickly became a hit in Japan and overseas. The method for maintaining and evolving this concept in successive product innovations is revealed in the relationship between Muji and its customers.

Product appeal

One feature of the Muji brand that appealed to customers was a strategic emphasis on "texture" in design and materials, while the private labels of other supermarket chains focused more on price strategy to undercut the national brands. Muji also differentiated itself by setting its quality standard at the level of Japanese department stores rather than that of the general merchandise supermarket, establishing a higher value brand image from the start. In fact, differences between Muji and other private brands in the supermarket business were few in the beginning; but its strategic emphasis on intelligent design and eco-friendly materials eventually distinguished it from the others. Muji was selling a lifestyle whose concept was clearly presented and easily understood, and the core concept was strictly maintained as the quality of design improved. There were four main elements in its branding strategy: balance of quality and price; emphasis on texture and simplicity in materials; focus on the basics; and creation of store layouts consistent with the brand image.

Balancing quality and price

Price is an important factor in any decision to purchase. Muji sets prices relative to quality, always looking for the right balance. As a general rule, daily items are sold at prices 30 percent to 40 percent cheaper than the equivalent national brand of similar quality. The more expensive luxury items can also be sold at more reasonable prices because they have no designer label. This is in keeping with the Muji objective to "eliminate excess without sacrificing quality or functionality."

Texture and simplicity

Muji design focuses on simplicity and the use of natural colors and materials of good quality. The message is that Muji offers quality goods at reasonable prices because it eliminates wastefulness in the production process. Simplicity in design is aimed at conveying the texture and qualities of the material. Both in-house and outside designers are engaged in product planning to achieve the right "feel" in a product.

Focus on the basics

Muji's focus on the basics, emphasizing the use of natural materials, is a clear message of the brand that is strictly enforced. Colors are restricted to natural colors such as white, black, brown, and blue, and textile prints are either in checks or stripes. Materials, design, and pricing follow strict guidelines to maintain the core concept. The color and textile limitations may give the impression that Muji clothing is rather dull, but customers say they find it is easier to combine and coordinate Muji designs with other styles of clothing, and this is its attraction as a basic lifestyle product. Customer reviews on the Internet also describe Muji products as "simple," "not decorative," and "not tiresome." This simplicity is viewed as an aesthetic feature of high quality design.

Conceptual axioms in product development

There are four basic axioms of the Muji concept that are absolute guidelines for product development. If a product does not meet even one of these guidelines, it will not be developed. All existing products are also regularly reviewed for adherence to the guidelines. They are represented by the "four Rs,"[8] which explain the deeper meanings implied in each guideline. This meaning is often difficult to articulate but is understood on a tacit level by all employees engaged in the continuous planning process. The four Rs are as follows (see Figure 6.2):

- Raw: the raw material feel – emphasis on sensation, no brand;
- Recombination: all-purpose – emphasis on intelligence and freedom;
- Reasonability: easy to understand – emphasis on logic and comprehension;
- Reconditioning: not damaging to the environment and health – in tune with the times.

6.2.4 Making use of internal and external knowledge

What is notable about Muji's method of product development is the process of gathering knowledge externally from customers and collaborators and incorporating this knowledge into a concrete product. Ryohin Keikaku has built a system for connecting knowledge and ideas with product concepts and planning for continuous creation of new products in response to the changing environment, such as changes in customer needs and the manufacturers used in outsourcing. Ryohin Keikaku collects ideas from customers

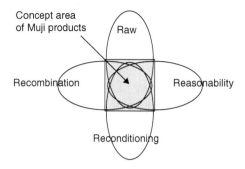

Figure 6.2 Conceptual diagram of product positioning of Muji products
Source: Based on internal material of Ryohin Keikaku, modified by the authors.

and manufacturers and makes use of the knowledge and skills of outside designers to continually accumulate knowledge in design, manufacturing, and sales. Thus, its knowledge base is widely dispersed in the complex relationships of people in its organization and in the outside companies it interacts with. It collects and synthesizes this knowledge of the parts into a whole that exemplifies the Muji brand and is actualized in concrete products. It is this system that allows Ryohin Keikaku to maintain its competitive advantage as a producer of retail goods.

Information from the customer

Ryohin Keikaku pays close attention to the views of customers as a source of primary ideas and information. The company actively solicits customer feedback when adapting or terminating products or making improvements in business operations. Feedback is usually received by electronic mail, both domestic and international, and varies from opinions on products to inquiries about the Muji camping facility. This is a powerful tool for direct communication with customers. All employees above the level of manager have access to incoming messages, which are stored in the original form in which they were received to ensure they are not misinterpreted or distorted. The online store Muji.net receives nearly 100,000 email messages annually, which are classified according to content and reported internally. The information is used in product development in conjunction with sales results and observations about trends for more comprehensive analysis. The information flow is continuous, from the customer to product planning and development and back to the customer again, with new products and more customer feedback for the next round of product planning. This process also takes place on the Web. Muji.net has a page that invites Muji Club members to propose new products. These proposals may generate several product ideas that are then posted on the page for broader feedback, before finalizing the product's features. The final product is then made available on the

Web for members to pre-order. Once the number of orders exceeds 300, the minimum break-even point, manufacturing begins. The advantages of this method are that customer preferences are grasped and channeled into product planning quickly, with the pre-order system providing a quick projection of sales trends. Customer satisfaction is more assured because customers participate. Muji.net publishes the names of some customers who have pre-ordered to share their feedback with other potential customers.

Some of the flagship products that originated from customer ideas submitted on the Internet include the "cushion-sofa that conforms to your body" and the "shopping bag with outside pocket."

The cushion-sofa has a different type of cloth on each face, which varies the spring resistance depending on whether you use the cushion while lying down, or as a sofa for sitting on. It is made of both rough sailcloth and soft stretchable material, and is meant for daily use in the typical Japanese household where one room often serves as both a sitting room and a bedroom.

The "shopping bag with pockets" is for daily use and originated from ideas submitted by housewives. Muji.net collected ideas on the Net community and sent out questionnaires to 1,200 individuals. It then selected 30 of the respondents to try out the sample bag and incorporated their recommendations in the final specifications for production. This shopping-bag line included six different prototypes in different shapes and made of different materials. It was carefully designed with ingenuity to allow for more convenient shopping. For example, it has a stopper inside the bag to avoid spillage from a bottle, a waterproof insulator pocket for holding cold items, and handles attached on the inside of the bag for easier grip.[9] The value this shopping bag provides is not just that it is easy to use but that it also represents an ecology-oriented lifestyle; by using this bag customers can help reduce the wasteful use of disposable plastic or paper bags and contribute to resource preservation and protection of the environment.

Survey of changing needs

Since household goods are its main merchandise, Ryohin Keikaku continuously surveys the changing living conditions of people in its target market to uncover the seeds of new product development. These surveys examine the items in people's living spaces and how they use them, both independently and in combination with other items. Analysis of these factors often leads to new product development. This observation process is aimed at gaining a good grasp of what elements are essential for functioning effectively in existing living spaces. For example, the Muji "mattress with legs" is covered with sofa cloth on one side. The idea for this product originated from observations that college students living in studio apartments spend most of their time at home sitting on their beds making mobile phone calls or playing computer games.[10]

Using the knowledge of manufacturers

Muji products vary widely and production relies on a specialized knowledge of raw materials and manufacturing technologies and processes. Ryohin Keikaku relies on its manufacturers for this expertise. Employees in charge of product planning make regular visits to the manufacturers and work with them to identify new opportunities for product development. They call such visits "wandering around"[11] and they are common practice in the product planning phase. The manufacturers are strong in their areas of specialty but often weak in product development and marketing knowledge. There may be cases where a manufacturer is not aware of how to combine technologies for more efficient production, or is not even fully utilizing its own technologies. Ryohin Keikaku brings its market knowledge to the manufacturing process in the development of new products by combining it with a manufacturer's technologies, or coordinating with several manufacturers in an alliance.

Expert advisory board

Advisors, both internal and external to the company, play an important role in creating concepts at Muji. They form an "advisory board" that includes art directors and creative directors working on planning, conceptualizing, and design. The contributions of expert advisors have been significant in establishing the Muji brand. The advisors see the company from the outside and this helps strategic planning and product development by providing more objective evaluation of new products and sales campaigns.

All Muji products provide basic functionality, which is unchanging, with variations in detail according to customer preference and changing trends. The basics are universal, the variations change according to context. Muji predetermines the size of products such as tableware or unit furniture so it suits the average customer's living space. The notion of interchangeable modules applied to all Muji goods extends to its wood-frame house. The basic frame doesn't change but allows for a continuously changing lifestyle space within.

In summary, the value of Muji branded products is a result of the creative and organizational process of coordinating and combining knowledge that emerges in various *ba*, and integrating that knowledge into the unified concept of the Muji brand expressed in its products. To develop a new product line, the knowledge of various stakeholders is combined with original ideas, while maintaining Muji's core concepts of simplicity, good quality and natural taste. The effect is to increase product sophistication as customer tastes evolve, while enhancing brand loyalty.

To maintain and preserve the brand concept, products must continuously meet strict criteria established in quality control and improvement processes. This starts with a report reviewing all existing products, as is done in the product development phase. The product line is then assessed according to the four Rs (Raw, Recombination, Reasonability, Reconditioning). A final review determines whether there is an even balance between product quality and price.

Ryohin Keikaku uses a trial-and-error method of gauging product longevity, where customer response can suggest that the product may be reaching the end of its life. The company identifies the cause of obsolescence and embodies this understanding in a new product. This has the advantage of achieving market response quickly and directly. On the other hand, it puts pressure on the company to develop new products continuously. Unlike with patentable technologies, anybody can enter the household goods market and imitate Muji, so, to maintain competitive advantage, it must continually provide new products with the tangible value in design and materials that its customers expect.

6.2.5 Repositioning and redeveloping the concept

Muji's growth is the result of its ability to synthesize a universal concept with changes in the environment. The concept of "lower priced for a reason" is universal. What has changed is the variety of product lines and the greater focus on product design. Muji expanded from the supermarket brand of early days, offering a unique balance of quality and price, to become an ever-expanding line of products geared to changing consumer lifestyles, with elegant and intelligent design added to the brand image. By maintaining this basic concept while evolving the products to add value, Muji has retained its loyal customer base.

Nevertheless, mistakes were made during aggressive domestic and international expansion in the latter half of 1990 that resulted in dilution of the brand. This required a repositioning and redevelopment of the core Muji concept and the construction of an organization that could support it. In the fiscal year ending February, 2001, Ryohin Keikaku's operating profit had fallen 12.7 percent from the previous year, the first decline since the company's founding, while sales revenue rose only 8 percent. In January the same year, the company had chosen Tadamitsu Matsui from the ranks of senior managers to become president and representative director.[12] Matsui was charged with the task of turning things around and he started by analyzing the causes of Muji's business slump and revising its strategy.

Matsui determined that the major cause of the company's decline was the rapid expansion to open new stores with bigger floor space and the creation of an expanding range of products that led to dilution of the original brand concept. In addition, continued annual growth prior to the decline had made employees complacent. He restructured the company along two main lines, reformulating the concept of *Mujirushi Ryohin* to reposition Muji in the market, and cutting costs and waste to make operations more efficient.

Repositioning the Muji concept

To restore and reposition the Muji brand, the company needed to have a solid grasp of the brand image that already existed in customers' minds, as conveyed through its products. The customer had clearly grasped the original message of Muji products, which was to eliminate waste in packaging. The cornerstone of Ryohin Keikaku's strategic success was in preserving that message while continuously improving product design and concepts.

Strengthening design

Early on, Ryohin Keikaku had understood the value of design in the development process, and in 2002 it sought to strengthen its alliance with top designers outside the company. Muji formed an alliance with Yoji Yamamoto Co., Ltd, led by the designer of the same name, and launched new product lines in furniture and clothing on the theme of "natural warmth." Yamamoto joined as an advisory board member and also directed the design team in development of the new products.

Ryohin Keikaku reinforced its design division by establishing a team of "go-between" designers at the company in household goods.[13] This team played a pivotal role in connecting top designers from outside to the in-house merchandising team and to marketing managers to implement the Muji design concept. The department of household goods is divided by product category into seven groups, each responsible for work done by an outside designer as well as by merchandising staff. Merchandising staff might come up with ideas, but they would have difficulty conceptualizing and externalizing these ideas because they were not experts in design. The "go-between" design team connected internal merchandising staff with outside designers, acting as a kind of knowledge translator. In addition to coordinating, the team might also do some actual design work depending on the theme. This activity is supported by the Ryohin Keikaku advisory board. Japan's famed product designer Naoto Fukasawa is a member of that board, advising on research and development in household goods.

International partnerships with reputable designers

Ryohin Keikaku has a number of global projects aimed at strengthening the value of its products. Among these are World Muji, which engages famous designers in Muji product development. In April, 2003, the company launched a line of furniture developed together with top, overseas designers such as Enzo Mari from Italy, Sam Hecht from the United Kingdom, and Konstantin Grcic from Germany. The designers' names were not on the products but fans of Muji became aware of their involvement through Internet blogs. They created sofas and tables up to five times more expensive than the prices of other popular Muji furniture items. But excellence in design and materials gave these products a texture and appeal that drew customers regardless of price. The aim was to compete on the basis of the aesthetic value of the product itself rather than on name value.[14]

Muji designer products are now highly regarded internationally. In 2002, Ryohin Keikaku set up a booth in a shop attached to the Museum of Modern Art in New York(MOMA) offering goods with high artistic value, and began selling Muji brand products in the MOMA store itself in 2004. In March, 2005, five Muji products were awarded the gold prize at the iF Design Awards in Germany, for excellence in industrial design. It was the first time that a non-manufacturing company had won so many gold prizes. The event served as a showcase to the world of the quality of design at Ryohin Keikaku. Shoji Ito, director of the Product Planning Department, said that entering Muji products in the iF Design Awards was not expected to lead directly to more sales or higher value for the brand. "Rather, we wanted to be sure our products would be accepted overseas and to see how Europeans would evaluate them."[15] He said the award of five prizes was too good to be true and is significant in the transformation of Muji from a subjective value standard into a universal standard with worldwide support.

Restructuring the business system

After becoming president in 2001, Matsui visited stores around the country to communicate directly with Muji store owners and regional managers and solidify his grasp of the reasons for the business slump. He said he aimed to have a frank exchange of ideas, while also reiterating the vision of Ryohin Keikaku and seeking improvements. "There is no set answer to what Ryouhin is," he told the store owners and managers. "But ask yourself the question and you will see infinite possibilities."[16]

Matsui described his restructuring plan as an effort to share valuable knowledge throughout the company and "build up a rational business system based on clear logic in routine operations throughout the system."[17] He said he was successful in resolving 80 percent of the problems by targeting a variety of operations where decision-making was mainly guided by individual intuition and experience, and transforming that into a process that was visible, measurable, and resolvable.[18] Since then, the variety of know-how (tacit knowledge) and experience in the company has been accumulated and transformed into shareable knowledge accessible throughout the organization (explicit knowledge). It took about two and a half years for the effects of restructuring to show positive business results. Settlement of accounts ending February, 2008 showed a record high in net sales and net income on a consolidated basis, at 162.0 million yen or 1.5 million US dollars and 10.6 million yen or 0.1 million US dollars respectively.

Matsui's reforms not only re-established the Muji brand concept but reshaped the organizational systems that support it. He set rules for store operations and new store openings, increased the efficiency of logistics systems, and cut inventory by shortening the supply cycle. He also changed the organizational structure, redefining responsibilities and shifting reporting lines, in order to strengthen product development capability and enhance sales efficiency. He launched the reforms by establishing targets and creating a concrete plan of action to achieve them in all areas. During this process, he utilized both in-house knowledge and the knowledge of outside consultants and companies and their best practices. More importantly he was able to adapt that knowledge to Muji's particular situation and ensure understanding prevailed at each level of the organization during visits to the frontline. The director of the household goods department, Takashi Kato, commented on Matsui's efforts to restructure the organization: "We step into the factories to which we entrust production, and we work together with them as business partners to change the field." Kato said: "If we just arranged the deal from headquarters in Tokyo and left the rest of the process up to our partners, we would have no control over the cost structure."[19]

Up until 2001, steady growth at Ryohin Keikaku had been supported by their superior concept and its implementation, but gradually the company fell into the trap of overconfidence. It had also failed to design and execute expansion in accordance with the original vision and concept, and lost the capability to respond to changing trends in customer demand. Muji realized, after the fact, that it had lost the delicate balance between brand concept and the organization that supports it. Matsui led the transformation of Muji by going back to basics and seeing the company from the customer's point of view, while coordinating and combining a variety of knowledge within and outside the company to evolve the brand concept. Muji's turnaround worked because of this successful management of the evolving, organic relationship between the company and the business ecosystem.

6.2.6 The dynamics of Muji

The effort to maintain the original Muji concept, while evolving it in-line with the times, is reflected in the Muji slogans. During the early phase of Ryohin Keikaku the slogan was "lower priced for a reason," emphasizing that the elimination of wasteful packaging enabled the company to offer high quality goods at reasonable prices. Since 2005, Muji has begun to focus on a more far-reaching universal value with the slogan "this product is enough for me," emphasizing reasonable demand and finding satisfaction in the basics, as an alternative to conspicuous consumption. The company says the Muji concept will continue to be the compass for its products, emphasizing fundamental values and their universality.[20] In effect, Muji has maintained the original concept of naturalness and simplicity while enhancing both the message and the quality of design. It is a consumption style where selection is not based on clear brand preference but on evaluation of material texture and an affinity with simplicity in design that has universal appeal. The Muji literature describes this as an "ultimate flexibility" that speaks to everyone because it leaves space for the imagination, like the concept of *wabi* in Japanese tea ceremony or the way of organizing the stage in Japanese theatre.[21]

It is difficult to maintain an original concept over a long period of time. Twenty years have passed since the birth of Muji, and it has survived, despite the difficulties in 1999. The original strengths of the brand strategy were the close cooperation with partner companies and customers and the creation of a system to support this exchange, which enabled continuous product innovation. The brand is now confronting the paradox of having to continue to satisfy the basics with high quality, long lifecycle products, while also offering attractive new products that reflect the changing times.

While the restructuring of a business system is generally a standardized, logical process, restructuring a brand that has suffered dilution is significantly more challenging. This is because a brand is not created by a company alone but emerges from a shared understanding between the company and its customers. The key to successful restructuring of the Muji brand was timing. The company took appropriate steps early to restore the message when it started to become ambiguous in the product. By maintaining critical focus on design in product development, they were able to avoid irrevocable brand dilution. The universal appeal of the basic product concept was confirmed when Muji was honored at the iF Design Awards.

Important factors for recovery at Ryohin Keikaku were its use of knowledge from inside and outside the company to improve its products and business operations, and its revival of dynamic processes through use of the Internet to link it to the next cycle of growth. More importantly, it was able to restore the original Muji concept.

The designer Kenya Hara was on the advisory board at the time and described the Muji concept this way: "We are free to see with our imagination because there is nothing there at that moment. In simplicity there is the flexibility to match any context."[22] Ryohin Keikaku has expressed the value of Muji as an "empty container." The container can accommodate a variety of values such as rationality, simplicity, reasonable pricing, and preservation of the environment, but ultimately it is the customer who decides what values are to be accommodated. The value of Muji is determined in the relationship with its customers. The moment the company insists on a specific value regardless of the customer, the essential value of the brand will be destroyed (Akamine, 2007).

Muji products reflect each customer's image of what the products are, seen in the open spaces of design that leave room for the imagination. This is a Zen notion of seeing existence in nothingness and freely creating meaning in space, according to the context (see Figure 6.3). While *Muji* products have grown up in Japan, their global acceptance and unique positioning in the world stems from their grasp of the universal value of satisfying the basics in design and functionality.

Figure 6.3 Muji advertisement: Muji bowl in a traditional Japanese *Shoin* room (left) and Zen garden (right) at Ginkakuji (Jishoji) temple in Kyoto
Source: Ryouin Keikaku (2005).

Unlike patented technologies and know-how, general merchandise is more difficult to differentiate for competitive advantage, as new product lines are quickly duplicated by competitors. When Muji filed suit against a manufacturer and a retailer of a product that resembled its best selling polypropylene storage cases, the court did not accept that the design was a Muji original.[23] As this case demonstrates, the strength of Muji is not simply in the physical value of their products. Market acceptance of the products is also based on their aesthetic value, in terms of the messages they convey and the meanings they hold for individual consumers. In fact, Muji is a rare case of brand support for daily-use products because of their aesthetic value. It is neither a luxury brand nor a national brand, but rather is positioned in-between. As a retail brand without its own production facilities, Muji has still managed the whole process, from idea generation and product development, to manufacturing, logistics, and feedback, all the while maintaining the flexibility to match the changing times and relentlessly pursuing improvement in product quality and production lead-time.

Sales revenue at Ryohin Keikaku dropped for the first time in the company's history in 2002 because Muji had become rigid, sticking to past methods that had been successful. At the same time, the core concept was being diluted in a rapid expansion of product lines. Muji overcame these setbacks under the leadership of Tadamitsu Matsui, who was able to identify important, internal knowledge assets for sharing across the company, while combining that with the external knowledge of customers, manufacturers, and collaborators, to accelerate organizational reform and business improvements. He took bold steps to strengthen the Muji concept and recover the organizational strength needed to support it. In the area of product development, he maintained the original Muji concept but evolved it with the times, with enhanced design suited to an international market. Muji's competitive edge was maintained through a continuous, dynamic process of product development, synthesized with the knowledge and experience gained in a variety of business relationships.

6.3 Implications

In this chapter, we have examined two retail companies, Seven-Eleven Japan (SEJ) and Ryohin Keikaku (Muji), whose brands are widely accepted in their domestic markets and are expanding globally. A key factor for their success is their relentless pursuit of meaning and value creation for the customers through dialogue and practice to realize their vision to meet and provide values to the rapidly changing needs of the customers. Both companies have no production capability of their own; they collaborate with outside partners to develop and manufacture products through the sharing and synthesis of knowledge about production, the market, and customers in *ba*. In our view, these companies create value in a processual way.

Seven-Eleven Japan was the first to introduce the convenience store business model in Japan and developed its own unique style of store management. SEJ has achieved its high level of performance through continuous knowledge creation to adapt to ever-changing market needs. Such knowledge creation is made possible by distributed *phronesis*, which enables store-staff to make the judgments needed in a particular situation and according to the particular time and place relevant to each store. The *phronetic* capability to make such judgments is fostered through never-ending dialogue and practice in the form of building and testing hypotheses. This is a process of converting a particular tacit insight into objective, universal theory and applying that theory to reality again to further enrich the tacit insight. This continuous cycle is driven by the knowledge vision and driving objective that define SEJ and its *raison d'être*, which is to adapt to market changes by seeing the essence in the flow of change that enables them to give customers what they want, when they want it, and in the exact amounts that they want it. SEJ has built its system on state-of-the-art IT data communications, distribution, and Field Counselor meetings to keep the process moving in a way that actualizes the vision and driving objective. Elements such as the POS system and *item by item management* are merely the tools for keeping this cycle of knowledge creation moving forward. The real key to SEJ's success is its store-staff, who learn to see and synthesize the particular with the universal to make correct judgments on a daily basis aimed at achieving a common good.

Like SEJ, Ryohin Keikaku also has the flexibility and mobility to transform itself to respond to the changing needs of customers. Looking at the process of recovery at Ryohin Keikaku, we see the importance to corporate identity of the effective development of a product concept and its succession. Muji's sustained advantage is not a result of "technological edge" or ownership of a sophisticated system of production. Rather, it stems from an awareness of process in brand imaging and product development. Rigidity in the organization led to a temporary downfall and brand dilution. Restoration of the brand and reform of the organization through a revitalized relationship with the customer enabled the company to regain its original dynamism. In particular, it was achieved through a product development process that pursued better design while adhering to Muji's unique value concept and responding to customer needs. Since there is no one, fixed concept that fits with an uncertain future, what is most important is the pursuit of an ideal.[24] The Muji brand has maintained its core ideal of "good quality at a lower price" while evolving in dynamic co-creation with the customer to evermore sophisticated design in its products. It was supported by a system of knowledge sharing and knowledge creation within the company and with the customers through dialogue and practice. As expressed in the Muji vision statement, it is "the customers [who] judge the value" of Muji, and while there is "one right answer," there are also "infinite possibilities if we continue to ask" what Muji should be.

In the knowledge creation process, knowledge is gathered from inside and outside the organization and synthesized into a concept that is vague and unfixed, but is enhanced in the flow of space and time until it is crystallized in a concrete product. This product, in turn, triggers the flow of knowledge sharing and knowledge creation among stakeholders in the business ecosystem. Ryohin Keikaku's understanding of this process is the underlying strength of the Muji brand.

What the designer Kenya Hara describes as the "emptiness of Muji" is not meant to suggest that there is nothing there, but that the brand is open to the customer's reflection and image of what each product should be. Through co-creation, sophistication of the product and customer response evolves in tandem and Muji is no longer just a product for consumption but

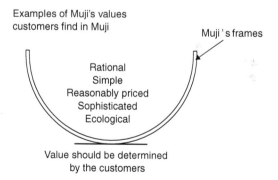

Figure 6.4 The view of Muji as an empty container
Source: Based on Akamine (2007).

an interactive experience of production with the customer. In that sense, Muji products themselves act as a *ba* with customers, encouraging them to feel the meaning of the product in empathy with the brand in an act of co-creation that reflects the "here-now" relationship of Muji with its customers globally (see Figure 6.4).

In summary, the two firms succeeded because of their flexibility and mobility to keep meeting to the changing needs of the customers. Both SEJ and Muji manage flow by interacting with their customers directly at the storefront and on the Internet to feel the changing trends, while working directly with their manufacturers to ensure they can respond to those trends in a timely and appropriate manner.

Notes

1. "Store-staff" is a SEJ term which means clerks in franchise stores, who are not direct employees of SEJ.
2. Ryohin Keikaku is no longer a division of Seiyu, which has sold all of its stock.
3. Interview with Tadamitsu Matsui, President and Representative Director, February 14, 2006.
4. Licensed stores are managed by Seiyu stores.
5. "Dokuji shiyou no jyutaku mo hanbai: Ryohinkeikaku net hanbai kogaisha" ["Ryohinkeikaku Muji.net store sells original houses"]. Nikkei Shinbun, June 29, 2000, p.11.
6. "Ryohin Keikaku oshu no 4 tenpo heisa" ["Ryohin Keikaku closing down 4 shops in Europe"]. Nikkei Ryutsu Shimbun, December 25, 2001.
7. Comments of Masanobu Furuta, Managing Director, in "Oroshiuri business wo jyushi" ["More attention to wholesale business"]. Nikkei Ryutsu Shinbun, February 7, 2002.
8. Based on internal material of Ryohin Keikaku.
9. http://ryohin-keikaku.jp/csr/060701.html
10. "Seika*tsu kuukan jindori gassen*" ["Fighting for life space"]. *Nikkei Ryutsu Shinbun*, October 28, 2003, p. 3.
11. MBWA management by wandering around.
12. Matsui was promoted to Chairman and Representative Director on January 8, 2008.
13. World Muji website: http://store.Muji.net/.
14. World Muji website: http://store.Muji.net/.
15. "Design award *ni katsu: Kaigai 3 sho wo jyusho suru Toshiba, Mujirushi ha iF sho*" ["Winning the design awards: Toshiba won three prizes, Muji won the iF design award"]. *Nikkei Design*, January, 2006, pp. 60–3.
16. Interview with president Matsui, February 14, 2006.
17. Ibid.
18. Ibid.
19. Ibid.
20. Based on the Mujirushi Ryohin booklet, *The Future of Muji*.
21. Ibid.
22. From a lecture at the Japan Productivity Center for Socio-Economic Development.

23. *"Mujirushi Ryohin no design ha naze hogo sarenakattaka"* ["Why Muji Design was not protected?"]. *Nikkei Design*, 2005.
24. A vision of Muji expressed by Ryohin Keikaku in 1996.

References

Akamine, T. (2007). *"Kankyouhairyo ha mujirushi ryouhin no kachi no ichiyouso"* ["Attention to ecology is only one part of Muji's value"]. *Business Research*, December, 55–63.
Iwanaga, Y. (2002). *Subete ha naming* [Naming is Everything]. Tokyo: Kobunsha.
Katsumi, A. (2002). *Suzuki Toshifumi no tokei shinrigaku*. [Toshifumi Suzuki's statistical psychology]. Tokyo: President Sha.
Senoo, D., Akutsu, S., and Nonaka, I. (2001). *Chishiki keiei jissennron*. [On Practice: Knowledge Creation and Utilization]. Tokyo: Hakuto Shobo.
Suzuki, T. (2003). *Shoubai no genten* [The Origin of Merchandizing]. Tokyo: Kodansha.
Suzuki, T. (2006). *Naze urenai noka, naze ureru noka* [Why Things Don't Sell, why Things Sell?]. Tokyo: Kodan Sha.
Suzuki, T. (2008). *Chourei bokai no hassou shigoto no kabe wo toppa suru 35 no jikigen* [Adaptable Conceptions]. Tokyo: Shinchousha.
Watanabe, Y. (2006). *Mujirushi Ryohin no kaikaku*. (Innovations of Mujirushi Ryohin). Tokyo: Shogyokai.
Yoshioka, H. (2007). *Seven Eleven oden bukai* [Seven Eleven oden Team]. Tokyo: Asahi Shinho.

7
Dynamic Knowledge Assets in Process

A person's cumulative experiences form an archive of personal knowledge. To share and effectively utilize this personal knowledge in an organization, the fluctuating relationships in the organization have to be managed and given direction. Moreover, this shared knowledge becomes an asset inherited by successive generations in the firm.

In this chapter, we shall focus on two companies. The first is the YKK Corporation, which effectively used its knowledge assets to reconceptualize the role of the simple garment fastener and achieve a global market share. The second is the JFE Steel Corporation, which succeeded in drastically turning around its business with a corporate merger that effectively integrated the experiential knowledge of two different corporate cultures.

7.1 YKK Corporation

7.1.1 Company overview

YKK Corporation is the world's leading fastener company, with 118 subsidiaries in 70 countries and a global market share of more than 45 percent as of December 2007. The strength of YKK resides in the exquisite balance it achieves between philosophy and practice in knowledge creation to respond to changes in the business environment. Founded in 1934 by Tadao Yoshida, YKK's unique management philosophy established a firm foundation for the business in just one generation, securing both domestic business growth and global expansion. Tadahiro Yoshida, Tadao's son, has combined his father's management philosophy with a more contemporary business approach. In this section, we examine the YKK management philosophy and practice, known for its emphasis on the social contribution of the firm.

The YKK Group encompasses three areas of business: Fastening Products, Architectural Products, and Machinery and Engineering. YKK Corporation is the headquarters for all three businesses and runs Fastening Products and Machinery and Engineering, which is responsible for research and development and management of YKK's so-called "total engineering solution." YKK

AP Inc. is the Architectural Products arm of the group and produces house interior and exterior products such as aluminum sash used in building construction. As of the fiscal year ending 2007, total sales revenues for the YKK Group were 658.2 billion yen or 5.48 billion US dollars. Of this total, fastening products represented 258.6 billion yen or 2.15 billion US dollars, and architectural products 391.1 billion yen or 3.26 billion US dollars, with 8.5 billion yen or 0.07 billion US dollars in revenues from other businesses. The profit margin for the group is 6 percent, although the fastening products business alone generates a profit margin of 14 percent, which is high for a mature industry.

YKK's global market share of the fastening products business is about 45 percent, making it a giant in the industry relative to competitors. The second largest company in the industry is Opti, with annual sales of about 10 billion yen or about 96.39 million US dollars. Close to 100,000 companies are YKK clients, with 53 "global accounts" that include the top brands Louis Vuitton, Ferragamo, Adidas, Nike, and Levi Strauss. These companies rely on YKK for timely delivery of high quality fasteners at competitive prices. YKK also provides products that are exclusive to individual clients, allowing them to enhance the value of their brand to the customer, like the gilded fastener created for Louis Vuitton. This practice has made YKK a brand in itself, prompting some apparel manufacturers to advertise their use of YKK fasteners as a mark of quality.

YKK's management philosophy – the "Cycle of Goodness" – is central to its business practice and is based on the thinking of its founder, Tadao Yoshida. The Cycle of Goodness assumes that "no one prospers unless they render benefit to others," and this is the basis of decision-making in all areas.[1] The philosophy is applied to enhance the quality of business operations in seven key categories: society, customers, products, technology, employees, management, and fairness, as illustrated in Figure 7.1.

This philosophy views the firm as a member of society, first and foremost, so the firm's *raison d'être* is to contribute to that society with "inventions and innovative ideas for continuous creation of value."[1] The value that is created brings profit to YKK in the process of benefiting customers, trading partners, and society. Tadao Yoshida felt strongly that the fruits of innovation should be widely distributed in society, rather than monopolized by the companies or the individuals. Since the value that YKK creates is for its customers and society first, employees are required to think from the customers' viewpoint, always. As a result, operations have developed in a way that enables the company to offer the best product and price, and in a time frame that suits the customer best. This way of thinking has been a key factor in the expansion of YKK's business and market share.

To sustain competitive advantage the company emphasizes in-house development and innovation in products and production technologies to build on its knowledge assets. YKK's products are innovative and of high

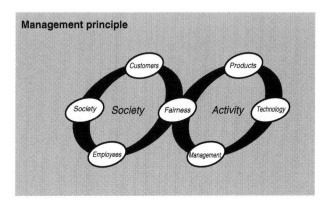

Figure 7.1 YKK management principles
Source: YKK Corporation

quality because of its unique production technologies. The company's insistence on developing a "total engineering solution" has enabled it to continuously accumulate technical know-how at every step in the manufacturing process. Today, no one can match YKK's level of accumulated knowledge in production, and these valuable knowledge assets are created and held by employees, so the people at YKK are considered the most important factor in value creation. The seventh key category of "fairness" was added to the list of quality objectives as the company aggressively expanded globally. YKK moves into overseas markets with the aim of becoming a part of the local social fabric. Rather than "breaking" into a local market, it aims to "build" a local company that contributes to the local economy and society.

While all of these characteristics are not, in themselves, unique to YKK, what is unique is the way in which they are interlinked and relentlessly pursued within the company, such that profitability becomes the by-product rather than the ultimate goal.

7.1.2 The founder's philosophy and business practice

YKK's founder, Tadao Yoshida, learned the international trading business at a chinaware company where he started working at the age of 20. When the company went bankrupt, he acquired its inventory, including that of a small subsidiary that produced fasteners. In 1934, at the age of 25, he established his own company producing and marketing fasteners. He learned from this experience that reliability is important to success and that this means putting the customer first and managing relationships among stakeholders. The experience of running his own business also opened his eyes to the global market, and by 1994 his company had grown to become YKK Corporation, short for Yoshida Kougyou Kabushiki Kaisha, translated as Yoshida Industries Incorporated.

Cycle of Goodness

Tadao Yoshida's management philosophy, shaped by his experiences in building the company, has had a lasting effect on YKK management style and corporate culture. His phrase, "Cycle of Goodness," is a quote from the biography of US steel magnate and philanthropist Andrew Carnegie, who strongly influenced his thinking (Yoshida, 1987). Tadao had grasped the essential meaning of business, not as a series of one-time deals, but as a flow of continuously expanding relationships in a "cycle." This required that the firm operate on the basis of a long-term perspective for the benefit of stakeholders and for society as a whole. From his early days at the chinaware company to the founding of YKK, the idea that he should "render benefit to others" was his basic rule in business, and it seemed like common sense at a time when reliability and credibility were considered the most important factors in business. He took the phrase "Cycle of Goodness" as the company motto when YKK started to expand overseas. It remains to this day, setting out the vision and principles of YKK's future expansion in ever-changing business environments, ensuring that employees understand that their long-term prosperity depends on the consideration that they give to benefiting others.

The Cycle of Goodness is realized as "the distribution of results among three," the "three" being the major stakeholders: YKK customers, business partners, and employees. The results are higher value products for the customer, prosperity for suppliers and distributors or vendors, and good salaries and bonuses for employees. It was Yoshida's belief that profits should be returned to the people who had made the effort to earn them. Profit was not only the product of capital investment but of the people who had worked to create the value that produced that profit. For this reason, YKK is not a public company even today, and their stock is held by employees and customers who earn dividends. Though it might be less costly to raise capital on the public exchange, Yoshida did not want management to be subject to the influence of investors who had no relation to the company. He thought the true owners of the company should be the people who work for it, and he viewed management less as a contractual arrangement and more as the sharing of feelings in human relationships among employees. He said, "a shareholder is someone who collaborates with the company; a supporter who shares our delight and struggles" (Kawashima, 2003: 122). Shareholders are expected to feel a unity with the company, and the holding of stock enhances their sense of participation in management. So only those people related to, and concerned about, the future of YKK are invited to become shareholders and share in the dividends when the company makes a profit. Based on the philosophy of the Cycle of Goodness, employees were encouraged to invest part of their salary and bonuses in the purchase of company stock. That investment was used to create further profitability that was then returned to employees in the form of interest dividends, establishing a virtuous circle in the flow of cash between the company and its employees. This flow becomes part of a larger flow in a chain reaction of activity designed to create value for the broader society. With investment from employees and customers, YKK is able to produce better quality products at lower cost, adding value to its clients' products and boosting demand and profitability all round, facilitating greater corporate tax contributions in support of services for the community. The flow of prosperity circles back to YKK with increased sales revenue and profit to the benefit of its stockholders, who are its customers and employees. This flow remains one of the main pillars of management strategy today.

Importance of autonomy

Tadao Yoshida sought to empower employees to make decisions at the frontlines of business, in keeping with his view of the individual as an autonomous human being in equal partnership with management. The only condition for autonomy was that they fully understand the philosophy and principles of the company, and he considered effective communication important to this understanding. When the company was still small, he made all employees attend management meetings so they would understand the management way of thinking and the process of decision-making. When he chose an employee to send overseas to develop new markets, language ability took second place to understanding of the company principles and eagerness to communicate them to co-workers in other countries. Yoshida would often send an enthusiastic young employee to start up a foreign-based venture, giving him or her his full trust and backing, and viewing the challenge as an investment in that person's future with the company.

Employee autonomy at YKK is supported by a culture that accepts and learns from failure in on-the-job training. Yoshida was known for saying to employees who were entrusted with big projects: "Even if you fail, I take final responsibility as president of the company...so do the job as you see fit" (Onishi and Shoji, 2007: 34). Yoshida believed that individuals learned best from their own failures and he encouraged them to analyze why they had failed. "If I know that an employee has done their best I do not criticize them for failure," he said. "Instead, I communicate the reasons for, and the meaning of the failure to other employees...so it will never happen again. Failure is our asset" (Yoshida, 1987: 360–1). In a culture that accepts failure, employees are empowered to make decisions at the frontline based on the particular situation that is "here-now." YKK encourages employees to accumulate experiences that will help them build high-quality tacit knowledge.

Staff and managers are trained to question the "why" and "what for" of every decision they make so they can act autonomously. Consciousness of the process of purposeful action is second nature at YKK. When faced with a difficult decision, the practice is to return to the basic concept of "render benefit to others." However, the emphasis on autonomous action does not mean that YKK has no management control. Business strategy and budget planning are considered very important to evaluate strictly and control the risk of failure. YKK has built a control system based on quantitative targets and an evaluation system based on achievement of those targets.

7.1.3 Key factors in YKK's development

One of the key factors for YKK's success in maintaining a high market share is its effective use of accumulated technologies, which have helped it to reconceptualize the "fastener," and ultimately redefine the company's *raison d'être* from the customer's point of view. The fastener was commonly viewed as a minor component of a garment in the apparel industry, but YKK reconceptualized it as something that could both "open and close." This triggered development of an expanded variety of functions for the product, such as waterproof and airtight fasteners. This would have been impossible while the fastener was viewed simply as a substitute for buttons. As *Forbes* magazine described it, YKK was about *"zipping up the world"* (Fulford, 2003). The static fastener became active "verb", which changes the relationship of space by opening and closing.

The effective permeation of YKK's management philosophy throughout the group is another key factor in its success, driving exhaustive development of superior technologies in manufacturing, from raw materials development to production process. YKK actualizes its philosophy in daily operations in the pursuit of technological excellence. Like the athlete of extreme sports, YKK pursues extreme technologies to redefine the limits of its product while producing higher quality at a competitive cost – and quickly, in response to any particular demand from its customers.

Technological development and added value

In the competitive world of business, a noble management philosophy alone does not deliver success. The value-added system that Yoshida put into place at YKK, characterized by the relentless pursuit of improvement in technology and product quality, has been a strong factor for sustainable growth.

From the beginning Yoshida emphasized the importance of building client and consumer confidence in YKK's products, and the need to develop technological capabilities in-house to do that. He said: "If we are to provide the best product with confidence, we can't leave any part of the process up to any other company. We should try to do it all by ourselves" (YKK, 1995: 74). YKK's "Total Engineering Solution", from raw materials to the finished product, is supported by in-house development of precision machinery for quality production and timely delivery. This comprehensive capability is its core strength and the key to its overwhelming global market share. For example, in 1978 YKK developed a machine that automated the process of sewing fasteners on jeans. At the time, jeans manufacturers, such as Levi Strauss, were buying fasteners in rolls and had to cut them to the necessary lengths to sew them on. YKK's machine, designed exclusively for its own fasteners, not only offered higher value to the jeans manufacturers who bought it, by automating their entire process, but secured a position for YKK as the client's sole supplier of fasteners. YKK is not just a *maker* of fasteners. They have accumulated and systemized both tacit and explicit knowledge from daily business operations and practices throughout the value chain.

Cumulative technologies

A fastener consists of three parts: the interlocking teeth called the element; the slider that zips the element together; and the tape on which everything is affixed. It seems like a simple product but the underlying technologies that support its production today are far from simple. They are the accumulation of many years of experience in choosing appropriate raw materials and modifying machinery and techniques to ensure stable, high-quality production at a competitive cost.

YKK's technological capabilities reside mainly in its Machinery and Engineering Group, which produces the machines and parts for all YKK factories around the world. Through in-house production and supply of machinery, YKK says it ensures that its products are of the same quality everywhere in the world. Its machinery is strictly guarded as proprietary technology. When a machine is scrapped, the dismantling is so complete as to ensure that the know-how embedded in the machine does not get into the hands of a competitor. YKK understands that quality control through superior technology is the source of its sustainable competitive advantage.

The activities of the Machinery and Engineering Group are an important knowledge-creation process of continuous externalization and accumulation of tacit knowledge among experienced engineers. Accumulated engineering knowledge is explicitly articulated, shared, and combined and then imbedded in precision automation machines whose quality determines the quality of the goods produced. YKK's Total Engineering Solution is the result of a knowledge-creation process developed in part by the repeated resolution of bottlenecks arising from continuous improvements in production processes that are unique to YKK. But in-house engineering of machinery was not always the case historically. In the beginning, YKK had relied on an outside vendor for machine parts, but in 1947 Tadao Yoshida realized that he would have to completely revamp production methods in order to match the quality of overseas producers. He had contacted a buyer in the hopes of exporting YKK products to the US, but when the buyer showed him a sample of the US-made product, he was astonished by the better quality and level of technology in production relative to his own. He then moved to total, in-house production so the company could exercise complete control over the quality of its products.

YKK launched the first step in the development of its Total Engineering Solution in 1949, with the construction of a copper pressing plant to produce fastener elements and sliders, and a textile looming plant to produce tape. It then replaced its manual production system with the introduction of four, chain-stitch machines imported from the US, and began full-scale automated production. Once fastener production was automated, an imbalance with other stages of production became apparent. While the demand for elements on the production line increased due to improved productivity, the use of "flat wire" metals[2] to make the elements resulted in unstable quality and much waste. Engineers switched to "profile wire" metals,[3] which enabled faster, more precise production. However, the use of profile wire shortened the life of the molds used to make the elements. YKK then decided to make the molds out of a new superalloy, and it automated new mold production by developing a precision grinding machine. Once this issue was resolved, another imbalance emerged, this time in slider production. There were 13 steps in the existing pressing machine in a production process that lagged far behind the speed of the new, chain-stitch machines, so a new slider production machine had to be developed in-house. In this way, previously outsourced production machinery was gradually replaced with technology developed and built completely in-house by the Machinery and Engineering Group. The company eventually built a spinning factory and an aluminum factory based on the same logic of quality control and utilizing the cumulative knowledge assets that had become exclusive to YKK.

The human resources of the Machinery and Engineering Group

YKK's continuous improvement in machinery and process relies on superior human resources. Close to 90 percent of YKK employees in the Machinery and Engineering Group working on the production line hold public certification of their technical expertise. The engineers will say that there is always something that can be improved, even though there are only three parts to the fastener. "I wish I could say that we are the most superior, but as long as we have competitors, there is always something we must do to remain competitive," said one engineer.[4] All employees in the Machinery and Engineering Group think in terms of business growth and work tenaciously to make improvements daily so they can always be half a step ahead. As the group closest to the production line, they are at the center of technical development at YKK. An engineer becomes known as "Mr Metal" when he has achieved a high level of experience and technological know-how in metal works, which he shares in on-the-job training. An engineer with this level of expertise can usually sense precision to the level of 10 microns, simply by touching.

Engineers can easily collaborate to produce better materials and product design and better production-line technologies to make a better product, integrating the various knowledge specialties with knowledge accumulated at the frontline of production. Every employee understands that the production line is the *ba* where explicit knowledge, based on logic, and tacit knowledge, based on intuition, are blended in technology and product development; and that this *ba* is the source of future improvements.

The practice of listening to the customer

YKK's success is also based on its thorough pursuit of the philosophy of "customer first," such that no benefit can be derived unless there is a benefit to the customer first. The priority is to respond quickly to customer needs and maintain a long-term relationship. Even if a total engineering solution allows the company to create a unique product, if that product is not accepted by the customer, it has no meaning. YKK recognizes that it must change and evolve continuously to meet changing customer needs. Its emphasis on thinking continuously about how to increase value to the customer may seem simple enough, but, approached honestly, it is hard work trying to fulfill every client's wants and needs.

The majority of YKK customers are leading apparel manufacturers, but getting their trust was long and difficult work. YKK has developed a particular way of constructing a long-term relationship with the customer. Employees will call on potential customers every day even if they don't get an order. The aim is to develop and maintain a daily communication that will give them a clue to what the customer needs and how to satisfy it. Former president of YKK Europe, Masaharu Ando, said that when he was sent to Europe 30 years earlier the elder Yoshida had told him: "You must visit the customer every day until they place an order." He did just that, and after showing up on the premises every day, communication would start to develop.[5] The customer might have a complaint about a product they were using, or might place a small order as a gesture. Ando said every visit was an opportunity to see things from the customer's point of view and show how YKK might have an answer to a problem. Eventually, the company's credibility grew along with their ability to target customer needs with a high quality product. By responding to the customer's every demand, the size of the order continued to grow until YKK became the client's sole supplier.

YKK's attention to technology and new product development is driven by its relentless adherence to the policy of "customer first." The ability to "indwell" with the customer has driven continuous innovation in both product and process to satisfy demands in quality, variety, cost, and delivery, quickly and precisely. As of 2007, YKK produced about 200,000 types of fastener in 5,000 colors (Onishi and Shoji, 2007). Customer preferences change quickly as fashion trends are short lived and product life-cycle in the apparel industry becomes shorter and shorter. At one time, a product was sold over two seasons so lead-time to production was one or two months. Now, it is an average of five days. Short lead-time is an important factor for inventory control. A client may want to wait until the very last moment to determine which design will be popular in a particular season. For example, the Spanish apparel maker Zara keeps an inventory for only 15 days, with just 45 days from design to finished product. YKK's in-house technological development has enabled it to create a new product mold quickly, sometimes in just two days, and start production immediately to keep to a delivery date. No other manufacturer can match this because they do not have this system and process and the accumulated technical know-how that supports it. YKK also sustains competitive advantage with its ability to supply products with stable quality to customers who are expanding their business worldwide. For example, when Adidas asked YKK to supply identical zippers for its markets in the more than 40 countries where it operates, YKK met the request by modernizing all of its 88 factories overseas and some factories in Japan (Fulford, 2003). This was possible because of its Total Engineering Solution approach.

7.1.4 Succession and renewal of management philosophy

Every company founded by a charismatic leader faces the dilemma of who will succeed that leader. While conforming to changes in the times, companies often lose track of their original *raison d'être* and become confused about what they need to do to sustain themselves. At YKK, the direction was to maintain the founding philosophy but change the organizational structure of the business, which did not match up the changing business environments. They undertook drastic reform based on their vision of an ideal future while avoiding overreliance on past experiences and successes.

Management succession

Tadao Yoshida's son, Tadahiro, assumed the presidency of the company in 1993, after serving as a vice president for seven years. At the press conference announcing his succession, he said he would continue to follow the company philosophy of the Cycle of Goodness. In 1994, he changed the company name from Yoshida Kogyo to YKK to demonstrate that the company was not just a patrimonial possession of the founding family but belonged to the larger family of YKK employees. Since then, Tadahiro has pursued a variety of reforms.

"Tadao Yoshida was a charismatic leader," said Tadahiro (Yoshida, 2003: 48). "His words were shared among employees like dogma. This helped form an organization where ordinary people could work at their maximum potential." But Tadahiro also believed that such strong leadership at the top overshadowed the strengths of other individuals at the company and he thought he would have to do something about this to ensure YKK could continue to survive after his father's departure. As a vice president, Tadahiro had already launched major reform at YKK, seeking to make it a more holistic organization, as it operated in so many countries with different customs and social norms. He understood that partial optimization would not get to the root of any problem. His primary goal was to put value creation into practice across the company.

Reaffirming philosophy

First, he put a fresh face on YKK's management philosophy, calling it the "Tadao Yoshida Spirit," and added new objectives that could drive the company in the new era. He summarized these objectives in the phrase: "YKK seeks corporate value of higher significance." The message was that the days of the sole charismatic leader were over and every employee should take on the responsibility of leading growth and adding value to the company. He summarized his father's management principles into six key words – customers, society, employees, management, technology, and products – and targeted each for improvement. He added a seventh keyword fairness (see Figure 7.1). Fairness meant respect for others and assumed that no issue could be resolved if one party was putting pressure on the other. He viewed fairness as an essential condition for pursuing business globally.

Organizational reform

Tadahiro also reformed the organizational structure to support global expansion. Since its founding, YKK had been operating on the basis that every employee was an equal part of management and that their proficiency was based on individual experience. However, as the variety of work increased and the balance shifted in labor supply and demand, that approach was no longer efficient or effective. Employees working autonomously in production and sales in various parts of the world became inefficient as a group. In 1985, then Vice President Tadahiro thoroughly restructured the former organizational model of distributed autonomy, combining production and sales into one unit and reforming the region-based organization into a divisional organization. In 1993, when he became president, the divisions were further strengthened along with the headquarters as the core of the group, so that strategic decisions concerning the entire group could be coordinated and integrated by the headquarters.

Tadahiro also strengthened the system of legal compliance. His father believed in the innate goodness of the human being in the Confucian sense. Tadahiro said: "If we all stand on the same basic idea of the innate goodness of the human being and then make our best efforts to pursue that goodness, then the organization will naturally become most effective. This is the ultimate organizational theory...Unless we truly share that spirit, we will never be a good company regardless of what we do or how we are as an organization" (Yoshida, 2003: 137–49). But he has also recognized the need to change with the times and expected that as the company grew larger, it would be prone to more mistakes and wrongful behavior. He also understood that human nature was both good and bad, and that an individual's behavior depended on their value system. If all employees shared the same values then a simple code of conduct would be enough, but as a global company they had to incorporate a variety of cultures and value systems while passing the global test of social reliability. To prevent any contravention of law, he strengthened the system for checking daily routines by establishing the Management Audit and Inspection Division.

Overall, Tadahiro's reforms have decentralized the businesses while streamlining the headquarters by focusing on group management. Indirect management functions such as accounting, human resources, and administration were transferred to a new, specialized subsidiary in 2003. Following global trends, YKK's principle of manufacturing in the consuming country no longer applies, and the new principle is to manufacture and procure wherever it is the most efficient to do so. This change reflects a larger principle of flexibility in management to centralize and decentralize according to the changing circumstances.

The relationship with overseas subsidiaries is also based on the philosophy of the Cycle of Goodness. Tadahiro Yoshida describes the relationship as follows: "We never siphon profits from subsidiaries to headquarters. We return [locally generated] profits to benefit the local economy. This is our principle and our discipline." Local benefits to employees, suppliers, and customers accrue as the local company prospers. "In other words, the local YKK firm does every aspect of its business within that society and this way the company provides a benefit to the society and becomes a part of that society," he said (Yoshida, 2003: 62). This builds local confidence in the company through community. A manager dispatched from headquarters has always been expected to "become a local" by taking up semi-permanent residency to ensure localization of the business while maintaining communication with headquarters. Many of those posted overseas have stayed 15 years or more and some for over 30 years.

7.2 JFE Steel Corporation

7.2.1 Company overview

As economies globalize and competition becomes more fierce, reform and restructuring of organizations and industries through mergers and acquisitions (M&A) have become more common. However, M&As are not always effective. This is especially true for large firms with long traditions, where a merger can lead to conflict between corporate cultures. The firms may have merged externally, but internally they remain apart, even though they are in the same industry.

The steel industry is currently undergoing major transformation worldwide, and the merger that has formed JFE Steel Corporation is a rare case of the successful joining of two highly competitive and distinct corporate cultures. That merger, between NKK Corporation and Kawasaki Steel Corporation to create JFE Holdings, Inc, has resulted in a remarkable business recovery for the group in addition to the more difficult integration of the two cultures.

Steel production has high barriers to entry and exit due to the vast amounts of investment required over a long period of time right from the start. It can take up to five years and several million dollars to get a new factory up and running in all processes of production, from making pig iron to rolling and surface processing of steel. It also takes a long time to implement reform, let alone integrate the operations of large facilities, so the benefits of doing so are not apparent in the short term. The merger that created JFE was able to scale these obstacles through continuous and open dialogue between the companies and the exchange of key personnel that facilitated an emergence of the knowledge and understanding needed to make the integration a reality.

The steel industry in Japan

In Japan, steel manufacturers both compete and collaborate, sharing technology to the extent that they are all functioning at a similar level of technological capability. This does not make it easier to integrate them, however, because their processes of manufacturing can differ widely, especially at the level of know-how in the factory. This know-how is a tacit, embodied knowledge that is not easily shared or transferred because the context for manufacturing differs from company to company, in operational methods and the organization of facilities. Computer control systems also vary and integrating this aspect is a huge commitment of time and effort. The industry has made continuous improvements in production processes, in building a skilled workforce, and accumulating know-how, all of which have improved productivity. But despite the computerized steel making process common to all firms today, it is improvements on the production line unique to each firm and the accumulated know-how of their workers that have had a more significant effect on productivity. Accumulated, experiential knowledge in a company is both visible and invisible. Workers on the production line are often organized into specialized teams, such as pig iron production, steel making, or rolling, and they tend to become attached to the division where they work and to the steelworks itself. Production operates on the basis of teams that integrate their variety of know-how with the production facility into a system. This is how unique culture and methods develop and are institutionalized in each firm, and these differences can be a major barrier to successful integration in the event of a merger.

NKK and Kawasaki Steel had these differences, but they found a way to integrate smoothly and with little conflict afterwards, paving the way for good business results in their new incarnation as JFE. This was partially attributable to the rise in global demand precipitated by rapid growth in China, but it does not explain why JFE has been able to improve profitability drastically more than other companies in the same business environment. At JFE, a synergy was achieved in the integration of knowledge from each firm, thanks to the sense of crisis felt about the changing environment and the ability of managers to engage in sincere dialogue about goals and objectives for the whole group.

JFE Group and the background to integration

JFE is a group of companies under the umbrella of JFE Holdings, Inc., established by the merger of NKK and Kawasaki Steel in September, 2002. There are five companies in the group, including JFE Steel and JFE Engineering (See *Figure 7.2*). Each company was established in April 2003. Consolidated net sales for the group reached 3,540 billion yen or about 33.7 billion US dollars in the fiscal year ending March 2008. The largest company, JFE Steel, had consolidated net sales of 3,203 billion yen or about 30.5 billion US dollars during the same period and is the fourth largest manufacture of steel worldwide.[6]

The backdrop to the establishment of the JFE group was a long recession in the steel industry which had worsened profitability at the original companies. By the end of the 1990s, employees at Kawasaki Steel shared a sense of crisis that the company could not continue as it was. The company was

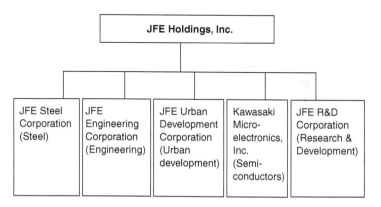

Figure 7.2 Overview of the JFE group
Source: JFE Holdings, Inc., Company Profile.

known in the industry for its severe cost controls, but even they knew they were reaching the limits of cost-cutting as a response to falling prices. NKK was also facing serious difficulties. While it had higher net sales than Kawasaki Steel, it had lower profitability and was lagging in other indices. Its stock price reflected this trend, and shares in Kawasaki Steel were higher than NKK for a period of time. NKK employees had been putting up with never ending wage cuts due to the slump in business. Eventually, their wages fell below those at Kawasaki Steel and both companies knew they needed to take drastic action.

In October, 1999, the Japanese automaker Nissan started to pare down the number of companies they purchased materials from. This was the final trigger for the merger of Kawasaki Steel and NKK. Nissan was restricting buying to those steel producers who would accept lower prices. The move became known in the industry as the Ghosn Shock, named for its new chief operating officer Carlos Ghosn. Prices in the steel industry collapsed and all the manufacturers suffered. In the fiscal year ending March, 2000, Kawasaki had a consolidated net profit of 12.4 billion yen or about 103 million US dollars, but NKK recorded a net loss of 45.9 billion yen or about 382.5 million US dollars. NKK shares hit their lowest ever, falling to 65 yen or about 50 cents per share on September 26, 2001. Both companies began to see that a merger was the only solution, but they were not in any hurry to do so.

Discussions between top management at the companies started with the idea of forming an alliance in areas where there was less likely to be conflict. After a long period of preparation, the holding company was established and eventually a full merger took place.

7.2.2 The process of the merger

In the beginning, Yoichi Shimogaichi, then president of NKK, and Kanji Emoto, then president of Kawasaki Steel, held a series of meetings and started organizing a flexible alliance. In April, 2000, both companies announced they would start looking at ways to increase efficiency in purchasing, maintenance, and logistics in their ironworks, and they began to collaborate. They started with streamlining logistics and inventory control through cooperation between neighboring factories: Kawasaki Steel's Chiba and Mizushima ironworks, and NKK's Keihin and Fukuyama factories, respectively. This eventually paved the way for a complete merger. By September, 2000, they had agreed on ten themes for an alliance in the three areas of management. At the time neither company spoke about a merger but internally both were preparing for that eventuality.

In April, 2001 they announced the merger, describing it as a two-step process. A holding company would be established by the transfer of shares in October, 2002. Both companies would come under the control of the holding company and would restructure and merge as equal partners by

April, 2003. An announcement dated December 21, 2001, stated the mission as follows:

> JFE Group is determined to become a world-class competitor with its strong customer base, advanced technology, high efficiency steel works and manufacturing plants, and will create an innovative corporate culture with a spirit for challenge. In doing so, JFE Group will pursue the following aims:
> (1) To strengthen its capability to fulfill customer needs on a global basis
> (2) To enhance credibility with shareholders and global capital markets
> (3) To provide more challenging opportunities for employees
> (4) To contribute to local communities and global environmental conservation.[7]

Production capacities at the time were 20 million metric tonnes at NKK and 13 million tonnes at Kawasaki Steel. Combined, they exceeded Nippon Steel's 29 million tonnes. The merger would make JFE the world's second largest steel manufacturer at that time. The group aimed to strengthen competitiveness by increasing its market share, eliminating indirect costs, and maximizing efficiency of investment in R&D and equipment. Total steel production in the Japanese market in 2001 was 126 million tonnes, 4.5 percent lower than the previous year. Nippon Steel held the top 25.6 percent of market share, compared with NKK at 12.6 percent, and Kawasaki Steel at 12.0 percent.[8] With a combined market share of 24.6 percent, the merger put JFE Group at a close second to Nippon Steel.

JFE Holdings Inc. was launched in September, 2002. The share allocation was even at first, but had to be revalued in-line with stock prices at the time: to one Kawasaki share equal to NKK 0.75. In April, 2003, the various divisions of each company were restructured into five business units, all with clear domains and focus (see Figure 7.2). A shipbuilding division was spun off from the JFE Group and merged with part of Hitachi Zosen Corporation to become the Universal Shipbuilding Corporation. This allowed each of the companies to concentrate on their own unique, core business domains, while the group focused solely on steel making.

7.2.3 Conflicting methods and cultures

Despite being in the same industry, NKK and Kawasaki Steel had vastly different management systems and corporate cultures. Their biggest concern from the start was whether or not they could get along. Differences in systems and culture could hinder integration of organizations and technologies. For example, the two companies were using different technical terms to express the same functions on the production line, so the first thing they had to do was create a common language to communicate in. There were more fundamental differences. NKK's production volume was higher than that at Kawasaki Steel, and NKK had been investing aggressively in facilities, equipment, and R&D, and had a high level of technological capability. However, its investments didn't always pay off and NKK management was not as efficient as that of Kawasaki Steel.

Before the merger, NKK group operated in the three main areas of steel, shipbuilding, and engineering. All three businesses were autonomous in terms of management and did not seek synergies within the group. NKK was also in other types of business, such as urban development and semiconductor manufacturing, with methods of operating that were quite different from the steel industry. In short, NKK was aggressive in R&D and diversification of its business, but not good at making a profit, with a corporate culture more focused on technological development than profitability.

By comparison, Kawasaki Steel was perceived as a bold company. It had been spun off from Kawasaki Heavy Industry to become an independent steel manufacturer with its own management strategy. Former CEO Yataro Nishiyama had helped establish Kawasaki Steel and had a great influence on its culture. The company strictly centralized cost control, which worked better than NKK's approach during the steel recession. Investment decisions were based on strict cost–benefit analysis: investments were not made unless profitability could be proved.

To achieve profit targets, the sales division communicated with production so both divisions took responsibility for planning to reach the goal. Sales staff participated in production planning and pursued a unique strategy (Takase and Imamura, 1990). A close relationship was fostered between manufacturing and sales, and sales and end-users, tied to the overall market strategy. At Kawasaki Steel, the aim of profitability was always made clear in every product category and a final decision to produce was made only after a thorough exchange of information with the sales divisions. The two companies were also vastly different in the way they operated their production lines. NKK put priority on the needs of end users and produced a variety of products to meet various customer needs. Kawasaki Steel's priority was efficient use of a product line by maximizing production volume to increase profitability. Kawasaki Steel was a typical "top-down" hierarchy, while the management style at NKK was more cooperative on the production line, emphasizing "working together" regardless of position or authority. In summary, it could be said that NKK was stronger in technology and R&D while Kawasaki Steel was stronger in management systems and sales capability. A merger to combine these strengths would only be successful if they could overcome the obvious conflicts in corporate culture and management systems.

7.2.4 The role of dialogue in the merger

The successful integration of NKK and Kawasaki Steel created synergies that showed financial results in a short period of time. The key to integrating these very different organizational cultures lies in the quality of dialogue achieved between the top managers of both companies.

A dialogue of leadership

CEOs Shimogaichi (NKK) and Emoto (Kawasaki Steel) met frequently to discuss how best to integrate their companies. Their first contact was on December 6, 1999, when Emoto called Shimogaichi on the telephone. Shimogaichi was concerned about the poor performance at NKK and its falling stock price, and was considering a merger as one possible alternative at the time. Ten days after their telephone conversation, they met in person, and they continued to have one-on-one meetings until the announcement of a basic agreement in April, 2001 (Emoto and Shimogaichi, 2004). During that time, the two CEOs built a relationship of trust that was so strong that the decisions and policies they implemented together have remained firm. They began by declaring their Four Principles of Integration, which became a clear standard of conduct for the merger. The first and most important principle was stated as follows:

> Management and employees should transcend the interests of their former company; should concern themselves only with the interests and development of the new company; and should act rationally and fairly when making decisions and taking action.[9]

The aim of the principles was to end unnecessary attachment to the former companies. Tetsuo Miyazaki, then an executive of Kawasaki Steel, said the statement of principles demonstrated "that systems of management or treatment of personnel would not be biased in favor of either of the companies. It declared that everyone should throw away the pride and ego of attachment to the former companies. The statement of principles was the only standard for determining what was best for the new company JFE. We all followed it simply and honestly."[10] If there was a major problem, the two CEOs would meet immediately to resolve it and this prevented confusion and anxiety from arising among the employees. Their leadership was effective in sorting out conflicts quickly, without hesitation or loss of valuable time, and served as a solid foundation for the merger's success.

For example, the companies had to decide which blast furnaces to eliminate to increase operational efficiency. A blast furnace is the strongest symbol of a steel company, so it would have been easier to compromise and stop one blast furnace at each firm. Instead, they decided it was more cost effective to stop operating the two blast furnaces at Kawasaki Steel in Chiba and Kurashiki. Both were shut down in May, 2002. By not choosing the obvious compromise, management sent the signal that it was serious about integration and this had a strong impact on employees.

By making the policy clear from the outset and not deviating from it during the integration process, the leaders ensured a smooth integration, made possible by the trust between management teams engaged in open dialogue throughout. Emoto described his relationship with Shimogaichi this way: "I feel like I have finally met my best friend at this age." Shimogaichi replied, "I feel the same" (Emoto and Shimogaichi, 2004: 60).

Timing is the most important factor in carrying out decisions. Emoto had waited cautiously for the best time to broach the subject of a merger. Since Kawasaki Steel had some profit in the first half of the fiscal year 2000, he knew that parts of the sales division were not likely to favor a merger at that time. Later, when steel prices started to fall, the sales division began to feel the pinch and that's when Emoto made his recommendation. He did not impose the merger from on high, but suggested in a training session of general managers that they examine their respective areas of expertise and the effects of an integration scenario early in 2001. It was an opportunity for the managers to think seriously about how integration would affect them and their divisions and to grasp the idea experientially.

Meanwhile, at NKK, Shimogaichi was promoting internal communication. Once the two companies had agreed on a full merger, he created opportunities for dialogue between head office and the factories involving a variety of people, from senior and middle management on down to rank and file workers. This enabled management to spread its message, but it also instilled a feeling of participation among the employees that made it easier for them to buy into the process (Emoto and Shimogaichi, 2004).

Promoting dialogue through reform

Creating operational efficiency in the organization in the short term was the biggest barrier to integrating the diverse corporate cultures. Management at each company sought to reform production, human resource allocation, and organizational structures with the consent of their employees. The aim was not to find a balance between the two systems but to determine a course of action based on what was best for the new company internally and for the customer externally.

Preparations began at JFE Steel before human resources and technologies had been integrated. Communication between the steelworks was reinforced by site visits and cooperation in business. When the integration was announced, major personnel changes were also announced, with directors in core areas of responsibility exchanged between firms. This accelerated communication and the exchange of knowledge in key areas for the successful merging of technologies.

Unifying the ironworks

Unification of the ironworks started with changes in management. To eliminate sectionalism related to former affiliations, the various ironworks were grouped together in two regions, each under a single management. NKK's Keihin plant and Kawasaki Steel's Chiba plant were put under the management of East Japan Ironworks, and NKK's Fukuyama plant was grouped with Kawasaki Steel's plant at Mizushima under West Japan Ironworks. Each manager overcame barriers of distance and culture to unify operations, promoting agility in decision-making and the sharing and standardizing of business practices. This enabled smoother use of production capabilities and increased flexibility to handle problems and fluctuating demand. Furthermore, the operational ratios improved around 10 to 20 percent, as production of particular products was concentrated at specific ironworks.

Transferring knowledge through human communication

Unification of control systems is nothing new, but JFE took the unprecedented step of unifying the two organizations and their technologies in a way that defied common sense in the industry. To merge technological capabilities quickly they not only transferred and exchanged technological information but also the people who had tacit knowledge or experiential understanding of that information.

To start with, in April, 2003, numerous general managers in charge of technology and production were exchanged among the ironworks. In production alone, 17 general managers were exchanged between corresponding sections of Kawasaki Steel and NKK. All general managers apart from deputy general manager were allowed the accompaniment of two staff. The number was limited to two to discourage the creation of a manager's group in the new environment. JFE continued to expand personnel exchanges between the former NKK and Kawasaki Steel. By 2005, the exchange of 350 middle managers was planned in various production processes from blast furnace work to surface pressing. Exchanges were mainly between neighboring ironworks, such as Kurashiki and Fukuyama in West Japan, and Keihin and Chiba in the East Japan Ironworks (see Figure 7.3).

The main purpose of the exchanges was to eliminate sectionalism and attachments to the former company, and to merge know-how in technology, production, and general operations to improve competitiveness.

Information sharing

Other big changes initiated by JFE were in cost control and information systems. Before integration the two companies were run on the basis of differing ideas about how to operate. Kawasaki Steel functioned according to a "sector system," which controls production, sales, and R&D horizontally, product by product, overseen by both the sales and production divisions. Meanwhile, at NKK each division was autonomous. As a result, its production division had access to detailed information on the cost of materials, but no access to pricing to analyze profitability. After integration, JFE retained Kawasaki Steel's sector system and encouraged everyone to learn

194 *Managing Flow*

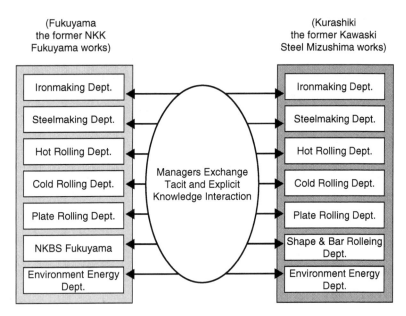

Figure 7.3   Exchanging personnel at the JFE West Japan Works
Source: JFE West Japan Works, April 2003.

it. For former NKK employees this shifted the focus to cost control in daily operations and helped them to understand the importance of managing expenses.

In information systems, JFE created a database that enabled employees to project profit margins by product and sales orders based on inputs from the technology, production, logistics, and sales divisions. The data could also be sorted by production site, providing feedback to improve production processes or technology. The database made it possible to track unprofitable products and identify the causes at each stage in the value chain. A list was created of the "Worst 30" products that needed improvement. The existence of a database eliminated guesswork and enabled managers and other employees to discuss production technology and processes based on real information with participation from the sales and R&D divisions. Finally, managers were able to take responsibility for implementing improvements according to plan.

The systematic sharing of information also supported cost cutting. The database was organized according to the accounting system at Kawasaki Steel, which was more superior in terms of cost management. But it also included some good aspects of the NKK system. By preserving the best parts of both companies in technologies and management systems, cost control and efficiency improved.[11]

Unifying sales divisions

Integrating the rival sales divisions of the respective companies was a delicate task. Sales know-how based on experience is a prized commodity and the level of know-how and management methods usually differ from one company to the next. This inherent rivalry can become a strong barrier to integration. A merger can also produce anxiety from the customer's perspective when changes in organization and operations are not made clear. How to deal with overlapping customers at NKK and Kawasaki Steel was an added complication. Customers were anxious about changes in logistics and payment methods due to the merger, and needed to be reassured. Only a quick unification process would erase these anxieties.

JFE considered all the issues and moved forward step-by-step in a way that clarified the principles behind each of its actions. The principles were to establish a system that was beneficial for the customer and proactive to improve profitability. No precedent was required for an action to be considered.

The head of the reformed sales division was chosen prior to integration, with deputies from both NKK and Kawasaki Steel. The aim of the new system was to promote information sharing within the division. A *ba* was established at the outset to build communicative relationships. Six months before integration, employees in charge of the respective sales divisions gathered to exchange information on logistics costs, pricing, payment methods, customers, and so on. This was followed by thorough discussions daily to finalize the details of the new system of operation. When there was a conflict about sales methods or systems of control that could not be resolved after thorough discussion, both options were tried and the results compared before a final choice was made.[12]

Most of the differences between NKK and Kawasaki Steel were identified and resolved prior to integration because of the *ba* established to cultivate open communication. It was also helpful that the sales divisions of the two original companies moved onto the same floor one month before integration.

JFE created a policy requiring sales staff to report every little detail of customer feedback. A database was installed to support this and facilitate sharing of all information within the sales division. The database recorded the details of every sales visit or customer-related activity and everyone had access to the information. By pursuing frank and open exchange in an environment of trust, JFE was able to encourage sales rivals to share their coveted expertise and disseminate this knowledge across the organization.

7.2.5 Synthesizing technologies through exchange of personnel

It had been characteristic of the steel industry that engineers operating the production line did not move from one plant to another, hence they had close-knit relationships. JFE intentionally broke with this practice in order to synthesize technologies and management.

The effect of exchanging personnel

The exchange of middle managers between the former companies had the great effect of promoting communication and integrating technical knowledge. The timing of this move was integral to its effectiveness. It was done immediately after integration when people were more willing to accept the changes that were occurring within JFE. Improved profitability in the business largely depended on improvements on the production line that would result from exchanging personnel. The exchanges broke down the organizational barriers of the former companies and combined their technologies to positive effect. The key to combining technologies was not simply the exchange of formal knowledge but the exchange of people who embodied that technological know-how and were willing to share their knowledge with former rivals. This achieved the more important objective of sharing tacit knowledge. What made this easier was the fact that the level of technological skill was much the same at Kawasaki Steel and NKK, as were the types of equipment and facilities in place. Many of the engineers at the formerly rival companies already knew each other from meetings of the technological society and industry associations. Some had even advised each other on technological issues they were facing. Engineers in the steel industry are not only attached to their company and their ironworks but also maintain relationships with other engineers in the industry who are working with the same type of technology. Due to the limited number of manufacturers making equipment and production lines for the steel industry, many of the companies were using the same equipment from the same manufacturer. Thus, they had all the basic technologies in common, making exchange of knowledge and technical know-how easier.

As with sales, the exchange of key personnel in the early stages of integration was an important factor in smoothing out communication. Another important factor was the sense of crisis in the industry felt by all employees. Everyone agreed that they needed to find a better way, and if this meant adopting the methods of a former rival because they worked better, so be it. While the basic sales approaches did not change much, the influence of the customer increased with the improved system of information gathering, storage, and dissemination. This resulted in an expanded product line-up leading to an increase in sales opportunities and market share.

Middle managers central to integration

Middle managers, ranging from manager to general manager, are the linchpins in organizations, because they are familiar with both the day-to-day details as well as the broader managerial picture. From the start of integration, it was the exchange of middle managers that brought new knowledge and viewpoints to the frontlines of production. Their pursuit of small, incremental change showed immediate results in reduced costs and enhanced efficiency, and was at least as effective in improving operations as the large scale technology exchanges, such as the super-OLAC[13] and the Large Block Ring Construction Method.[14] All of the middle managers we interviewed said they found that the production systems that were the core of each company were not so different. Neither were the people who operated them. But once the work of integration began, differences emerged. These issues were very specific to the worksite and could be examined there in concrete detail and resolved. Each issue was analyzed in terms of which company's method worked, and that was the method that was chosen. The continuous exchange of information and technological expertise in concrete problem solving eventually unified all processes. The cumulative effect of even marginal improvements in each division resulted in vast improvements overall in production. Here are some of the comments made by anonymous interviewees:[15]

> [NKK's] Fukuyama and [Kawasaki's] Kurashiki [plants] are similar, so they were competing with each other. But then they started coordinating operations in areas such as procurement, distribution, and facility maintenance. We didn't know what our competitor was doing until we actually saw in detail how their production line operated. We were stimulated to learn from them by exchanging technologies and methods.
>
> When we exchanged opinions about technological issues on the production floor, especially technical know-how, we could see if they were doing some things better than us, or if they were still doing things the old way and what they should change.
>
> I think exchanging general managers was a big thing. The general manager at Fukuyama came to Kurashiki and actually saw the differences between the two [companies]. Whenever we identified differences we did not accuse or blame each other. We just said, "this is how we do it, so let's try it and learn together." That is how we worked.

7.2.6 Profitable outcomes

The outcome of integration was improved profitability for the JFE group after the fiscal year 2003, helped by rising demand for steel products. That improvement was significant relative to the Japanese steel industry as a whole. In 2003, consolidated operating income at JFE was 250 billion yen or about 2.1 billion US dollars. That rose to more than 503 billion yen or about 4.8 billion US dollars in fiscal year ending March 2008, with debt falling substantially (see Table 7.1, Figure 7.4 and 7.5).

198 Managing Flow

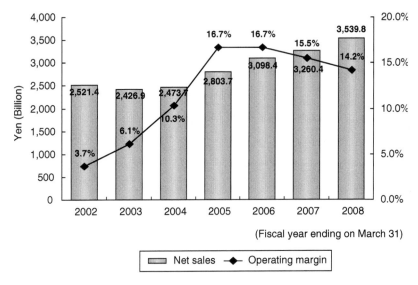

Figure 7.4 JFE holding's net sales and other operating revenue/operating margin
Source: http://www.jfe-holdings.co.jp/en/investor/zaimu/index.html

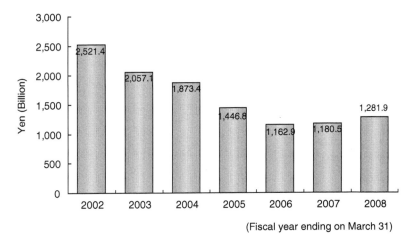

Figure 7.5 JFE holding's debt outstanding
Source: http://www.jfe-holdings.co.jp/en/investor/zaimu/index/html

Table 7.1 Comparison of operating profit over sales (%)

	2003	2004	2005
Steel Industry Average	5.3	10.1	11.6
JFE Group	8.8	16.4	16.7

Source: Web page of The Japan Iron and Steel Federation and JFE Holdings (consolidated).

Output increased along with profitability as the supply–demand balance improved and steel prices increased. These results were reflected in salary bonuses, boosting the motivation of employees and attracting media attention, which strengthened pride and unity in the company. In the end, every employee interviewed in every division said they felt strongly that the merger was a good thing.[16]

Moreover, JFE Steel's market share increased in Japan. Before the merger, Nippon Steel Corporation dominated, with other companies sharing what was left. After the merger, JFE became a major player alongside Nippon Steel. This also supported employee motivation at JFE. But profitability was not simply the result of JFE's expanded size resulting from the merger. The care shows that it was largely due to the change in the mindset of employees, who shared a sense of crisis about their future and were guided through integration in a process of intensive communication.

Exchanges of personnel between the two former companies, especially middle managers and engineers, not only eliminated old attachments, but resulted in improvements at the production site fed by new knowledge and new points of view. The role of middle managers was the key to realizing a smooth integration as they connected the broader management view to actual work processes. The exchange of middle managers created an environment for the transfer of tacit knowledge and the creation of new synergies.

Eisuke Yamanaka, General Superintendent at the West Japan Ironworks, described his experience this way: "When someone new came to take charge of the site, it was clear just by watching them how they would manage the situation. When you're evaluating staff, you have to set the hurdles high. If they're too low, anyone can pass."[17] Steel production had long been a major industry in Japan and had cultivated a highly skilled and capable work force. The architects of the JFE merger created an environment of knowledge sharing that brought out the hidden potential of many of these employees. They did not simply compare systems and choose the better of each. In an industry like steel that operates with huge machinery and equipment in a mosaic of interlocking processes, every improvement, no matter how minor, has to be integrated effectively into the whole. A bottleneck between the furnace and pressure and surface processing can throw off an entire production run and damage the product. This makes collaboration vital, on the production floor as well as between manufacturing and sales, and requires real and effective communication.

Fujimoto (2004) has observed that the strength of Japanese companies resides not in their use of the latest manufacturing technologies to mass produce goods, but in their manufacture of precision goods at a consistently high level of quality. If Japanese ironworks were simply making a product for mass consumption, then just using the latest machinery and equipment might be an advantage. Instead, they are manufacturing a high quality product for specialized use, such as the steel plate used in chassis production in the automobile industry. The quality of the Japanese product currently gives it a clear advantage over global competitors and the key is consistent quality control. The goal of the current JFE president Sumio Fudo has been to improve marketing and customer satisfaction by promoting information sharing and additional improvements in efficiency. This is in keeping with the JFE approach, which is not to choose the best of existing options but to identify best practices and combine them in new ways.

The JFE group was established not as a result of a hostile takeover bid, but through a partnership of rivals who were able to identify the shared values that would enable them to transcend differences in corporate culture and management to survive together. It is a common feature of M&As that the book value of the newly formed company is greater than the total value of the two original companies. Other advantages are in economies of scale, cost reductions through efficiency, increased bargaining power in the market, and synergy effects. According to Sato (1987), mergers and acquisitions in Japan tend to try to build complementary relationships, where the weaknesses of

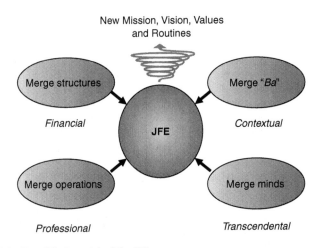

Figure 7.6 Simplified model of the JFE merger

one party are supplemented with the strengths of the other. At JFE, the original companies were able to locate these functional complements easier because they were in the same industry.

The new atmosphere created by their merger is different from that of the former companies that now make up the JFE group. You could call it a JFE culture. As M&A activity increases in Japan, the case of JFE provides insights into how to proceed with a merger in a way that effectively integrates the intangible knowledge assets of each firm (see Figure 7.6).

7.3 Implications

A person is always in the state of becoming, creating a new self at each moment of experience in daily life. Experiences differ by person, and these differences play an important role in knowledge creation. To create knowledge and utilize it as a management resource, personal archives of knowledge and experience have to be shared explicitly in human interaction. The knowledge arising from this process becomes internalized as organizational knowledge or wisdom. The prerequisites of the process are the creation and management of an environment or *ba*, where interaction at a deep, tacit level is possible, and the provision of an established principle or perspective for action that cultivates and maintains that environment.

The companies we have presented in this chapter are YKK, the world's top producer of fasteners, and the steel manufacturer JFE, whose successful merger of two different corporate cultures paved the way for a remarkable business recovery. Both casees illustrate how high-quality tacit knowledge is accumulated organizationally in a process of sharing personal knowledge and experience to create products and production technologies.

YKK was able to expand its business globally based on management principles derived from its founding philosophy, the Cycle of Goodness. Founder, Tadao Yoshida, believed in the innate goodness of people. He sought a virtuous circle in the human relationships that comprised his business and strictly maintained the principle of rendering benefit to all stakeholders, including the local community, as the guiding perspective in a dynamic business environment. Considering the range and complexity of the relationships between companies and their employees, suppliers, customers, and the larger society, he thought that the best way for a company to sustain itself and grow was to pursue its ideal self, and this would determine the company's value. He reasoned that if his company could satisfy its customers and other stakeholders, such efforts would naturally result in profits, a part of which should be invested in the future growth of the company with the rest returned to employees and society. YKK's continuing success is partially attributable to the effective transfer of this processual, integrative way of thinking through the generations of management and to overseas operations.

Processual thinking has also enabled YKK to rethink and expand its business in a mature industry. Initially, this occurred as a reconceptualization of the simple fastener, from that of a minor component of a garment in the apparel industry, a "thing" that could be substituted for buttons, to an "action" illustrated by its function to both "open and close." This notion of the fastener as an action that changed the space or relationships between things enabled YKK to develop a variety of innovative solutions for a greater variety of customer needs. At the same time, the company strived for superior quality and timely delivery, which led them to expand their focus to include the entire supply chain, from raw materials to the end-customer, as well as the environment and the community where supply was located. YKK views itself as a part of each environment, and seeks optimum solutions through trial and error, accumulating experiential knowledge in process. Its emphasis on quality in product and technology became the pursuit of a total engineering solution built on, and building, cumulative in-house knowledge of production that is now unique to YKK, and which is the source of its sustainable advantage.

Shared philosophy and cumulative knowledge has helped YKK achieve a global market share of 45 percent, outstripping all other competitors. The company is organized so that both the Sales division and the Machinery and Engineering division together "indwell" with the customer to address their issues. Both service and technology are offered to realize faster and better solutions for the customer. This promotes deeper communication inside and outside the company and the knowledge gained from such dialogue is fed into production for timely implementation of solutions.

YKK's shared philosophy of the "Cycle of Goodness", emphasizing "goodness" in dynamic relationships and cumulative knowledge assets, has been passed on successfully as an organizational discipline, and this has empowered employees to think and act autonomously. Knowledge emerges from experiences in actual practices, which are linked organically in deeply communicative environments of *ba* that enable the spiral of knowledge creation and promote the sharing and accumulation of knowledge organizationally to evolve value creation at the company. This process is illustrated in Figure 7.7.

The case of JFE offers a new way of thinking about how to proceed with an M&A at a time when global realignment of the steel and other industries is underway. Mergers are fraught with conflict, even those between companies in the same industry, so it would seem that merging a smaller company with a larger one might be more workable than merging equals. However, JFE effectively merged two similar sized companies with very different cultures of operation – NKK and Kawasaki Steel. This case is exceptional because frictions were anticipated and avoided, technologies and know-how at both companies were retained and effectively merged, and solid business performance ensued.

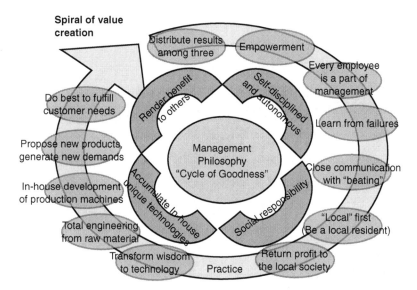

Figure 7.7 YKK Cycle of Goodness and Spiral of Value Creation

Often times an M&A means adding up the explicit assets of two companies to achieve economies of scale. In contrast, JFE sought to merge the tacit knowledge of employees and the innovative technologies embedded in practices at each company. This process was guided by a shared vision, purpose, and principles of action articulated by the companies' leaders and communicated in *ba* in a variety of forms, most notably through the exchange of personnel between the companies aimed at merging the tacit knowledge of middle managers. The success of this merger is the outcome of utilizing the knowledge assets of both NKK and Kawasaki Steel to create new knowledge of a higher quality at JFE to produce better quality products and services.

Both cases in this chapter illustrate how personal archives of tacit knowledge based on experience are effectively shared and utilized as a management resource to build and expand the knowledge assets of the firm. Top management plays an important role in designing and establishing organizational structures and goals to foster the transfer of such knowledge to contribute to better business outcomes.

Notes

1. http://www.ykk.com/english/corporate/m_principle.html
2. A wire whose section is rectangular shaped.
3. A wire whose section is "Y" shaped.

4. Interview with Masaharu Ando, August 21, 2007.
5. Ibid.
6. As of 2005, the largest steel producers were Arcelor Mittal, 110 million tons; Nippon Steel, 32 million tons; Bosco, 31 million tons; JFE Steel, 30 million tons.
7. http://www.jfe-holdings.co.jp/en/release/2001/011221-1.html
8. "Market Share, 2003 edition." *Nikkei Sangyo Shimbun*, 2002.
9. The other three principles were: fair and appropriate human resource management; decision making through discussions; and fairness between the two former companies.
10. Interview with Tetsuo Miyazaki, then the vice president of JFE Holdings, conducted on December 2, 2004.
11. Interview with Eisuke Yamanaka, then the General Superintendent, West Japan Works, JFE Steel, on January 26, 2005.
12. Interviews with Sales Division managers of JFE Steel, on February 1, 2006.
13. Super-OLAC (on-line accelerated cooling) is a technology developed by NKK. This system can uniformly cool down the steel plate on the production line the instant after it is pressed. This enables drastic reduction in delivery time, and steel of increased strength.
14. The Large Block Ring Construction Method is a technology developed by Kawasaki Steel for revamping its blast furnaces. The method shortens the blasting time, from the conventional 130 days to 6–80 days. The blast furnace body is assembled in advance by dividing it into three or four blocks, which are installed and welded together one after another from top to bottom. The construction method is proprietary to the JFE Group and offers a shorter construction period and lower repair costs.
15. Interview with employees of JFE Steel, West Japan Works.
16. Interview with Tetsuo Miyazaki, then vice president of JFE Holdings, conducted on December 2, 2004.
17. Interview with Eisuke Yamanaka, on January 26, 2005.

References

Emoto, K. and Shimogaichi, Y. (2004). "JFE Tanjo: Tekkou daitougou no kyodai project wo furikaeru" ["The birth of JFE: Looking back on the merger project of steel giants"]. *Financial Japan*, October 21, pp. 50–60.

Fujimoto, T. (2004). *Nihon no monodukuri tetsugaku* [Philosophy of Manufacturing in Japan]. Tokyo: Nihon Keizai Shinbunsha.

Fulford, B. (2003). "Zipping up the world: How Japan's YKK built a better fastener and caught its competition in the teeth." http://members.forbes.com/global/2003/1124/089.html, accessed November 16.

Imai, C. (1998). *NKK no gyokaku* [NKK's reform]. Tokyo: Diamond sha.

Kawashima, M. (2003). "Key person: Yoshida Tadahiro YKK daihyo torishimariyaku shacho" ["Tadahiro Yoshida, President of YKK Corporation"].*Weekly Toyo Keizai*, August 2, pp. 120–2.

Onishi, Y. and Shoji, N. (2007). "YKK shirarezaru zen no keiei" ["Not well-known YKK's management by virtue"]. *Nikkei Business*, January 15, pp. 26–44.

Sato, R. (1987). *M&A no keizaigaku* [Economies of M&A]. Tokyo: TBS Britanica.

Takase, T. and Imamura, K. (1990). *Kawasaki Seitetsu fukugo keiei senryaku no subete* [All about Kawasaki Steel's Complex Management Strategy]. Tokyo: TBS Britanica.

YKK Corporation. (eds). (1995). *The History of YKK: 1934–1994*. Tokyo: YKK Corporation.

YKK Corporation. (2004). *YKK Group Environmental and Social Report 2004*. www.ykk.com/english/corporate/eco/report/2005/pdf/2005e_04.pdf

Yoshida, T. (1987). *Yoshida Tadao Zenshu II: Keiei shisou* [The Complete Works of Tadao Yoshida II: Management Philosophy]. Tokyo: Yoshida Kogyo K.K.

Yoshida, T. (1988). *Yoshida Tadao Zenshu: Hyouden-hen* [The Complete Works of Tadao Yoshida: The Critical Biography]. Tokyo: Yoshida Kogyo K.K.

Yoshida, T. (2003). *Datsu charisma no keiei* [Free from Charismatic Management]. Tokyo: Toyo Keizai Shinpo Sha.

8
Leadership: Fostering Distributed Excellence in the Organization

In previous chapters we have discussed how a firm creates knowledge through dialogue and practice, guided by its knowledge vision and following a driving objective. We have also looked at *ba*, knowledge assets, and the ecosystem as the foundation for knowledge creation. The question remains: what drives the entire process? We believe it is a leadership capability that can coherently synthesize, direct, and implement the various elements that foster knowledge creation. However, in the knowledge-based firm, leadership is not exclusive to an elite few. It is distributed throughout the organization among individuals who can exercise *phronesis* to make decisions and act appropriately to each situation to realize a common good. Knowledge-based management requires management of both internal and external knowledge creation activities, case-by-case, because knowledge is created both inside the organization as well as in dynamic interaction with the external environment. In other words, companies exist in an ecosystem of knowledge. Therefore, leaders must be capable of immediate decision-making in response to the *ba* that continuously emerge and vanish both inside and outside the organization. This would be impossible in an organization where leadership is fixed.

The role of leadership begins with setting the vision and the driving objective, and ensuring the consistent understanding of these so the entire organization can understand and commit to them. A leader must also actively leverage *ba*, where it is possible to synthesize subjectivity and objectivity in order to move the organization from partial to total optimization. Unlike the traditional economic view of sequential determination, in which environment determines the structure and structure determines the agents, in the process-based view the agent, structure, and environment interpenetrate with each other in the *ba* that arise between them. This means activities of agents are not energized by the structure but by the *ba*, and the *ba* influence the structure. In such a *ba*, leadership takes the important role of creating and nurturing the environment. Specifically, the leader must do three things: build the kind of *ba* needed for the required activities; maintain and energize the *ba* to ensure continuous knowledge creation; and connect the varied and multilayered *ba* as needed. A leader also has to build and utilize knowledge assets efficiently and effectively and drive the continuous interaction between tacit and explicit knowledge through dialogue and practice.

In this chapter we shall show examples by presenting two cases of distributed *phronetic* leadership. The first is the remaking of the manufacturer Canon Inc. CEO Mitarai's leadership may seem charismatic, but he understands the importance of empowerment and autonomy for his employees. The second is the project to create the Toyota Motor Corporation's hybrid car, the Prius. Not only the top management but the middle managers play key roles in connecting and nurturing various processes and relationships. Both cases demonstrate that only a certain kind of leadership that is distributed can drive the process of organizational knowledge creation.

8.1 Canon Inc.

8.1.1 Company overview

Canon Inc, the once floundering global brand in camera and optics manufacturing, achieved a major turnaround leading to high profitability under the leadership of Fujio Mitarai, who was appointed CEO in September, 1995. The company experienced an extraordinary turnaround during his tenure. In 1995, Canon was heavily in debt to the tune of 840 billion yen or 7 billion US dollars on a consolidated basis. The ratio of interest-bearing debt to total assets reached a high of 33.6 percent. That ratio dramatically decreased to 5 percent by 2002 and 0.6 percent by 2007, fiscal year ending December 31. Cash flow improved, reaching 406.8 billion yen or 3.9 billion US dollars in 2007 from minus 22.5 billion yen or about 187.5 million US dollars in 1997. Net profit also increased from 118.8 billion yen or 990 million US dollars in 1997 to 134.1 billion yen or 1.1 billion US dollars in 2000, jumping to 488.3 billion yen or 4.7 billion US dollars in 2007 (see Figure 8.1 and 8.2).

This may seem like the typical story of a charismatic CEO turning the company around with strong top-down leadership, but that is not the full story of Canon. In addition to strong, top-down leadership, the distributed leadership cultivated by Mitarai's reforms has led to spontaneous knowledge creation and effective use of that knowledge at all levels of the Canon organization. Our aim is to show how effective leadership cultivated in *ba* turned Canon around from a company that was losing ground despite its strong technology, sales capability, and rich internal resources because it was functioning on the basis of partial optimization rather than total optimization in the deployment of these assets.

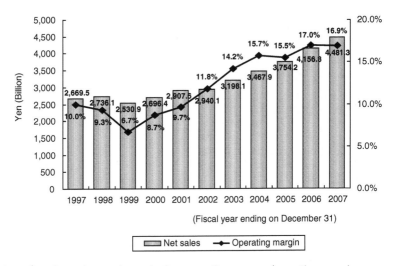

Figure 8.1 Canon's net sales and other operating revenue/operating margin
Source: http://www.canon.com/ir/historical/index.html

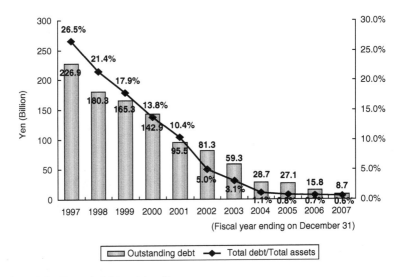

Figure 8.2 Canon's debt outstanding
Source: http://www.canon.com/ir/historical/index.html

8.1.2 Crisis at Canon

When Mitarai returned to Japan in 1989 after working 23 years at Canon USA, initially handling the areas of sales and accounting, he soon realized that the Canon Group was drowning in debt, still dependent on a management model of financing development with the debt. He had been urging financial reform at the company but no one was listening. The prevailing mentality was that all the company had to do was to produce a new technology product that would sell well, since Canon's past successes with new hit products had generated sufficient profits to keep the company going. However, the amount of time it took to get a product through development and onto the market was becoming longer and longer, and without sufficient equity it was becoming increasingly difficult to fund the basic research in technology needed to generate new products.

Mitarai had also noticed the damaging effects of sectionalism in the company, resulting from its organization into separate divisions. Starting as a camera company, Canon had grown into a large, multidivisional firm by developing and applying optical and digital imaging technology to produce a wide variety of products. Each division had full independence in operations, from personnel to making decisions about what projects to invest in. As a result, each division focused only on its own interests rather than the interests of the company as a whole. Each division invested in their own research and development to advance their own technologies, with no consideration of the overall balance sheet or the possible synergy effects of sharing technologies. There was no group-wide plan for raising capital, so each subsidiary had to raise funds on its own. While some subsidiaries had cash to spare, others were forced to borrow from outside at high interest rates. The same kind of inefficiency existed in the allocation of staff. While some divisions lacked qualified people, others had them in excess and didn't know where to put everyone.

Faced with the two major problems of raising capital and managing the divisions, Mitarai embarked on a reform of Canon with the slogans, "Seek what's best for the whole not the parts," and "Focus on profitability in cash-flow management." In 1996, one year after becoming CEO, Mitarai issued a policy document. He called it the Excellent Global Corporation Plan, and it set the clear financial goals of cutting the ratio of interesting-bearing debt to assets from 34 percent to 3 percent, raising the equity ratio from 35 percent to 60 percent, and raising profitability to 10 percent.

8.1.3 Restructuring Canon

To achieve such ambitious goals, Mitarai spearheaded a major reorientation of thinking in the divisions about profitability, advocating the strategy of "Selection and Concentration." He decided to pull Canon out of the personal computer business, which had been deficit ridden for decades. Canon exited seven other areas of business, among them FLCD (ferroelectric liquid crystal display), word processors, optical-magnetic disks, optical cards, and color filters for LCDs. These decisions were not welcomed. In fact, there was a lot of opposition, but they were accepted in the end because they came directly from the top with strict communication. Canon lost 73 billion yen or 608 million US dollars in turnover after closing these businesses, but it stopped the bleeding of 28 billion yen or 233 billion US dollars in losses.

More importantly for the future growth of Canon, the restructuring freed up important resources, not just capital but also human resources, that were being expended on projects with no future. Preserving the Japanese custom of lifetime employment, those who had worked in the businesses that had been closed were not laid off but transferred to other divisions. For example, engineers who had been working in the computer division were transferred to another division to work on computer technology, specifically, on development of the SOC or system-on-chip, a technology for integrating multiple functions on a single integrated circuit. Their efforts generated the NADA or Network Adaptive Digital Architecture, a control mechanism used in multifunction copiers. Similarly, the engineers who had worked in FLC display were put to work on sensors and developed the CMOS (Complementary Metal Oxide Semiconductor) sensor for digital cameras and scanners. Both NADA and the CMOS sensor are key technologies at Canon today. In short, rather than losing a valuable knowledge asset of experienced and knowledgeable employees, as has often been the case in the restructuring of companies, reforms at Canon improved the flow of knowledge internalized in employees to support innovation in the company.

8.1.4 The balance sheet tells the management stories

The effect of bold restructuring based on top-down decision-making was drastic, but it might have been a limited, one-time effect if not for the continuous company-wide effort to improve Canon. Mitarai considers the balance sheet more important than the profit-and-loss statement because it shows assets and liabilities accumulated over the years, while the profit-and-loss statement only shows figures for a particular year. Mitarai says a careful reading of the balance sheet reveals the story behind the figures. He said "to improve management is to improve the balance sheet" (Oguri et al., 2003: 25). He continued, "the profit and loss statement could be controlled rather easily to produce superficial profits, but to improve the balance sheet, it takes a long period of time." Focusing on the balance sheet requires setting a clear goal and making a plan in long-term perspectives because as a manufacturer it takes time to earn profit out of newly developed products. To be capable of supporting long-term investments, long-term debt must be minimized and equity must be increased. With the experience in finance from his work in the US, Mitarai recognized the importance of the balance sheet, and knew by heart how to read and manage one.

To improve the balance sheet and to keep pushing the organization, Mitarai set financial targets as goals. These were the key performance indicators of net sales, the ratio of gross profit to net sales, R&D expenses as a ratio of net sales, operating profit relative to net sales, daily inventory turnover, and the ratio of debt to total assets. However, this was not just a matter of producing cold numbers. Mitarai created and told stories of achieving his goals that referred to the kinds of means to achieve those goals. For him, the process of planning and achieving the goal is the story of management: where the key players are the figures. He remembers all the important indicators with the narratives, and whenever the situation changes he changes the plot and a new story will be created. This way, the numerical targets also served as a starting point for discussions at meetings aimed at translating policy concepts into concrete reality, in terms of improvements in routines on the factory floor and in collective understanding of individual roles and responsibilities. "It is important to state a goal as a concrete figure because then it becomes clear what you have to do to reach that figure," said Mitarai (Katsumi, 2006: 35). When a Canon employee sets a numerical target as a goal, he or she is asked by his or her supervisor to also develop a scenario or a narrative about who should do what, in which situation, to achieve it. According to Mitarai, "each person must have the capability to not only set a concrete numerical goal, but to create the story to realize it. That capability becomes the source of Canon's strength" (ibid.). In that sense, numerical goals are also tools for making everyone at Canon think about and understand the process of reaching the goals.

In his long tenure at the US subsidiary, Mitarai also learned the importance of cash-flow management. While the balance sheet tells the results of investment and the profit-and-loss statement tells the reasons for the results, cash flow helps to grasp the process of investment and the results. Before the cash-flow statement was made mandatory in Japanese accounting regulations in 2000, Mitarai introduced the concept as a means to improve the balance sheet and accelerate improvement and innovation. Throughout his tenure, he continued to communicate the meaning of this concept throughout the organization. Cash-flow management at Canon is not only about improving numbers in the financial statement but is the objective driving every employee to think continuously about how he or she can contribute in his or her particular job to improving cash flow in the entire company. Cash-flow management aims for optimal use of overall resources in all parts of the company by making it clear how much value (cash inflow) each part creates and what amount of resources it consumes (cash outflow) to create value at a particular time. Aiming for total optimization of resource-use requires that employees see themselves and their work in relation to other functions and divisions and in relation to the company as a whole. It also makes them conscious of time, or how to create value sufficient to offset cost in a certain period of time. Cash-flow management rejects the kind of thinking that says "one day, the investment will pay off". This is not to deny that investment for the future is needed, but to emphasize the need for clearly articulating the story of how such a future is to be realized. Recognizing that excessive focus on cash-flow management can easily fall into a pattern of cost-cutting only, the company has established a mid-term plan to identify new business domains and accumulate the required technologies. To that end, Canon plans to increase R&D expenditures from 8.2 percent of net sales in 2007 to up to 10 percent by 2010.[1]

Another means Mitarai introduced for improving the balance sheet was consolidated statements for settlement of accounts as the standard for evaluation, to make the overall financial situation of the group companies more transparent. Because Canon operated in a group of companies where the parent company was responsible for R&D and production and the subsidiaries were responsible for sales and services, this evaluation system was especially effective. Under the old system of distinct divisions, managers only monitored non-consolidated figures, mostly of their own business domain, which did not reflect the performance of the whole Canon group. The consolidation of figures changed the relationships between divisions and subsidiaries in the company, forcing them to see themselves in relation to the whole company. With the new emphasis on group performance, each division focused not only on its own performance, but also made an effort to enhance the performance of the entire Canon group. Finally, all parts of the organization learned to think and act as one company instead of as many, single companies within the group. Mitarai said "cash flow management and evaluation by consolidated statements are inseparable and closely related with each other in realizing the goal of improving the balance sheet" (Oguri et al., 2003: 27).

8.1.5 Installing cell production system

To improve cash flow, Canon either had to increase net profit or decrease assets not directly contributing to gaining free cash flow. The department that was most utilizing the cash was the production line, where parts, work in process, and finished goods were piled up. To reduce these inventories, Mitarai introduced the revolutionary cell production system proposed by one of his frontline subordinates. Unlike the conventional conveyor-belt system of streamlined production, where each worker progressively completes very specific tasks and then hands the work over to the next person on the assembly line, cell production consists of a self-contained team or cell of multiskilled workers (or sometimes just one worker) who are responsible for significant portions, or sometimes even the whole, of the assembly process. Mitarai had observed the shortcomings of conveyor-belt production of camera lenses shortly after joining Canon and had been looking for a more innovative system. One day, he heard from a division manager about a Sony factory that was doing something different. He immediately went

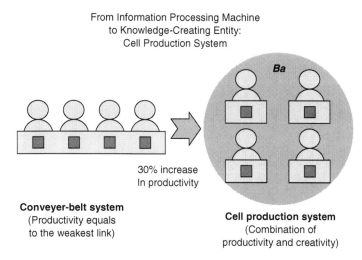

Figure 8.3 Image of cell production system

there to see it and instantly understood the merits of cell production and brought it to Canon. The results were stunning. Five years after introducing cell production, Canon had freed up the equivalent of 22,000 jobs and reduced the total amount of work in process at any one time from 20 days to 4 days. In addition, removal of the old production lines and warehouses freed up 870,000 square meters of space, reducing rental space by half. The surplus in space and human resources was absorbed by other business operations (see Figure 8.3).

Another merit of the cell production system is flexibility in production. The number of cells can be increased or decreased to synchronize production with fluctuations in demand. At the Ami plant in Ibaraki prefecture, where copiers were produced, lead-time under the old system had been three months. After cell production was introduced and skills improved, lead-time gradually fell to one week. Production and sales had previously spent a lot of time negotiating which department should assume the risk of a production run, based on sales forecasts made three months earlier. Today, there is no such risk. This flexibility also made it easier to introduce a new product to the market. For example, in 2005, Canon introduced 17 new models of digital camera in just one year. This would not have been possible with the traditional fixed assembly line and belt-conveyer system. Speed of production is a very important factor in marketing new products in the camera industry in Japan, where the retail price of a digital camera usually falls to half just two months after it goes on the market.

Greater efficiency and flexibility at Canon was not achieved only by eliminating conveyer belts and reducing the amount of work in process among line workers. The essential value of the cell production system is that it allows each worker to see his or her work in relation to the whole process and effectively utilizes each worker's knowledge, which continues to accumulate through experience. The traditional conveyer-belt assembly line or Ford system of production was built on the assumption that there are limits to individual capabilities and that this does not change. Even when a worker's skill in his or her particular capability improves, that skill cannot be used to the fullest because the worker can only work as fast as the speed of the line. In contrast, advances in a worker's skill in cell production system are immediately reflected in overall efficiency.

Nevertheless, cell production system was not an immediate success at Canon. Efficiency and flexibility were achieved only after production workers started to re-evaluate the production process on their own. Using the wisdom of their experience they created procedures for realizing the maximum benefit of the cell production system. They shared the problems they were facing and worked by trial and error. Tools and jigs were adapted by workers to suit cell production methods. Mitarai called it "Chie-tech" or Intelli-Tech because it was developed on site from the shared knowledge and creativity of employees. Compared to the high-tech tools and jigs once considered essential to an efficient production line, Chie-tech was substantially cheaper and more effective. And the effect on production reform overall was huge, with every worker volunteering to invent new, handy, low-cost tools, stimulating greater inventiveness on the job. The value of inventiveness on the shop floor was soon recognized in other parts of Canon. If assembly workers found some parts of a product difficult to assemble, engineers and designers would visit the factory and consult with workers to devise a Chie-tech tool that would make assembly easier, rather than resorting to costly changes in the design of the part.

Such innovation based on worker knowledge is possible because the cell production system allows workers to see the manufacturing process as a whole, and to see themselves as a part of the whole company rather than the manufacturing process alone. Production workers came to know and understand the entire process, rather than just one part of the process on the assembly line. This triggered them to think about improvements in terms of total optimization, and each individual's ideas and methods were apparent in the overall result. In cell production, workers are intrinsically motivated by a feeling of achievement and self-actualization, which accelerates efficiency. The knowledge of each individual worker is engaged on the production floor and all activities there are based on workers' knowledge. Worker initiatives on the spot can change the arrangement of cells, production tools, and even production procedures. Every experience can be a source of new knowledge and every second can be a moment of innovation. The stimulation of individual thinking and team atmosphere creates a *ba* of knowledge sharing and deep communication that improves effectiveness.

Such innovation, based on knowledge at the frontline, is supported by two systems at Canon for fostering, maintaining, and sharing the important technological knowledge of individuals. These are the "Canon Expert System" for production employees based on the German meister system, and the "Master-Craftsperson System" for technical experts. These systems cultivate the capabilities and enthusiasm of workers and are key to the success of cell production. The Expert System ranks four levels of mastery in production up to the level of "Super-Grade Expert." For example, one Super-Grade Expert alone can assemble a high-end copier machine with more than 3,000 parts in just 14 hours, memorizing all 2,000 pages in the manual describing the procedure. Assembly of such a machine formerly required the effort of about 70 workers. A worker at the level of Super-Grade Expert is sometimes dispatched to other divisions to make optimal use of their expertise. For example, three Super-Grade Experts were sent to the R&D department to help design copier machines with fewer problems in the production phase. Super-Grade Experts are rewarded with better wages and a special badge, and they can sign their names on the products they assemble.

The term "Master-Craftsperson" applies to those employees with excellent technique in specific areas such as polishing lenses, precision processing, painting, and coating. One Master Craftsperson will hand polish the master lens to be used as the standard of quality for inspection of high-precision lenses for steppers, the machines used to expose the ultra fine circuit patterns in semiconductor devices. Such a person can sense by hand a difference of one micrometer or one millionth of a millimeter in the accuracy of the lens. There are 24 such Master-Craftspersons at Canon as of 2007. Each one is asked to choose their successors (usually two) and train them one-on-one over a two-year period. These Expert and Master-Craftsperson systems ensure that technical knowledge and expertise at Canon is both nurtured and passed on to the next generation.

8.1.6 "Communication, communication, communication!"

Not surprisingly, Mitarai's drastic reforms met with resistance at every level of Canon. To overcome this and keep the whole organization moving towards reform, he emphasized the importance of communication, noting that it is more powerful than authority as a tool for getting people to work. "It is very important that someone is convinced about why they need to do a certain job in order for them to grow. For that to happen, bosses must have the ability to convince workers. I myself kept trying to convince people in order to encourage individuals who would tackle reform at the frontline. That's who created today's Canon," said Mitarai (Katsumi, 2006: 33). He said the only way to convince people was to communicate the message over and over again. The more frequent the communication, the more convinced and consenting people will be. Leaders have to be able to communicate their intentions and the reasoning behind it, and make sure everybody in the organization understands and commits to it.

Mitarai had learned about the importance of communication between management and employees while working overseas, and he often encouraged staff to look at issues from each other's point of view. He said he has always believed that his most important task at the helm of Canon is to change people's mindsets and behavior by effectively communicating the vision of the company and his ideas for implementing it.

Mitarai built a variety of *ba* to promote communication that would tear down the walls between divisions and subsidiaries and overcome the prevalence of partial optimization. He first set up a management reform committee, which he headed. He divided the committee into eight subcommittees according to management tasks. Each subcommittee was led by a senior manager of a division, and each manager was responsible for reforming a part of the business that was not their own to encourage cross-divisional communication and collaboration. This forced them to cooperate fully, even if it meant sacrificing the short-term interests of their own divisions. Mitarai urged the managers to see themselves as responsible for Canon as a whole, rather than as representatives of their particular divisions. Everyone in the company was encouraged to express their opinions and ideas freely and to follow up on them independently. The increased communication and interaction in *ba* in the various subcommittees soon started to break down barriers between the divisions and groups in the company and generate a new way of thinking. One typical example of the process was the project to unify product codes. When Mitarai took up the presidency, there were about 200,000 variations in product coding. He chose the head of Canon's human resource division to manage the subcommittee on global logistics innovation and take on the job of rationalizing the coding system. The project was completed successfully in two years, overcoming the resistance of various divisions by synthesizing their concerns.

The three most important communication forums at Canon are the management strategy committee meeting, the management meeting, and the board meeting, all headed by the CEO. The management strategy committee meets to identify and discuss various managerial issues, while the management meeting decides how to resolve such issues. The board approves decisions made by the management meeting. The management strategy committee meets monthly and also when urgent issues arise. Rather than passive listening to one-sided presentations and reports, the meeting is meant to encourage lively discussion and the exchange of knowledge and opinions. Managers from the divisions and units try to elicit as many different opinions as possible. The management meeting is weekly and attended by all executives and managers from the relevant divisions to develop a concrete plan of action based on the goals set by the management strategy committee. The board must give final approval to all decisions taken. All three meetings take place in one hour over lunch. According to Mitarai:

> All my meetings are during the lunch hour. Since everybody has to eat lunch, attendance is 100 percent. We eat lunch in five minutes and spend the remaining 50 minutes in heated debate. We're using the "free" time already allocated for lunch. (Takeuchi and Nonaka, 2004: 24)

The meeting room is small, so everyone has to sit close to each other. This is aimed at creating a "melting pot" atmosphere for lively discussion. Through the discussions in these *ba*, Mitarai could tacitly share his perspectives and values on why and how the improvement of the balance sheet is important, why and how the cash-flow management and cutting inventory are exciting, and why and how the profit loss is bad for the company.

In addition to these formal meetings, Canon has forums for cultivating mutual understanding and trust in *ba* in more informal settings. Canon executives meet at the so-called *"asa-kai"* or morning meeting from 8 a.m. to 9 a.m. everyday. No agenda is set for the *asa-kai*, so participants can bring their most urgent "here-now" issues for discussion. Executives can talk about whatever is on their minds that morning, even if it is trivia from the morning newspapers. The atmosphere is relaxed and informal, so directors who have other important business are not expected to attend. The meeting is also not expected to produce final decisions. However, when a critical issue arises from the flow of sharing on a variety of topics, the informal nature of the *asa-kai* can instantly turn formal. Participants will discuss and sometimes decide something on the spot and execute the decision once the meeting breaks up at 9 a.m., or they might send the matter to the management meeting for further discussion. Mitarai believes it is important that board members meet briefly and talk face-to-face at least once a day. The relaxed atmosphere is meant to encourage creative thinking, improvisation, and engagement. The informal nature of the discussion helps executives make sense of differences of opinion and allows them to share contexts and information that may seem unrelated to their own immediate business concerns. As an important place of knowledge sharing it helps speed up the decision-making process at Canon.

Occasionally, decisions are made at the *asa-kai*, but even if they are made later, all those affected by the decision have prior awareness of the matter from the morning meeting. Mitarai's successor as president, Tsuneji Uchida, describes the importance of top management providing leadership through timely decision-making, and he says the fast exchange of information at the morning meeting assists this process. "Even if you're only 60 percent sure, you have a responsibility to make a decision," he said, adding that if you think too much, "you'll miss the timing and lose out" (Uchida, 2007: 86). This emphasizes the important timing and time-saving function of the morning meeting as a place for sharing knowledge, context, and the will to act.

In addition to the *ba* at the level of top management, there are also various *ba* that are nested and interlinked, engaging employees, customers, suppliers, collaborators, and other stakeholders such as global leaders in the company. All of the *ba* at Canon are organically connected and related, promoting both closer and wide-ranging dialogue and relationships throughout and beyond the company. Canon's multilayered system of *ba* is a whole world of people connected through small-world networks (see Figure 8.4).

To share knowledge and information about company policy throughout the organization, executive managers from all departments across Japan come together at headquarters once a month. Managers at these meetings review policy and the status of projects and are directly informed by their CEO about ideas and plans for the future. Summaries of the meetings are circulated on the company intranet.

Mitarai has often stressed the importance of direct communication with frontline employees to share vision, knowledge, and information. He says the only way for the CEO to get a feel for what is going on at the frontline is to have as much contact with employees as possible by talking with them face-to-face. One of the main opportunities for him to do this is his annual visit to every R&D laboratory and factory in Japan. During these visits he

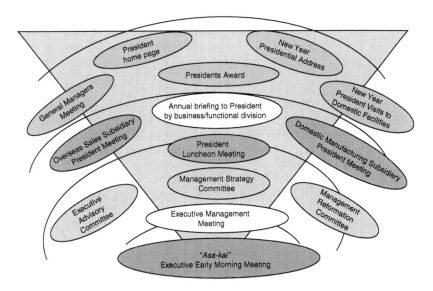

Figure 8.4 Canon's organic configuration of "multi-layers of *ba*"

speaks for about two hours each time and then meets with every employee, or everyone from assistant manager up, depending on the size of the office. Twice a year, when bonuses are paid, he personally hands out salary statements and chats with 800 selected managers. He has also maintained various, traditional reward systems at Canon that recognize and evaluate business achievements. He views these rewards as tools of communication, such as the President Award, given to an individual or group that has contributed a new invention or other kind of innovation to the company. Mitarai publicly commends the award winner with an honorarium to show that upper management acknowledges the contribution of each employee. Another reward is the "gift money" handed out at special events to celebrate milestones and other achievements. Mitarai attaches a message with the cash, communicating to the employee directly and in a concrete way that shows that management recognizes the value of their effort.

Such methods not only help Mitarai communicate company policy and his vision to the entire company, they also help him to pick up more contextual knowledge in each place, which guides him in strategic decision-making. He knows that "seeing is believing," and often stresses the importance of seeing things with your own eyes. For example, when perception of the large risks associated with changing production methods slowed the company-wide shift to cell production, even though it was ordered by top management, Mitarai took all 12 members of the management strategy committee to the Nagahama Canon subsidiary where cell production was operating full scale. Once they could see how it was working they understood the benefits, and this accelerated the introduction of the cell system to Canon's other plants. However, sometimes seeing is not enough. Mitarai said he also visits the frontline to check on the results of his strategy and make adjustments if necessary:

> There are those who claim to be frontline-oriented by just going to the factories without setting any goals or making any suggestions. These people are just doing factory tours and they will not discover anything. Because I have set the goal, I can check, by looking at the results at the frontline, if there is a problem, if the process deviated from the goal somewhere, or if the goal setting or strategy was wrong from the beginning. (Katsumi, 2006: 38)

8.1.7 Managing flow for becoming an excellent company

The case of Canon clearly explains managing flow in the actual business operation. At Canon, seemingly static and analytical numbers and figures are dynamic and narrative; they are made into the key players of management stories. At Canon, resources including cash, inventory, and of course human resources are considered as processes. Mitarai remembers by heart all the financial targets of every division, because the numbers are an important part of his management scenarios. As a result of intensive communication at various *ba* nurtured by CEO Mitarai, all the managements and employees are asked to create scenarios and tell the management stories with a shared understanding of why and how the balance sheet, cash-flow management, and evaluation with consolidated statement are important for becoming an excellent company. Uniqueness of Canon's management resides in the leadership of one CEO who managed and distributed flow by creating lively and dynamic *ba* within the firm.

8.2 Toyota Motor Corporation – Prius project

8.2.1 Project overview

Toyota Motor Corporation has emerged as a global leader in auto manufacturing, exceeding General Motors Corporation in auto production in 2007. It is best known for continuous production innovation, and its unique Toyota Production System has long been studied by academics and practitioners alike. Many overseas competitors have adopted Toyota practices such as *"kaizen"* (continuous improvement), *"mieru-ka"* (visualization), and *"just-in-time manufacturing."* The creation of the Prius hybrid car, however, has demonstrated that in addition to incremental, continuous production innovation Toyota is capable of technological breakthrough as well.

Prius, which means "prior to" in Latin, is the world's first mass-produced hybrid vehicle. It went on the market in December, 1997 and has received numerous awards for its innovative product concept and technologies, including Car of the Year Japan (1997), the North American Car of the Year (2004), and Car of the Year in Europe (2004). Toyota President Hiroshi Okuda has called the Prius an epoch-making automobile, and an automobile for the twenty-first century.[2] Toyota claims that the Prius boosts fuel economy by 100 percent and engine efficiency by 80 percent. It says the car emits about half as much carbon dioxide, and about one-tenth as much carbon monoxide, hydrocarbons, and nitrous oxide, as conventional gasoline-powered cars.

The Prius was a breakthrough for Toyota in three ways: as an innovative product, as new technology, and as a knowledge-creating process. First, it is an innovative product: the first mass-produced hybrid passenger vehicle in the world, it virtually created a new market for itself. It was also innovative in the sense that it did not fit with any of Toyota's existing product lines. At Toyota, each product is designed to complement another so that all product lines have a consistent, Toyota brand image. The Prius does not fit this picture. From the beginning, the project was designed to give Toyota engineers a new perspective on developing a car. Second, the Prius consists of many innovative technologies, in the engine, the electric motor, the battery, and the brake system, and the technology applied to combine these into what is now called the Toyota Hybrid System. Through development of the Prius, Toyota not only acquired new skills in electronics technologies to complement existing mechanical expertise, it also acquired the ability to integrate these effectively into a new production process, an achievement that is important for the future of the company. In keeping with its emphasis on *"yokoten"* or horizontal deployment, Toyota has put its hybrid technology to use in a wide range of vehicles, including the Lexus. The hybrid technology is expected to help Toyota gain a stronger foothold in the European market. It is also offering the technology to other automakers, for economies of scale.

The third breakthrough for the Prius was its creation in a new process of product development, and in record time. It usually takes about four years for Toyota to develop a new model in an existing product line, which is still one of the shortest production cycles in the industry. The Prius, which is a totally new design based on new technologies, took only 15 months from the design freeze to the start of production. To achieve that speed and level of innovation the engineers frequently had to take unconventional approaches to the work. The hybrid drive system was still in the research phase when the Prius was being developed, so both research and development were going on at the same time.

The social context for hybrid development was a rising concern about the impact of fossil fuel emissions on the environment, and rising oil prices. Building the Prius required forming a product development team with the necessary technological skills to create a product in short order. Given the wide-ranging expertise and complex, multiple technologies applied in modern automobile manufacturing today, the effort demanded a massive accumulation and creation of new knowledge. The successful transformation of this knowledge into the Prius demonstrates the impact of superb leadership in knowledge-based process management that is the strength of Toyota and the source of its ability to continuously generate innovation (see Table 8.1).

8.2.2 Background of the development of the Prius

In the early 1990s, the market for automobiles both in Japan and overseas was in recession, and although Toyota had a high market share in Japan, profitability was declining. Top management at Toyota felt a crisis was imminent, and they thought the company had become too big and inflexible to deal with the situation quickly and effectively. Toyota was also facing problems in product development. For 30 years, it had employed a system in which a chief engineer (CE) was assigned project leader and was responsible for the entire process of product development, from planning to the final check before going to market. Hence, each car reflected the unique personality of the CE responsible for its development. But by the 1990s, Toyota had

Table 8.1 Distributed leadership at the Prius project

	Top Management (Meta-funtional)	Knowledge Producers (Uchiyamada)	Knowledge Managers (Funtional)
Vision	Be a car manufacturer in the 21st century Sense of crisis	Concept making: A car for the 21st century	
Knowledge assets	Realized that Toyota had no knowledge of EV/Hybrid technologies	Knew other engineers (who knows what)	Deep knowledge of own engineering and technology fields
Create *Ba*	G21 room EV department Reorganization	G21 room Mailing lists Task forces	Various departments and sections
Energize *Ba*	Created chaos: "Double the fuel efficiency" and "Release Prius one year earlier than the plan". Backed-up the projects to gain commitment Gave G21 autonomy	Showed guidelines Shared information Saw from multiple view points Gave autonomy to task forces	
Connect *Ba*		Brought in people from various departments	
Promote SECI	All S, E, C, and I	E and C	S and I

more than 120,000 engineers, and the number of models was increasing more than ever. This created several problems. First, the time it took to coordinate the various departments and sections involved in product development dramatically increased. The technologies were subdivided and specialized to such a degree that engineers spent 30 percent of their working day in meetings to coordinate with other departments. Second, it had become difficult for a CE to put his personality stamp on a car. Product development had become more systemized, and each department more conservative, making it difficult to develop innovative new products. For example, in engine design, the engine department could tell the CE to choose from one of three existing designs, instead of developing a new engine that best suited the new car concept. In fact, a CE could create a new car simply by assembling existing components from the various departments.

The other challenge Toyota was facing was global warming, which was becoming one of the overriding issues of the twenty-first century. Increasing public concern about the environmental effects of fossil fuel consumption and the spike in oil prices was sending automakers around the world in search of a cleaner alternative to the internal combustion engine. Top management at Toyota had long been aware of the demand for cleaner air and greater fuel savings, a consideration made explicit in the Toyota Earth Charter of 1992 calling for lower-emission vehicles. Toyota President Fujio Cho had summed up the company's intentions this way:

> It bothers me when I'm told that Japan has not contributed anything in 100 years of automobile development. Unfortunately, the starting lines were different, so nothing can be done about that. With respect to the environment, however, the starting line is the same for everyone. Toyota will make every effort so that we can hear that Japan's technology has contributed much to the environment.[3]

Toyota had been working to reduce emissions in internal combustion engines (ICEs) and was already one of the leading automakers in terms of fuel efficiency. It started to focus more seriously on alternative technologies in 1991. These efforts were stimulated partly by the Zero Emission Vehicle (ZEV) program implemented by the State of California in 1990. Toyota managers quickly realized that car manufacturers needed to be able to respond to increasingly tougher environmental standards.

That same year, Toyota launched an advertising campaign in Japan called "Dr Dolittle," featuring a provocative phrase for an automotive company: "One day I realized that we don't need a car." It then posed the question: "What is a good car?" In a series of advertisements that followed, environmental concerns and safety issues were explored to answer this question. Not only did the series gain attention and positive responses from customers, it also gave Toyota employees the good feeling that they were making an effort on environmental issues, stimulating internal discussion about them. Around the same time, some of the engineers at Toyota started several voluntary groups to study technologies to develop more environmentally friendly vehicles. One group conducted a systematic study of hybrid technology combining a gas engine with an electric motor. A senior manager called this spontaneous development a Brownian movement, an analogy to the continuous, random motion of certain particles leading to diffusion throughout the organization.

The engineers also had been motivated by a sense of crisis. They knew that Toyota did not have the technologies to make the main components of an electric vehicle, such as a battery, motor, converter, and inverter. Toyota prides itself as an automobile *maker* whose core capability is producing engines, and this shortcoming posed a serious threat. Toyota has a tradition of producing the more important components internally to accumulate the necessary subtechnologies. Even components that eventually would be outsourced were first produced internally so Toyota engineers could understand the basic science, the production process, and the cost of the components. But the company had no such experience with electric vehicles, meaning it could be reduced to a mere assembler of components supplied by outside companies when the next generation of engines, such as the electric motor or hybrid, replaced gasoline-powered engines. For this reason, it was decided that development of the hybrid system would have to be completely in-house.

This coincided with a policy from top management recommending that the company "return to the basics of manufacturing." In January 1993, then president, Tatsuro Toyoda, announced that managers should focus on the question of what it means to be a manufacturer. At the end of that year, Eiji Toyoda, who was then chairman emeritus, emphasized in a speech to employees the importance of going back to the basics of manufacturing. Senior management had understood that the company was short on knowledge assets that could ensure the future of the firm. They had agreed to provide the necessary resources for research into electric vehicle technologies and had formally established the Electric Vehicle Development department in 1992. Toyota developed several electric vehicles, including the RAV4 EV in 1997, but none of them were commercially successful: high costs and a low operating radius were still unresolved problems with battery-powered vehicles.

8.2.3 Developing the Prius [4]

The first phase: creating a new concept for the twenty-first century

The Prius project started in September, 1993 as a small study group called G21, short for Generation 21st century. The group was formed by Yoshio Kanahara, then executive vice president, and it had strong backing from Shoichiro Toyoda, the president. At first the group met once a week while continuing their regular jobs. They knew they were working on a special project because Eiji Toyoda, the chairman, was heard to have said that it was something he would do himself if he were a bit younger. The mission of G21 was to figure out what a car for the twenty-first century should be, but the aim was not just to create a new concept for a car that could be mass marketed. Toyota wanted the G21 group to create a new process of product development as well. High-level support for the group from the start bolstered their commitment and the sense of urgency to come up with a comprehensive plan in just three months. The G21 issued a final report to management at the end of 1993, proposing that the car for the twenty-first century have the following features:

1. An extended wheel base to allow for more interior space;
2. Higher seats to make it easier to get in and out;
3. A height increase of 1,500 mm to make the car more aerodynamic;

4. A 50 percent improvement in fuel efficiency compared to other vehicles in the same class (the target was 20 km per liter);
5. A smaller engine and more efficient automatic transmission.

The report did not specifically propose development of a hybrid car in this embryonic stage because the group was still thinking in terms of conventional vehicle development. The next step would be to come up with a more detailed blueprint for the vehicle.

The second phase: building ba to realize the concept

The second phase started in January 1994 when Takeshi Uchiyamada was asked to lead the project and build a new car as well as a new process for developing a car. He was a specialist in harness and noise and vibration control and had never led a new-model development project. This was considered an advantage for developing a path-breaking vehicle because Uchiyamada would not be bound by the dominant way of thinking and established product development routines. He also had a strong social network connecting him to people with the knowledge and skills the project needed. Two years earlier he had been charged with reorganizing Toyota's research and development laboratories. He said this forced him to rethink how to break down the automobile for research purposes and gave him a broad knowledge of the technologies Toyota was working on and who was developing them. When he was assigned to lead the new project, Uchiyamada visited several departments at Toyota, including their Higashi-Fuji Research Center for advanced technologies, to find out exactly what technologies Toyota had.

The G21 project deviated in many respects from ordinary product development at Toyota. The goal to develop a path-breaking vehicle completely in-house meant there was virtually no interaction with external parties, but this enhanced the core group's focus and commitment to making full utilization of internal knowledge resources, and strong top management support ensured the team had relatively free access to those resources. Uchiyamada said he had a free hand, "unbound by any of the usual corporate and engineering constraints; freedom from component sharing and commonalities, marketing considerations, and product hierarchy."[5] Moreover, the core team was working solely on one product of its own design. Normally a new model, such as a Corolla, was developed according to a pre-established concept, and the job of the development team was simply to decide what improvements to make and requisition the necessary parts for assembly. Uchiyamada was charged with developing a totally new product and in record time, so he needed a small team of engineers who were self-sufficient in their technological know-how but also able to think about the car as a whole system and not just in terms of their particular technological specialty. He put together ten engineers representing skills in all the necessary areas so they could choose the best technologies in each to suit the car, from body, chassis, engine, and drive system, to production technologies. Each of them had about ten years' experience and all were in their early thirties – old enough to be skilled, but still young enough to be flexible.

The first thing they did was find the physical space they needed to do their work. They procured a room as base camp and brought in personal computers and two CAD (Computer Aided Design) systems. It was the first time that an entire product development team had worked together in one room, sharing and combining their knowledge on the spot. It meant that every member of the team had a more detailed overview of the project, which sped up decision-making, and this subsequently became standard practice. Uchiyamada had also established behavioral guidelines at the outset which he had written down and always carried with him. These included items such as: the technology should be evaluated by everyone, regardless of their specialty; think in terms of what is best for the product, not your department; don't just criticize, propose; share information; speed is important so don't wait till tomorrow; don't be concerned about rank or seniority when discussing technologies. The guidelines jettisoned the usual rigid hierarchies in favor of more open sharing of knowledge and ideas so problems could be resolved through constructive criticism and cross-functional collaboration.

"Equal access to information" was another of Uchiyamada's rules. Team members learned from each other by working closely together. Information was promptly disseminated using an electronic mailing list, the first time at Toyota that the computer had been used this way. When problems arose, the usual practice in product development had been to report it to a superior who then took it to the chief engineer, who subsequently informed the other engineers who might be affected. This took a long time and delayed action to solve the problem. The Prius engineers could send emails to each other on the list immediately after discovering a problem and get a quick response about how to solve it. Eventually, 300 people were on the mailing list.

Pushing to make a leap

After six months, the team had an overall description of their twenty-first-century car. It would have to be safe, appealing to female drivers, low-polluting, and efficient. The team considered high fuel efficiency critical because of projected oil crises in the future and rising public consciousness about environmental issues. Focusing on the human user at the center of design considerations, the team aimed for *optimum interior and minimum exterior* design. After examining scientific research on the best physical posture for sitting, they envisioned a small sedan with seating for four adults, powered by a 1.3 or 1.5 liter direct-injection engine, delivering 50 percent better fuel efficiency than existing, comparable vehicles.

However, senior management rejected this plan as too conventional and reset the goal posts, urging the team to seek more radical solutions beyond existing technologies. Executive Vice President at the time, Akihiro Wada, in charge of research and development, called for doubling the fuel efficiency. Wada re-emphasized that the G21 team was meant to do something that had never been done before. The new criterion to double fuel efficiency forced Uchiyamada to consider the hybrid system. But it was still in the research phase, and he was not sure if the technology would be ready on time for the Tokyo Motor Show in October, 1995, when the G21 concept car was scheduled for unveiling. The G21 team did not have sufficient technologies or resources. A new study group called BR-VF[6] was launched in February, 1995 to develop a hybrid system. It was led by Toshihiro Fujii, the head of the Electric Vehicle (EV) Development department.

Connecting ba: mobilizing varieties of knowledge

At an executive meeting in June, 1995, the BR-VF team presented a hybrid system that could double fuel efficiency. With this, senior management decided to commercialize the hybrid car and launch it by the end of 1998. It was named the Toyota Hybrid System (THS). The G21 team was allocated a code, 890T, giving it official status as a commercial product development project, and Fujii's hybrid team moved into its second phase.

Now, Uchiyamada had to build a fully fledged team. He went to each department – brakes, electrical systems, and the rest – looking for the engineers he needed. Top management was solidly behind the project, so Uchiyamada could commandeer whoever he needed without strong objections from other managers. "Okuda (the president) was very concerned that sectional rivalries would develop, so he encouraged everyone to cooperate fully," said Uchiyamada.[7] Eventually, about 1,000 Toyota personnel worked on the car, most of them on a part-time basis.

Given the time constraints for developing the Prius, everyone had to understand each others' work to carry out their own tasks effectively. Toyota is known for "concurrent engineering," where resident engineers (REs) are stationed at the manufacturing plants to solve any problems with a new vehicle in production as soon as they arise. The Prius was an extraordinary example of simultaneous engineering in reverse, where production engineers from the manufacturing plant came to participate in product development. This would ensure that there were fewer problems when the car reached the manufacturing stage. During development all things are in flux, so, to understand what the considerations are and how decisions are being made, engineers have to be able to actually see and feel the flow of each part of the process. This enables them to make sense of the process as a whole and to identify and solve potential problems in the early stages. A variety of departments joined forces to develop the Prius. The Second Engine department was responsible for the engine, the Drive Train Technology department developed the transaxle for the hybrid system, the EV Development department was responsible for the battery and motor, and the Second Vehicle Technology department was responsible for the brakes. The Second Testing department was responsible for product evaluation, and for production technology the Unit Production Technology department, the Production Technology Development department, and the IT engineering department were all involved. The inverter was developed and produced by the Second and Fourth Electronics Technology departments and the Hirose factory in Toyota City.

Since the hybrid system consists of several components that have to function together seamlessly, the engineers had to be able to work closely together and combine their areas of expertise in a similarly seamless manner. Engineers in charge of the engine had to also understand motor, generator, and battery technologies and communicate effectively with those technical engineers. It was possible to improve the engine only to worsen fuel economy and the effectiveness of other components. And since the hybrid system was still in the research phase, problems had to be analyzed, starting with identifying the component that was causing the problem. This required engineers to overcome the boundaries of their own specialties and understand the interrelated whole.

In May, 1995, Toyota decided to develop and produce its own integrated circuit technology called IGBT, which is central to the inverter for the hybrid system. The company could have purchased this from outside vendors, and there were those who thought that it should. However, IGBT was considered a basic technology for a hybrid car, so Toyota decided to produce it on its own, thereby retaining control over one of the car's key technologies. The battery was developed in cooperation with Matsushita Battery Industry. Toyota's EV Development department had been co-developing a nickel hydrogen battery with Matsushita for the RAV4 EV, Toyota's prototype electric car. The Prius battery was based on this technology, but had to be much lighter and smaller, about one-tenth the weight of the battery for RAV4 EV. Also, heat was a serious problem because the battery would be placed next to the engine.

In October, 1995, the Prius concept car was unveiled on schedule at the Tokyo Motor Show. It was the first public mention of the name Prius, and by November prototypes had been made and tested. Engineers worked day and night to find and correct problems with the prototypes. The Product Audit room, which is responsible for evaluating a car from the viewpoint of users, ran the car through the test course. On the first day, it wouldn't even start, then it stopped after moving one meter. Rather than evaluate the car's performance, the Product Audit room staff just focused on getting it to run. The engineers responsible for various components gathered to find and fix the problems. For 50 days the Prius prototype couldn't be driven due to an engineering fault that was preventing communication between the engine and the motor. By December, 1995, the car was able to move about 100 meters. "At the time, my first reaction was 'It moves!'" recalls Uchiyamada.[8]

It was around this time that the president of Toyota, Hiroshi Okuda, had asked Wada what was the scheduled date for release of the Prius. When he was told December, 1998 he said it was too late. As Wada recalls, Okuda said: "Couldn't it be one year earlier? It is important that we release it early. This car may change the future of the auto industry, not to mention the future of Toyota" (Itazaki, 1999: 90–1). Okuda and Toyota Chairman Shoichiro Toyoda insisted on launching in December, 1997. According to Uchiyamada, the approaching meeting of the United Nations on climate change in Kyoto in 1997, which established the Kyoto Protocol on global warming, was another reason to launch earlier. In January, 1997, Toyota launched an "Eco-Project" to publicize the environmentally friendly hybrid car and push for quicker realization. This put even greater time pressure on the team to meet the new deadline.

To meet the new launch date of December, 1997, the G21 team was renamed Product Planning Project Zi in January, 1996. Toshihiro Ohi joined the team to speed things up for the launch. He was another heavy hitter, with 15 years experience in product planning and commercialization for cars such as the Tercel, Starlet, Corsa, and Sainos, and would be responsible for seeing the Prius through to commercialization, overseeing development of production technology, actual production, sales, and public relations. In addition to a strong social network, he brought the vital knowledge needed to orient commercialization to consumer needs.

Besides the hybrid technology, aerodynamics, maximum interior space, and ergonomics were all important in the vehicle. It had to be large enough to house the hybrid technology and also be comfortable for passengers. The Second Design department presented several designs for the exterior and Uchiyamada was not satisfied with any of them. They were extensions of existing designs of Toyota cars, conforming with conventional wisdom in Toyota car design. Uchiymada wanted the Prius to be a new look for a new era. He insisted that even if the car appeared unconventional, users would get used to it as long as the essential design was sound. After several designs were scrapped, Uchiyamada held an open competition of all the designers in Toyota.

The preliminary competition for exterior design was held in February, 1996. Seven teams presented more than 20 designs and two were entered in the final competition. One was from the design department at Toyota headquarters, and the other was by Calty Design Research, Inc in California. The in-house design was an extension of existing models, while the Calty design by Irwin Lui was more futuristic. The judges were Toyota executives and 100 employees and they chose the Calty design. It was officially chosen for the Prius exterior in September, 1996. As the design of the first-generation Prius, it was short and upright and distinctive among contemporary small sedans.

In March, 1996, the BR-VF team was reorganized to complete the hybrid system. New members joined the team from various departments such as the First Engine, Second Engine, and Third engine departments, the Vehicle Technology department, the Second Power train department, the EV Development department, and the Higashi-Fuji Research Center. The team worked on fuel efficiency and emissions. They also had to resolve problems such as vibration and controls for switching the engine on and off. Uchiyamada set up problem-solving teams made up of people working on each of the technologies, and gave the team leaders the authority to resolve problems in their own way. Since the subtechnologies in the hybrid system were complex and specialized, team members were drawn from the relevant departments to contribute their specialized knowledge. Uchiyamada maintained a flexible organizational structure and would willingly restructure to adapt quickly to changing circumstances. He made extensive use of the trial car to put results into practice. Seeing the thing in reality helped in understanding what worked and what didn't.

In December 1996, Toyota, Matsushita Electric Industrial Co., Ltd, and Matsushita Battery Industrial Co., Ltd established the joint venture, Panasonic EV Energy Co., Ltd, to produce batteries for the Prius. Matsushita Battery would produce the cells, Toyota would produce the modules and holders, and Panasonic EV Energy would assemble them. Toshihiro Fujii, director of Toyota's EV Development department became vice president of Panasonic EV Energy. At the running test for the Prius, battery performance was below 30 percent. The poor battery performance was causing the test car to stall after running the course just once or twice. Fujii inspected the production line for the battery from top to bottom and found that the source of the problem was a huge gap between Toyota and Matsushita Battery in their understanding of quality control. Matsushita Battery produced for the consumer market, where a certain percentage of defects was almost expected. Consumers could live with one dead battery, but the battery for the Prius contained 240 cells. One defective cell could kill the whole battery and the car along with it. To improve quality, Toyota's philosophy and methods of quality control were introduced into every aspect of design, development, and manufacturing of the battery. Nevertheless, it still took a long time to improve battery performance to a satisfactory level.

In July and August of 1997, endurance tests were conducted in Japan, the US states of Nevada and California, and New Zealand, running the car for long hours under extreme conditions of heat and cold. The engineers from Panasonic EV Energy observed the tests, collected data, and talked with the evaluating team. This helped them to understand the high standard required of a car battery for the Prius and produced a sufficient level of anxiety among them to want to get it right. Thereafter, quality control at Panasonic EV Energy became more thorough, and the performance of the battery improved.

Over the course of development, the Prius project team took pains to thoroughly document each stage of the process and the know-how that was acquired. This would be stored for sharing across the company, reflecting the priority at Toyota on organizational learning and fulfilling the additional task assigned to the project team to produce a new process for innovation along with the new product.

The Prius market launch

The Prius was officially unveiled to the news media in a test drive at the company's Higashi-Fuji Research Center in October, 1997, and the first car rolled out of the factory in December the same year. Toyota president Hiroshi Okuda announced that the Prius was born out of the challenge to change. As the world's first commercialized hybrid car it was welcomed with such surprise and curiosity that Toyota had to host three press conferences in Tokyo alone. The extensive media coverage combined with the car's reasonable price resulted in a back-order of 3,500 vehicles. The company quickly decided to raise production from 1,000 to 2,000 units per month. The Prius was awarded the 1997–1998 Car of the Year Japan, plus numerous other awards for its innovative concept, design, and technologies.

The decision to keep design and production in-house proved beneficial. The concentration of knowledge in one place enabled development and modification of the hybrid system in a shorter period of time. And it allowed Toyota to accumulate new knowledge and skills, amounting to more than 300 patents. At the time of the Prius launch Toyota's closest rival, Honda, was an estimated three to four years behind in hybrid development. For the second generation Prius, Toyota was able to improve and simplify the technology. "We have been able to significantly reduce the cost of the major components and the hybrid's sophisticated support systems through in-house R&D," said the chief engineer for the second generation model, Masao Inoue.[9] The knowledge gained from the hybrid was put to use across all the main developmental domains, in alternative energy, such as compressed natural gas, as well as in diesel and gasoline engines, and electronic vehicles.

8.3 Implications

Our studies of the turnaround at Canon and Toyota's development of the Prius hybrid car provide vivid examples of *phronetic* leadership in practice. In both cases, leaders promoted innovation by making decisions and taking action that was timely and appropriate to the particular situations they faced. They were able to recognize the flow of change and grasp its essential meaning to generate ideas. They mobilized their organizations to create knowledge by building and connecting *ba* and by fostering *phronetic* capability in others.

8.3.1 *Phronetic* leadership at Canon

There is no doubt that the drastic reform of Canon was made possible by the strong leadership of Fujio Mitarai, but it was not a matter of a charismatic leader single-handedly turning the company around. Rather, it was Mitarai's mobilization of all Canon employees to pursue knowledge creation at all levels of the organization that achieved the turnaround. The case of Canon shows how distributed *phronetic* leadership builds a resilient organization that is able to adapt and change. We can track Canon's successful reformation by looking at it in relation to the six abilities that constitute phronetic leadership.

The ability to make a judgment on "goodness"

Canon's reform began with a series of drastic decisions, such as its exit from several businesses and its introduction of a cell system of production. Drastic action requires belief in certain values and a commitment to succeed. Without a guiding belief and commitment to it, no one is willing to take the risk of decision-making about a future that is wide open. The values underlying belief define "goodness" for the decision-maker so he or she can make "good" decisions. The fundamental value that guides Canon is its corporate philosophy of *kyosei*, the Japanese expression for living and working together for the common good. The company views imbalances, such as those in trade, in income, and in the environment, as hindrances to *kyosei* and sees its mission as addressing those imbalances in pursuit of an ideal of global harmony working toward the future.[10] Based on the concept of *kyosei*, Mitarai describes the mission of management as follows: to ensure a profitable return to shareholders, to stabilize and improve the working life of employees, to make a social contribution, and to create the financial capability within the company to invest in growth (Mitarai, 2006: 29).

The ability to share contexts with others to create ba

Reform is not possible by way of drastic decision-making and ambitious goal setting alone. Decisions must be actualized and goals must be reached, and these require the commitment and mobilization of knowledge at all levels of the organization. Mitarai created and utilized a variety of *ba*, from that of executive committee meetings to regular visits to the frontline, to share context that would help him to make decisions that were timely and to foster commitment to knowledge creation. From *asa-kai* meetings with executives at the local bar to regular factory visits, Mitarai emphasized close, direct communication in *ba* as the most effective way of sharing context.

The ability to grasp the essence of particular situations/things

For Mitarai, "change" is the ordinary state; every second is different from a second ago. Changes in the environment must be foreseen, and even the smallest signs must be read carefully. The firm then has to re-imagine itself and start the process of change, sometimes on a smaller scale, sometimes across the entire operation. This calls for imagination, planning skills, and an ability to read the changing times, according to Mitarai. It is the ability to grasp the essence of a particular situation. For example, Mitarai has emphasized the importance of using concrete figures to set goals and control results, but he urges that one must look behind the figures to understand their essential meaning, and this is done by observing what's actually going on in the work place. By assigning a concrete figure to cash flow, for example, one can grasp in the moment an understanding of a particular situation that is in constant change (Oguri et al., 2003). Accounting figures represent the noun form of the verbs of ever-changing business at Canon. Just looking at the nouns, however, can prevent one from seeing the process dynamics, so the nouns have to be converted back into verbs by seeing the "story" behind the figures as it is created and unfolds.

The ability to reconstruct particulars into universals and vice versa using language/concepts/narrative

A *phronetic* leader has to be able to conceptualize the essence of a particular situation as a universal idea, and vice versa, so that essence can be communicated effectively to others and applied in other situations. Mitarai, in particular, is known for his ability to modify his message to fit the context of an interaction. His broad-based application of the basic accounting concept of cash flow as an effective tool of knowledge-creation demonstrates his ability as a leader to translate an objective policy guideline into particular functions and behavior that are easily understood by all employees.

The ability to use well any necessary political means to realize concepts for the common good

This is particularly crucial in times of reform and transformation. Reform normally meets with active and passive resistance as people are inclined to avoid change and hold to precedent. A clear communication strategy can help overcome this tendency by convincing opponents and cultivating cooperation. In other words, the task of the leader is to be able also to transform the mindset and the behavior of employees. Mitarai played this role well. He made top-down decisions quickly using the power of his position as CEO. At other times, he took a softer, more interactive approach, discussing options with everyone first to seek consensus. He describes his approach as follows: "First, you have to set goals that everybody understands. Then I go and talk to the employees. Then I go to the shop floor and the frontlines to see whether my ideas are being implemented. If not, I ask people to do so directly. This process has to be repeated continuously" (Katsumi, 2006: 38). In other words, Mitarai first used his considerable communication skills to explain thoroughly the goals to employees in ways that were understandable

234 *Managing Flow*

and convincing to them, and whenever that understanding was not reflected in the work, he took direct action to correct it.

The ability to foster phronesis in others to build a resilient organization

To get the Canon Group moving forward efficiently and as an organic whole, the company had to be streamlined and power centralized to some degree, but headquarters did not seize all the power. Mitarai says one has to think global and act local, stressing the importance of local knowledge and decision-making based on local circumstances. This cultivates distributed leadership. For the whole group to be successful, everyone from headquarters to the business units and the subsidiaries must agree at a fundamental level, and it is the role of the leader to elicit this agreement. Asked who might qualify to succeed him as leader, Mitarai says the person should not be selfish. "All the candidates for the next leader have a similar level of business skill, but the basis of leadership is unselfishness and fairness. An unselfish person can see things from the broader perspective and balance optimization. Even subconsciously, he or she should not think about personal advantage," he said (Mizushima, 2005: 218–9). This is the basis of *phronetic* leadership.

8.3.2 Distributed *phronetic* leadership in the Prius project

The successful knowledge-creation process that emerged in the development of the Toyota Prius is clearly traceable to the *phronetic* practices of key individuals in a distributed leadership environment. As shown in Figure 8.4, both upper and middle managers played important roles in the various phases of development. Among middle managers there were two types of leader: knowledge producers and knowledge managers. Knowledge producers like Uchiyamada were at the intersection of vertical and horizontal information flows, interacting and facilitating interaction within the organization to create knowledge. Like the movie producer, the knowledge producer knows who has what knowledge that can be put to use, while also having a broad range of knowledge themselves. Knowledge managers, on the other hand, are the middle managers who have accumulated tacit knowledge in their own specialization, which is narrowly focused but deep. Without knowledge managers such as Fujii, who had accumulated expertise about electric vehicles before the Prius project even began, it would not have been possible for Toyota to develop the hybrid system in such a short period of time.

The role of leadership begins with setting the vision and the driving objectives, and ensuring the consistent understanding of these so the entire organization is committed to them and can be mobilized to realize them as a manifestation of a common good. The Prius was borne of the efforts of Toyota to review and redefine its product, starting from a blank slate. Despite

Toyota's comfortable financial position, upper management was aware of issues that could undermine the company's future, such as bureaucracy and declining innovativeness in the organization, as well as environmentalism. The provocative phrase in their "Dr Dolittle" advertisements suggested the obsolescence of the automobile as a clear and present danger at a time of skyrocketing oil prices and growing concern about the environment. The policy to "return to basics as a manufacturer" represented senior management's vision of a sustainable future for Toyota as a car manufacturer. To realize that future, the essential question, "what is a good car in the twenty-first century?" had to be explored, and management gave this task to the G21 study group. The vision was translated into a concrete concept by middle management. Starting with the first-generation Prius, Uchiyamada discarded all pre-established beliefs and practices in Toyota car manufacturing and pursued an idea of the essence of a new car emerging from new practice.

When the Prius was first proposed, it was widely believed that Toyota would not be able to recover production costs at a selling price of 2,150 thousand yen per unit.[11] It was Okuda, the president, who had made the final decision to go ahead with the Prius, even though the projected cost was high. Okuda was confident that the development and manufacturing engineers would be able to cut costs, and in fact costs continually declined as production proceeded, increasing the profit margin. Okuda's decision was in-line with the corporate philosophy of Toyota: "contribute to the creation of a prosperous society in the making of automobiles." "What is most important is how much the people of Toyota can contribute to the happiness of people in the global society by making automobiles," said Okuda. "The Toyota Production System is only a technical tool to support this" (Okuda and Zhu, 2007: 80–1). He also said, "profit is important but social responsibility is equally important; companies today must pursue both. A company that does not achieve both is not an excellent company. We must act on truth, goodness and beauty" (Okuda and Zhu, 2007: 65). This statement comes from personal experience. Okuda describes how he once set the goal of reaching one trillion yen in operating profit, but the company never achieved it even though everyone worked hard for it. "That's when I really felt that we needed to think in a way that we could contribute to society as a corporate citizen. We shouldn't put profit above everything...Then, with this mindset, our operating profit surpassed one trillion yen" (Okuda and Zhu, 2007: 85).

A company's knowledge assets form the basis for knowledge creation, so it is up to senior management to develop these assets in-line with the company's knowledge vision. While assessing their inventory of knowledge assets, senior leaders form a strategy to maintain and build them for efficient and effective use. More importantly, they must know what kind of knowledge the company lacks relative to the knowledge vision. To continue as a car manufacturer, not just an assembler, Toyota had to build its knowledge of electric vehicle technology. This led to creation of the EV Development department, and eventually the hybrid technologies. However, the building of new knowledge assets at Toyota was not solely a result of strategic planning by senior management. It also occurred as a "Brownian movement" of middle managers forming their own study groups because they shared the sense of crisis about the future of Toyota as a manufacturer. In that sense, the building of knowledge assets at Toyota is also a process of middle-up-down management, where middle managers exercising *phronetic* leadership break down the vision of top management into concrete concepts that are realized in synthesis with the reality on the frontline.

Knowledge producers who find and utilize knowledge assets are crucial because large organizations often don't know about all of the resources they have at their disposal to create and exploit knowledge. Uchiyamada had a vast knowledge of the assets dispersed around Toyota because he had worked to reorganize the company's R&D functions. Upon becoming chief engineer of the hybrid project, he immediately took an inventory of Toyota's knowledge assets by visiting the R&D labs. This "know-who" helped him put together a group of engineers with the right mix of technological know-how to build and connect the necessary *ba*.

Both senior management and the project leaders were able to communicate a vision of the future and guide it to realization by mobilizing knowledge assets through dialogue and practice in *ba*. They built communicative environments of *ba*, characterized by openness and responsiveness to different viewpoints, and to change. Uchiyamada demonstrated a keen sense of how to do this when he established rules for discussing the technologies that discarded hierarchical conventions and eschewed sectionalism. Team members were able to transcend their specialized fields to cooperate more effectively. The collaborative spirit of *ba* was also evident in the early and efficient cooperation between the development team and production and software engineers, all of this bolstered by strong leadership at the top.

A leader facilitates the building of *ba* by providing the necessary conditions of time, space, sensitivity, and opportunity. Top management and knowledge producers build *ba* in the physical space of a meeting room, in the cyber space of a computer network, or in the mental space of common goals, so participants can share "here-now" experience. To develop the Prius, these spaces were the project room that brought the team together in one physical place, and the mailing list enabled quick dissemination of information and response. A leader must also choose the right mix of people and promote their interaction to build *ba*. Uchiyamada knew which people had the right kind of experience for the team because he began with a clear set of criteria for choosing them and knew what their competencies were. Within the *ba*, leadership supports creativity that encourages interaction and energizes the *ba*. It is not easy to keep a *ba* continuously creative. To accomplish this, a leader must not only make a deep personal commitment to the *ba* as a participant, but also facilitate concept development and realization, drawing on metaphor and models, and stimulating the ideas of others.

To create knowledge in *ba*, the *ba* must be energized by all participants, which gives energy and quality to the SECI process. Leaders need to create the necessary intellectual and psychological conditions for *ba*, such as autonomy, creative chaos, redundancy, variety, love, care, trust, and commitment. Uchiyamada's rules of conduct played an important role in energizing *ba* to develop the Prius. The pressure exerted by top management to double the fuel efficiency and move the release date one year earlier showed a sense of timing and a desire to break with dominant thinking and seek radical change. The creative chaos that ensued triggered a rewiring of various *ba* within the company, transcending the defensive behavior of sectionalism and competition for turf. Top management provided a sense of urgency and direction by emphasizing that the future of the company depended on the completion and success of the project. Project leaders conveyed this urgency to the various *ba*, continually repeating and emphasizing the primacy of the underlying purpose.

Furthermore, different *ba* form for different objectives, and they connect with each other to make up a greater *ba*. To manage this creative activity, leaders have to facilitate interactions among the various *ba* and their participants, guided by the knowledge vision. The case of the Prius shows how knowledge creation depends on multiple layers of *ba* connected organically to a greater *ba*. The entire organization is itself an organic configuration of *ba* in motion, the *ba* arising like distant and disconnected fractals that leaders must differentiate and interweave to build knowledge that can be synthesized in the larger *ba*. Even in a culture of open, organizational learning like Toyota's, the level of interdisciplinary collaboration and knowledge sharing for the Prius was unprecedented. Almost all of the necessary knowledge and expertise already existed within Toyota, cultivated by knowledge managers. But it was spread out among the different groups and departments. Uchiyamada connected *ba* to bring together all the pieces under a shared vision. His successful integration and direction of so many different technologies and fields of expertise toward a common goal was his greatest achievement as team leader. The urgency, the focus on a single product, and the strong top management support enabled the core product development team to utilize a variety of organizational resources fast and effectively, connecting numerous *ba* under a coherent, overarching vision that helped individuals transcend self-interest to pursue the goal (see Figure 8.5). While the various *ba* were unified by a single vision, they were also self-organized and autonomous in their actions to reach targets. Shared contexts in *ba* were enriched due to the relative freedom in utilizing organizational resources, the focus on one product, and the close, cross-functional interaction.

238 Managing Flow

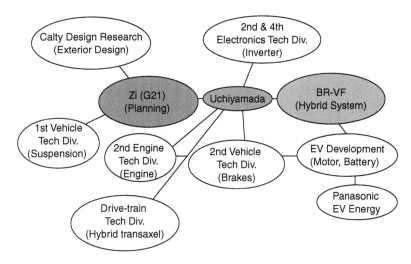

Figure 8.5 Various *ba* of the Toyota Prius project
Source: Nonaka and Toyama (2007).

In summary, for development of the Prius, a variety of new knowledge emerged simultaneously in the various *ba*. Each participant brought to *ba* their unique experience, such as expertise in a particular subtechnology, and they shared it with other participants while acquiring new experience working with others in the "here-now" context of *ba*. Knowledge emerged from the process of integrating and making sense of these experiences and that knowledge expanded continuously in the ever-changing relationship of interconnected *ba*. The Prius project can be seen as a process of building a dynamic community of knowledge. To build such a community, leaders need *phronesis* to make judgments appropriate to managing the relationship among the various *ba* and their participants, and this process, in turn, cultivates *phronesis* among the various participants in *ba*.

For distributed *phronetic* leadership to prevail, leaders must foster such leadership capabilities in the next generation. The Prius project was important for Toyota for building the kind of *ba* that generate the high-quality experiences necessary to foster *phronesis*. Toyota frequently uses pilot projects to test the future management potential of employees. One such employee was Satoshi Ogiso, who was with the Prius project from the start of the G21 group, through development of the second generation Prius. He was only 32 years old when he joined, but was given a high level of responsibility with the aim of cultivating his leadership skills. The accumulation of tacit knowledge in an organization in various domains, which can be shared and carefully rewired, is crucial to the process or *way* of knowledge-creation management. Like the *Toyota Way*, it is not a fixed or predetermined way of doing things but is in constant change, adaptation, and evolution, true to the learning organization and the knowledge-creating company.

Notes

1. http://www.canon.com/ir/housin2007/index.html
2. Toyota Motor Company (2001).
3. http://worldbenefit.case.edu/innovation/bankInnovationView.cfm?idArchive=303
4. This section is based on Kanazawa and Toyama (2001).
5. Interview with Takashi Uchiyamada, August 16, 1999.
6. "BR" stands for "business reform," which was a project on business operation reform that had been underway since 1993. "VF" stands for "vehicle and fuel," respectively.
7. Interview with Takashi Uchiyamada, August 16, 1999.
8. Ibid.
9. "Tokushuu 2: Hybrid de sekai hyoujyun wo tsukame" ["Special report 2: Setting hybrid as global standard"]. *Nikkei Ecology*, November 8, 2003, pp. 40–1.
10. http://web.canon.com/about/philosophy/index.html
11. Toyota said it set the price at a level that customers would consider affordable. Toyota has never revealed the cost of producing the Prius, but it claims to have recovered its investment in the end, considering all the beneficial effects that production of the car brought with it.

References

Itazaki, E. (1999). *Kakushin Toyota jidosha* [Innovate Toyota Motors]. Tokyo: Nikkan kogyo shinbun sha.
Kanazawa, S. and Toyama, R. (2001). "Zenshateki torikumi toshiteno Prius kaihatsu" ["Whole organization committed to Prius development"], in D. Senoo., S. Akutsu., and I. Nonaka. (eds). *Chishiki keiei jissennron* [On Practice: Knowledge Creation and Utilization]. Tokyo: Hakuto Shobo, pp. 145–78.
Katayama, O. (1998) *Toyota no houhou* [Toyota Method]. Tokyo: Shogakukan.
Katsumi, A. (2006). "Hatsukoukai! Mitarai-shiki 'settoku to shounin no leadership'" ["First to public! Mitarai method of 'leadership with persuasion and approval'"]. *President*, May 1, pp. 32–9.
Mitarai, F. (2006). "Mitarai Fujio 'Tsuyoi Nippon'" [Fujio Mitarai: Strong Japan], in T. Tsumuji (ed.). Tokyo: Asahi Shinbunsha.
Mizushima, A. (2005). *Canon "hitozukuri" no gokui* [Canon: The Secrets of "Raising People"]. Tokyo: Nihon Jitsugyo Shuppansha.
Oguri, M., Suzuki, G., and Fujii, H. (2003). "Suuji-ryoku no kitaekata" ["How to enhance the accounting capability"]. *Weekly Diamond*, January 22, pp. 24–8.
Okuda. H. and Zhu, J.R. (2007). *Chikyu kigyo Toyota ha chugoku de naniwo mezasunoka: Okuda Hiroshi no Toyota-ism* [What global-company Toyota aims at in China: Toyota-ism of Hiroshi Okuda]. Tokyo: Kadokawa Gakugei Shuppan.

Takeuchi, H. and Nonaka, I. (2004). *Hitotsubashi on Knowledge Management*. Singapore: John Wiley & Sons (Asia).
Toyota Motor Company. (2001). *Evolving to Achieve Maturity and Diversity toward the Hybrid Era*. http://www.toyota.co.jp/en/enviroment_rep/01/pdf/p72_77.pdf
Uchida, T. (2007). "Sotozuke kioku souchi: Sagashi mono ni tsuiyasu muda ha 1 nenkan de 6 shuukan" ["External memory devices: Time wasted for searching lost items totals to 6 weeks in a year"]. *President*, April 16, p. 86.

9
Conclusions

In this book, we have tried to present new developments in the theory of organizational knowledge creation. Widespread interest in the theory during the past 15 years, both in academia and in business (Nonaka et. al., 2006), has led to significant progress in understanding the process in which organizations create knowledge. Despite these advances in research and practice, the theory was not yet fully developed as a dynamic and comprehensive framework for managing the knowledge-based firm because we had not yet fully understood the characteristics of knowledge as a resource.

Starting from the common assumption today that knowledge is the most valuable management resource, scholars of knowledge-based management have been trying to develop theory that explained how firms create sustainable, competitive advantage by acquiring, utilizing, and building knowledge resources. While this work recognizes some of the characteristics of knowledge, such as intangibility, it does not examine the fundamental nature of knowledge, treating it instead like just another resource. Thus, it has been blind to the most important characteristic of knowledge: that it is a resource that is created by human beings in process and in relations with each other and the environment. This fundamental characteristic of knowledge demands that any theoretical discussion of the knowledge-based firm must deal with the human factors of subjectivity and values, and this is done by incorporating a process-relational viewpoint. Knowledge-based theory of the firm has to reveal the process in which individuals with different values and perspectives relate with each other and with the environment to create knowledge. This book is our attempt to present a framework of that process to further describe the dynamics of organizational knowledge creation and broaden the perspective on the theory of the firm and its role in society.

9.1 New developments

To clarify our view of knowledge as a resource that is created by human beings in relationships, we have elaborated the theory along the following lines.

Human factors in knowledge creation

Since knowledge is created by human beings, any theory of the knowledge-based firm has to address the reality of human beings as individuals, each with his or her own feelings, ideals, dreams, values, and perspectives. Conventional economic theory has simplified the firm's behavior in terms of production functions, describing human behavior as a utility function. Such simplification has been necessary to explain the complex reality of the modern economy, and its explanatory power has been convincing. But this has been a quest for objective science in management theory built on assumptions inherited from economic theory that profit maximization is the ultimate goal and that human behavior is guided by utilitarianism. As a result, this theory is inadequate to understanding management of the knowledge resource. Human beings differ in their values and perspectives and it is these differences that foster new knowledge. Individuals are driven by their dreams and ideals in relentless pursuit of knowledge to be happy. Similarly, organizations of people envision their own future and create knowledge to actualize that future. We place these human factors at the center of our expanded theory of knowledge-based management in a framework that explains the process in which individual subjectivities are shared, objectified, and synthesized to create knowledge. This process is guided by ideals, dreams, and the vision of the future that an individual or a firm seeks to actualize.

Knowledge as process-relational

Since knowledge is created by human beings in relationships, knowledge-based theory of the firm has to broaden its perspective from the static, atomistic, substance-based worldview typical of conventional economic theory, to a view of the firm as a dynamic entity in flow. The substance-based view fails to understand the significance of human relationships in knowledge creation. Human beings do not exist independently of each other and the environment, but are the relation and accumulation of their unique experiences at a particular time and space. We aim to move one step forward in developing a comprehensive theory of the knowledge-based firm by incorporating process philosophy, which views the world as a series of events in relationship rather than as a combination of separately existing *things*. The integration of process theory with organizational knowledge-creation theory helps us to build a comprehensive framework for understanding the context of a firm in a particular time-space, and their mission, vision, and values in relation to a business ecosystem evolving in *ba*.

Process theory views the world as an *extensive continuum*, where all that exists is indivisible, interrelated, and unbounded in time and space. Human beings are interrelated in an *extensive continuum*, with their own past and future as well as that of others. The individual stands in the present moment holding past experiences within and unites with experiences of the self and others to transcend the self to a new unity. From this perspective, the firm as an entity exists in the flow of constant change and transcends itself to create a future. Rather than *being*, firms are in the constant state of *becoming*. Knowledge creation in the firm is a process that synthesizes past and present events toward an open future; it is an activity to create new value. Firms create their vision of the future and make decisions to realize that future in the present by taking risks, while being affected by past situations and experiences. All the firms in our case studies regard the state of "change" as an ordinary process of business operations. While standing on past experiences, they see their future as open in front of them, and by committing to their ideal of the future they are relentlessly driven to actualize it.

In the atomistic view of the individual as *homo economicus*, people are interconnected only by contract and the firm is treated as a collection of contracts. In the process-relational view, people are what they are, in large part by virtue of their relations not only with their own body and their personal past, but also with those around them, those they care about, and the communities with which they identify (Cobb, 2007: 577). This model of "person-in-community" as an alternative to the model of *homo economicus* applies to individuals and organizations sharing common values and goals in a business ecosystem, and that amounts to more than just the expectation of personal profit. Of course, firms cannot continue to exist without profit. However, as some of the firms in our case studies repeatedly emphasize, profit is a *result* of the firm's pursuit of excellence and ideals, not a *purpose*. What these firms pursue ultimately is the happiness of the community and themselves. This causes them to continuously question their *raison d'être* and seek their own, absolute value in the context of their relationships in the community and society. They have built unique communities of individuals driven by their own beliefs, shared dreams, and a vision relentlessly pursued to create unique value leading to happiness in the community and then profit.

Knowledge creation as phronetic process

Management is a process whereby individuals with their unique accumulations of experience envision a future and then make their best decisions and take the best action at a particular time-space to actualize that future. Contrary to the conventional view of the firm, in the process-relational view there is no universal formula for management because firms differ and the situations they face differ in accordance with the way they relate to those situations, past and future. To manage effectively is to be able to grasp the essence of each unique situation and place it in the flow of daily events and experiences with a sense of timing for the right actions needed to build the story of the firm's future. Firms exist in complex relationships in a business ecosystem where it is difficult to identify direct causes of events because many of the factors leading up to those events are hidden. As in the "butterfly effect," a business ecosystem can be compared to a three-dimensional jigsaw puzzle. The pieces connect to each other directly, but also indirectly to pieces that are elsewhere in the puzzle. The puzzle may seem static, but misplacement of one piece affects all of the other pieces because they dwell together in interaction. Effective management of the puzzle demands sensitivity, imagination, and the insight to grasp essential meaning in the complex and dynamic relations of the business ecosystem. In this complex and ever-changing environment the firm faces many contradictions that must be managed, not as *either or* propositions, but as *both and* for the creation of integrative solutions. This higher level resolution is supported by dialectical thinking that transcends dichotomy to synthesize contradiction. For many of the firms in our case studies, contradictions of creativity versus efficiency, diversity versus coherence, social contribution versus profit, and keeping tradition while changing with the times, are an everyday occurrence resolved through knowledge creation. Of course, such synthesis is not easy, but it is achievable by pursuing an understanding of the essence of contradiction through continuous questioning of present circumstances and underlying premises.

How do individuals actualize such management? In this book, we have looked to Aristotle's concept of *phronesis* or *practical wisdom* to describe the kind of value judgments and timely action needed to create knowledge that is relevant to particular situations. *Phronesis*, in this sense, is less a *kind* of knowledge than a *way* of knowing and acting that is essential for effective leadership. By cultivating *phronesis* at every level of the organization, the firm fosters distributed leadership in people and processes that accelerates knowledge creation. Life in its state of constant change is energy-consuming and requires the accumulated collective energies of everyone in the firm. Change is encouraged and accelerated by the firm's vision, guided by its driving objectives, and powered by distributed *phronesis*. Distributed *phronesis*, therefore, is the essence of strategic management in the knowledge-based firm, which cultivates synthesizing capabilities through dialectical reasoning and the practice of wisdom.

9.2 Future challenges

This work is our first step in building a theory of the knowledge-based firm from a process-relational point of view. We recognize the need to enhance the theoretical discussion in several areas, such as on issues of political power in process, structure and the organization, justification costs, and the measurement of results to improve the accuracy of analysis from a process point of view. We are grateful for any constructive criticism that will help us develop the theory further.

To build and illustrate the theory, we have relied on case studies because we find the method of historical narrative or storytelling the most useful for grasping context in relationships and the processes between events. A criticism of narrative is that it cannot exclude subjectivity in the selection of events to be related and unified. In our view, subjectivity is the more important element, since the self, as subject in process, is created anew at every moment in the continuing effort to give new meaning to past experiences in relation and in unity with the experience of the "here-now."

We do recognize the limitations in our narrative of each firm. Of course, it is impossible to describe every context, decision, and action relevant to each. We have selected what to write about in each case on the basis of subjective judgment and such description quickly becomes outdated in the flowing, changing world. This is the limitation of converting verb to noun, but if the verb-noun conversion is done well, there are many things such narrative can tell. Like Whitehead's description of philosophy as a poem, a good case describes both universal principles and the most particular and concrete facts. We hope that we have been able to convey the poetry of actual 'here-now' events in language that sustains universal meaning beyond those particular events.

We also recognize limitations in the selection of cases. All the firms studied are Japanese. We would like to emphasize that our theory is relevant not only for Japanese firms, but for all firms, regardless of national origin. We selected these Japanese firms because of convenience of access to the data needed for case study. All the firms examined operate globally with their own creative routine or *kata* of knowledge creation. We know that there are many other excellent knowledge-creating firms around the world. To develop robust theory, there is a need to examine companies originating in other countries and operating in a greater variety of industry segments. We aim to accumulate such case study for further testing and development of the theory.

Despite these shortfalls, we feel certain that a process theory of the knowledge-based firm offers the most comprehensive understanding of the firm as a future creating entity which synthesizes contradictions in constant change. We believe that effective management emerges in the distribution of timely judgment and action among human beings who embody practical wisdom (*phronesis*) by sharing with others their individual, aesthetic values in actual, "here-now" experiences in the ever-changing flow. This means that effective management is not an issue of controlling skills, but an issue of how we live as human beings. In that sense, management is not a tool, but a way of life.

The theory is always becoming, but we hope it contributes to better understanding and management of the knowledge-creating firm, whose continuous self-creation in pursuit of excellence and ideals is ultimately a pursuit of human happiness.

References

Cobb, J.B., Jr (2007). "Person-in-community: Whiteheadian insights into community and institution.," *Organization Studies*, 28 (4), 567–88.

Notes on Authors

Ikujiro Nonaka is Professor Emeritus in the Graduate School of International Corporate Strategy at Hitotsubashi University in Tokyo, Xerox Distinguished Faculty Scholar, University of California, Berkeley, and Distinguished Drucker Scholar in Residence at the Drucker Institute, Claremont Graduate University in Claremont, California. As originator of the Knowledge Creation Theory of the firm his research is centered on knowledge creation management to foster the next generation of business leaders.

Ryoko Toyama is Professor in the Chuo Graduate School of Strategic Management at Chuo University, and Visiting Professor in the Graduate School of Knowledge Science at the Japan Institute of Advanced Science and Technology. Her research is in the fields of strategy, technology management, and knowledge management.

Toru Hirata is Professor in the School of Economics and the Graduate School in Human and Socio-Environmental Studies at Kanazawa University. His research is in the field of Knowledge Management related to technology and intellectual property strategy.

Collaborators' biographies

Susan J. Bigelow is a journalist and research fellow in the Graduate School of International Corporate Strategy at Hitotsubashi University. Her research is in communication theory and comparative philosophy concerning aesthetics and technology.

Ayano Hirose is a D.B.A. candidate in the Graduate School of International Corporate Strategy at Hitotsubashi University under the supervision of Ikujiro Nonaka. Her research is in the field of knowledge creation and management in social and community based organizations.

Florian Kohlbacher is a research fellow at the German Institute for Japanese Studies in Tokyo and a former visiting researcher at Hitotsubashi University in the fields of knowledge management, international business and marketing.

Index

absolute value 92
accumulated technologies 179
action
  embodied 46
  plan of 114–16
  synthesis of 33
"actual entity" 10
actuality 21
added value 179–80
advisory boards 163–4
alliances 45
ambition 94
analogies 23, 60
ARICEPT 74, 76–8
Aristotle 3, 14, 55–6, 62, 65
assets, *see* knowledge assets
autonomy 178–9

ba 33–42
  ability to create 57–8, 233
  ba-centered management 119, 133–4
  building, on Toyota Prius project 225–6
  business ecosystem and 46
  for communication 216–19
  connecting 227–31
  direct dialog in, at SEJ 146–9
  factors behind activation of 37–9
  importance of 119
  KUMON method 120–32
  leadership and 236–9
  leveraging of 206–7
  Mayekawa example 107–20
  meaning of 33–7
  organization as organic positioning of diverse 39–42
  social 127–8
balance sheet 210–12
becoming 11, 243
brand imaging 171
Bread Factory Kaizen 116–20
Buber, Martin 31
bureaucracy 8
business ecosystem 45–6, 119, 133, 243–4
butterfly effect 47, 243

Canon Inc. 30, 60, 62, 63, 207–20
  balance sheet 210–12
  cell production at 212–15
  communication at 215–19
  company overview 207–8
  crisis at 209
  flow management 219–20
  phronetic leadership at 209–20, 232–4
  restructuring 209–10
capital
  intellectual 42
  structural 42
cash-flow management 211–12
cell production 212–15
change, adaptation to 141, 215–19
co-creation 110
  of *ba* 116–20
  of knowledge with customers 116–20
co-existence 108
cognition 46
combination 23–4
common good 56, 62–3, 127–8, 233–4
communication 215–19
communities of practice 36–7
community 43
competitive advantage 175–6
consciousness 24
context 33–42, 57–8, *see also ba*
contradictions, synthesis of 29, 30–1
corporate culture differences 189–90
corporate vision, *see* vision
cram schools 120, 126
creativity 11, 98
cumulative technologies 180–1
customers 51, 113
  co-creation of knowledge with 116–20
  indwelling with 20, 112–13, 117, 119, 133–4
  information from 161–2
  listening to 182–3
  surveys of 162
  thinking like 147–8
  understanding needs of 149–51, 170
Cycle of Goodness 177–8, 185, 201, 202

247

Index

decisions, value-based 3
deductive logic 23
design 165
dialectic dialog 30–3
dialog 43–44
  dialectic 30–3
  direct, in *ba* 146–9
  of leadership 191–2
  promotion of, through reform 192
  role of, in mergers 190–5
distribution system 154
doppos 110–11, 113–16
driving objectives 29–30, 72–87
Drucker, Peter 60
dynamic model, of knowledge
    creation 26–47

ecosystem of knowledge 45–7
eidetic intuition 22
Eisai 28–9, 70–87
  company overview 70–1
  human health care (hhc) 72–87, 103–4
  knowledge creation
    department 81–5
  philosophy 71–4
  understanding and internalizing *hhc*
    philosophy 74–81
Eisai Korea Inc. 86
Eisai Research Institute of Boston, Inc. 86
Eisai Thailand Marketing Co., Ltd. 86
embodied action 46
employee autonomy 178–9
employees, enjoyable environment
    for 96
endogenous motivation 38–9
environment
  business 45–7
  firm structure and 39–42
episteme 54
essence, ability to grasp 58–60, 232–3
aesthetics 12–13, 27
excellence 3
experience 21
explicit knowledge 19, 22–6, 30–1
extended enterprises 45
extensive continuum 36, 242–3
external knowledge 160–4
externalization 22–3, 30

failure 97, 178
firm structure, environment
    and 39–42
flow management 219–20
fresh food management 155
Fujisawa, Takeo 88, 97, 98–9

Genba 97–8
Genbutsu 97–8
Genjitsu-teki 97–8
global vision 92–3, 104
golden mean 62
goodness, ability to judge 55–7, 232

harmonious flow of work 96
Hegelian dialectic 31
homo economicus 12, 43, 243
Honda, Soichiro 59, 61, 87–8, 98–9, 102
Honda Motor Co. 20–1, 28, 32, 56, 59, 65
  company overview 87–8
  company principle 92–3
  corporate philosophy 88–92, 104
  maintaining vitality at 102–3
  management policies 93–8
  organization and activities 98–102
  research and development 99–102
  respect for the individual at 89–91
  Three Joys 91–2
horizontal deployment 221
human factor, in knowledge
    creation 2, 242
human health care (hhc) 72–87, 103–4
  in daily operation 87
  global spread of 85–6
  organizational mechanism for 81–5
  projects 76–81
  understanding and
    internalizing 74–81
human interaction 7, 8, 11–12, 43
human resources 2, 42, 181–2
human resource training 82–3
hypotheses 23
hypothesizing, testing, and verification
    practice 142–6

imagination 60
individuals
  respect for 89–91
  socialization of 20–1, 43

inductive logic   23
indwelling   20, 112–13, 119, 133–4
information
  access   23–4
  from customers   161–2
  gathering   149–51
  vs. knowledge   7
  sharing   193–5
information technologies (IT)
  information access and   23–4
  investment in   1
information-processing machine   2, 8
innovation   96–8, 147, 214–15
intellectual capital   42
interaction, *ba*   33–42
internal knowledge   160–4
internalization   24–6
international partnerships   165–6
intrinsic motivation   38
item by item management   155

JFE Steel Corporation
  company overview   185–8
  merger process   188–97, 202–3
  outcomes of merger   197–201
  role of dialog at   190–5
jigsaw puzzle   31
joy   91–2, 96
judgments, about goodness   55–7, 232
"just-in-time manufacturing"   220

kaizen   220
kata   43–4
Kawasaki Steel   188–97
Kawashima, Kiyoshi   94
kigyouka keikaku   111–20
kinetics   44
knowledge
  characteristics of   6–15
  context of   33–42
  as aesthetic   12–13
  explicit   19, 22–6, 30–1
  external   160–4
  vs. information   7
  through hypothesizing, testing, and verification practice   142–6
  internal   160–4
  mobilizing varieties of   227–31
  as process-relational   9–12, 242–3
  subjectivity of   7–9
  tacit   18–26, 30–1

knowledge assets   42–5
  at JFE   185–201
  leadership and   207
  at YKK   174–85
knowledge conference   83
knowledge creation   2
  ba-centered management and   119, 133–4
  co-creation with customers   116–20
  as dynamic process   2–3, 10, 26–47
  future challenges   244–5
  human factors in   242
  importance of *ba* to   133–5
  motivation for   38–9
  new developments in   241–4
  as *phronetic* process   53–67, 243–4
  through practice   13–14
  role of leadership in   53, 206–7
  SECI model of   18–26
  as social process   11–12
  spiral of   25–6
  theoretical framework   18–47
  value and   7
knowledge management   1, 1–2
knowledge sharing   45, 193–5, 214–15
knowledge survey   84–5
knowledge transfer   193
knowledge vision   27–9
knowledge-based economy   1
knowledge-based firms
  need for new theory of   1–5
  process theory of   14–15, 27
knowledge-based management   2
knowledge-based theory   6–7, 9–12
knowledge-creation department   81–5
KUMON
  community relationship building   128–9
  company overview   120
  regenerating   127–9
KUMON method   120
  characteristics of   131–2
  creation of   120–1
  globalization and   130–1
  instructors in   126–7
  learning system   121–7
  materials and methods   123–6
  philosophy   122–3
Kumon, Toru   120–1, 130
kyousei   108

250 *Index*

leadership
  ba and 236–9
  Canon example 207–20
  dialog of 191–2
  phronesis and 53–67
  power and 62–3
  role of in knowledge creation 53, 206–7
  team 101–2
  on Toyota Prius project 220–31
liberal arts 60
logic 23, 32
logical analysis 23
logical syllogism 65–6
Lorenz, Edward 47

management philosophy
  at Honda 93–8
  at SEJ 141–2
  at YKK 175, 179, 184
management succession 183–4
management theories
  dominant 1
  need for new, for knowledge-based firms 1–4
managers meetings 147
market activity, dynamic nature of 46
Matsui, Tadamitsu 164
manufacturers 163
Mayekawa Manufacturing 107–20
  ba-centered management 119, 133–4
  co-creation with customers 116–20
  company overview 107–10
  doppo organization 110–11, 113–16
  importance of *ba* at 119
  kigyouka keikaku 111–20
merger process 188–97, 202–3
metaphors 23, 60
mieru-ka 220
mission statement
  of Eisai 72–87
  KUMON 120
Mitarai, Fujio 60, 62, 63, 207, 209–12, 215–19, 232–4
motivation, for knowledge creation 38–9
Muji
  company overview 156–7
  dynamics of 167–70
  expansion of 157–9

  knowledge use at 160–4
  product development 159–60
  repositioning and redevelopment at 164–7
  vision statement 171
multiple perspectives 100–1

Naito, Haruo 73–4
narrative 4, 23, 60, 114–16
network economy 45–7
Nicomachean Ethics (Aristotle) 56–7
NKK 188–97

objective knowledge, interaction with subjective insight 60–2
objectives, driving 29–30
Ogiso, Satoshi 238
Okuda, Hiroshi 229, 235
Olympus 28
open-source software 23–4
operational innovation 147
opportunity losses 142–3, 149
organizational change, existing models of 11
organizational reform 184–5
outsourcing 45

particulars, ability to reconstruct universals to 60–2, 233
personal magnetism 62–3
personnel exchange 195–7
philosophy 56
phronesis 3, 4, 14, 53–67
  abilities constituting 55–65, 232–4
  ability to foster 63–5, 234
  concept of 53–4
  exercising 65–6
  knowledge creation and 243–4
  at SEJ 170
phronetic experience 60
phronetic judgment 55–7, 232
phronetic leadership 54–5, 62–3
  Canon example 207–20, 232–4
  on Toyota Prius project 220–31, 234–9
phronetic management 4
physical resources 6–7
Polanyi, Michael 9, 18
political power 62–3, 233–4
positivism 46

power allocation 39
practical syllogism 65–6
practical wisdom, see *phronesis*
practice 33
  changing mindset through 74–6
  hypothesizing, testing, and
    verification 142–6, 172
  kata of 43–4
  putting ideas into 76–81
pragmatism 24, 33
praxis 24–6
price, quality and 159
primary experience 21
process-relational view 2, 9–12, 14, 99, 242–3
product appeal 159
product development 25, 151–4, 159–60, 170
profit maximization 28
pure experience 21

quality, price and 159

reality 21
  objective 9
  unitary 11
reflection in action 24, 33
reflective practitioners 24
research and development 96–8, 99–102
resources 2
  human 2, 42, 181–2
  knowledge as 6–7
  physical 7
rhisomic model 11
routines 43–4
Ryohin Keikaku, see Muji

Schon, Donald 24
SECI model 18–26
  combination 23–4
  externalization 22–3
  internalization 24–6
  socialization 20–1
secondary experience 24
self, losing the 119
self-centered worldview 119
Seven-Eleven Japan (SEJ) 29, 30, 33
  company overview 138–41
  direct dialog in *ba* 146–9

distribution system 154
globalization of 154–6
information collection 149–51
management philosophy 141–2
phronetic capablity 170
practice at 142–6
product development 151–4
success of 170
sharing context, see *ba*
situations, ability to grasp
  essence of 58–60, 232–3
social *ba* 127–8
social capital 58
socialization 20–1, 43
soft dialectic 31
steel industry 185–7, 188
storytelling 60
strategic analysis 45
strategic planning 111–16
structural capital 42
subjective insight, interaction with
  objective knowledge 60–2
subjectivity 2, 7–9
Sugiura, Hideo 92–3
supply chain 154
support systems 149
surveys 162
Suzuki 29–30
Suzuki, Ichiro 44
synthesis
  of action 33
  of contradictions 31–3
  of technologies 195–7
  of thought 31–3

tacit knowledge 18–26, 30–1
Takaki Bakery 116–20
team leadership 101–2
team merchandising 151–3
technological development 179–80
technologies
  accumulated 179
  cumulative 180–1
  synthesis of 195–7
theoretical framework 18–47
  dynamic model 26–47
  SECI model 18–26
theory 95–6
third industrial revolution 1

thought, synthesis of   31–3
three *gen* principle   59, 65, 97–8
Three Joys   91–2
Three Realities Principle   97–8
Thurow, Lester   1
time, effective use of   96
total system   108
Toyota   32
Toyota Motor Company   66
Toyota Prius   220–31
   ba and   236–9
   background of   221–4
   development of   224–31
   market launch   231
   phronetic leadership on   234–9
   project overview   220–1
training by application   83
training programs   24
   at Eisai   74–6
   human resource   82–3

Uchiyamada, Takeshi   225–6, 229, 235
uniformity   8
universal rules   13
universals, ability to reconstruct particulars to   60–2, 233

value
   absolute   92
   added   179–80
value judgments   3
vision   27–9
   Eisai   70–87
   Honda   88–93
   KUMON   120
   Mayekawa Manufacturing   108
   Muji   171
visualization   220
vitality   102–3

Wada, Akihiro   227, 229
Whitehead, Alfred North   2, 9, 10

YKK
   business practices   176–9
   company overview   174–6
   corporate philosophy   176–9
   expansion of   201–2
   human resources   181–2
   key factors in development of   179–83
   succession and renewal at   183–5
Yoshida, Tadahiro   183–5
Yoshida, Tadao   176–9
youthfulness   94–5

Made in the USA
Lexington, KY
24 June 2018